T0167347

"Stick 'em up"

"Stick 'em up"

Michigan Bank Robberies
of the 20s and 30s

Tom Powers

West Branch, Michigan

Stick 'em Up: Michigan Bank Robberies of the 20s and '30s

Copyright © 2017 by Tom Powers

All Rights Reserved.
No part of this book may be used or reproduced in any form without written permission from the publisher, except in the case of brief quotations embodied in critical reviews and articles.

Published by
Thunder Bay Press
West Branch, Michigan 48661

ISBN: 978-1-933272-59-7
Library of Congress Control Number:

20   19   18   17   16   1   2   3   4   5

Book designed by Julie Taylor
Cover designed by 7ninedesign/Greg Kretovic
Maps by Timm Rye

Printed in the United States of America

This book is dedicated to Michigan police officers who have fallen in the line of duty. Unfortunately and sadly, they are too many to mention here, but the 570 names (as of this writing) of the fallen can be found online at the Officer Down Memorial Page, Michigan Line of Duty Deaths at http://www.odmp.org/search/browse/MI

Other Thunder Bay books authored by Tom Powers include:

In the Grip of the Whirlwind: The
Armistice Day Storm of 1920

Michigan Rogues Desperadoes & Cut-throats:
A Gallery of 19th Century Miscreants

Michigan State and National Parks: A Complete Guide

Special thanks to the Flint Public Library, the Library of Michigan, Mancelona Township Library, Lapeer County Library, and the Clarkston Community Historical Society & Heritage Museum.

Table of Contents

Introduction

*L*ike a kid caught stealing in a candy store, when I began researching and writing this book, I wasn't prepared for the consequences. As a student of Michigan history from my college years, through thirty-plus years as a public librarian and author of a few books on Michigan history and travel, I thought there wasn't an aspect of our state's history with which I didn't possess some passing familiarity. I couldn't have been more wrong when it came to the two lawless decades following World War I when bank robbers (cut from the same daring and deadly cloth as Missouri's post-Civil War Dalton and James gangs) wreaked havoc on Michigan banks.

The first armed robbery of a bank in the United States is believed to have occurred on February 13, 1866, when Jesse and Frank James stuck up the Clay County Saving Association in Liberty, Missouri. The more I researched and read on the topic, the more it seemed the Wild West had come to Michigan in the 1920s and 30s. By the mid-1920s Michigan ranked among the country's eight highest states for bank robberies. Tommy gun wielding gangs shot up Holland, South Haven, and other towns; the Detroit Police at one point threw up their hands and admitted they didn't have the men or resources to stop the bank robberies plaguing their city. In rural Michigan some gangs specialized in descending on small towns at night, clipping telephone lines to cut the villages off from the outside world, and holding the entire town captive while the gang's safe cracker broke into banks and fed the safe a cocktail of nitroglycerin that blew the doors off the steel box.

In nearly all cases, either rural or urban, the police and local constabulary were outgunned by bank crews who favored Tommy guns and sawed-off shotguns. And in almost every case, the bandits were better mounted. Just as the bank robbers of the 1870s made sure they rode fine horses that could outdistance and out last the local sheriff's nags, the bandits in the two decades after the War to End all Wars drove bigger and faster cars than the local lawmen. Early in the Roaring Twenties, their likely choice for a getaway vehicle was a big touring car, usually a Cadillac, that boasted a ten-foot-long wheelbase. The touring car was rugged, fast, and powerful enough to make even the worst roads passable while the cops drove Model Ts or As that putt-putted after them and got bogged down in the era's rutted, muddy back roads. In 1932 Ford introduced an eight-cylinder engine that simply left other cars in its dust. It not only became a favorite of southern moonshine transporters but the 'pick of the litter' for bank robbers. The car inspired so much admiration in Bonnie Parker's partner in passion and crime he wrote a fan letter to its maker:

Mr. Henry Ford
Detroit, Mich.
While I still have got a breath in my lungs I will tell you what a dandy car you make. I have drove Ford's exclusively when I could get away with one. For sustained speed and freedom from trouble the Ford has got ever other car skinned and even if my business hasn't been strictly legal it don't hurt anything to tell you what a fine car you got in the V-8.
Yours Truly,
Clyde Champion Barrow.[1]

The Michigan State Police, in part, owe their existence to the wave of bank robberies that swept through the state in the two decades after World War I. The force, originally called the Michigan Constabulary, was brought into existence during the war to discourage labor disputes and keep the machinery of war pouring from Michigan plants. The mounted troopers were also tasked with protecting roads, bridges, and infrastructure from sabotage. With the war over, the state police didn't even have to go looking for a new role. When Michigan went dry better than a year before the rest of the country, the state cops were handed the job of halting the tidal wave of rum-runners who traveled north from Toledo to Detroit on what was known then and now as Dixie Highway. When Prohibition became the law nationwide, Canadian booze poured across the Detroit River as if the Motor City was the terminus of a booze pipeline the size of the Trans-Alaska Crude-Oil Pipeline. From the Michigan side of the Detroit River, rum-runners set out on regular routes throughout the Midwest delivering 80 proof gold. U.S. 12 between Detroit and Chicago became a conduit on wheels for Chicago-bound booze, and the Michigan State Police worked tirelessly to dry up that major bootlegging route.

With state troopers in cars instead of mounted on horses and finally equipped with Tommy guns so they weren't outgunned by the booze transporters, the Michigan State Police were also ready to meet the rising challenge of bank robbers hitting small communities across southern Michigan. But a roving squad car was often out of contact with the state police post for hours. To keep the troopers current and abreast of crimes, bank robberies, and the sighting of alcohaulers, patrolling troopers would stop every hour and call into their post for updates. When this proved cumbersome and time consuming, the post devised a method of calling ahead to certain locations on a route and, whether a store or gas station, whatever message was left for the trooper would be passed on by putting a certain shape and colored poster in a designated window.

The 'Staties' best weapon against bank robbers came into being on October 1, 1930, when the state police radio went on the air and patrol cars were equipped with receivers. When word went out over the police radio network just minutes after a bank robbery, state police cruisers and motorcycle officers could converge on the possible getaway routes like German submarine wolf packs closed in for the kill on Allied convoys during WWI. The state police became so good at flooding the area around a bank robbery with patrol cars it has been said it was one of the reasons famed bank robber John Dillinger never tried to rob a bank in Michigan.

The most surprising discovery made during the research for this book was the regular and common practice of everyday citizens taking up arms to stop bandits from robbing their hometown banks. This occurred even when it was known banks were insured against loss by federal law. Armed mobs shot down bank robbers in several Michigan towns or instantly formed a posse and gave chase. In reading contemporary newspaper accounts, these impromptu vigilantes often chased bank robbers with all the enthusiasm and professionalism exhibited by the mob that chased Dr. Frankenstein's monster. And they were often just as deadly.

Vigilantism was rife in the state, and starting in 1927 it was promoted, supported, and even funded by the Michigan Bankers Association. The state association created a committee to study the rise in bank robberies and review methods already put in place by their sister organizations in Illinois, Indiana, Iowa, Wisconsin, Minnesota, and Kentucky. The Michigan bankers found that banker associations in the aforementioned states sponsored and encouraged vigilante organizations that immediately reacted to bank robberies by hunting down the bandits with deadly force.

After the inauguration of the Vigilante Plan in Indiana, bank robberies fell by 84%, and the amount of money stolen dropped by 79%. Bank robberies became tougher in those states because of organized vigilante groups, and in turn this encouraged bank robbers to focus on Michigan where there was less preparation or pushback. Michigan became, at least briefly, the preferred bank robbing venue for bandits.

The Vigilante Plan followed in most states was built around the county sheriffs. The vigilantes were sworn in as deputy sheriffs and often given arms and equipment supplied by the county banking organizations. A few even received some training. Rewards were posted for the capture of bank robbers that usually averaged $1,000. In a few rare cases the offer was hiked to $2,500 for a dead bank robber. Yes, there was a monetary reward for instant justice and the hell with due process. Vigilantes in some counties were given .45 caliber pistols and Karg rifles that could reach out and drill a mortal hole through a man 1.5 miles away. The vigilantes were encouraged to keep speedy cars parked and available near banks and develop a system of localized road blocks that could be in place within 15 minutes of a bank robbery. The Ironwood Daily Globe on October 12, 1927, reported 80 of Michigan's 83 counties had operating vigilante committees and all were supported by the Michigan Bankers Association.

It must be said that these vigilante organizations proved much more effective in rural areas than urban ones. Folks in cities seemed to take bank robberies as street theater and just stood and watched as gunfire erupted and bullets laced the air around their heads. It was even mentioned by several newspapers that unarmed city people would often run toward the sound of gunfire instead of away. And when city watchers did take action against bank robbers, it simply descended into a mob giving chase, or more likely, a curious mob chasing the police who were chasing the bank robbers.

The country cousin vigilantes took to chasing bank robbers with much more gusto, dedication, and a penchant for bloodletting. This frequently resulted in bloody shoot-outs and on at least one occasion a tragic case of mistaken identity. News of a bank robbery in a small community brought a pouring forth of well-armed farmers and merchants that in an odd way seemed the equivalent of a high society fox hunt for more down-to-earth common folk. Instead of "Tally Ho," one was more likely to hear, "Let's get them sombitches." And of course, in the latter case, the foxes discouraged pursuit by shooting back.

If there is some calcified adage from an ancient and honored Chinese fount of wisdom who said something about how the wheels of justice grind slow but exceedingly fine, the oriental sage who made the pronouncement was never present in a Michigan courtroom in the 1920s and 30s. If Lady Justice was supposed to be deliberate, reserved, balanced, thoughtful, slow, and yes, even demure, she dropped the robe and sometimes stepped out dressed to hit the fast lane in the Michigan courtrooms of the '20s and '30s. It wasn't due process so much as just do the process and be damn quick about it. The drive up window of today's McDonald's, even at one in the morning, could be slower in filling an order than the complete court proceedings that found a bank robber guilty and sentenced to life imprisonment. And the proceedings were often held late at night to "protect" the guilty.

The 23 bank robberies told here were chosen because they each tell unique stories while at the same time are characteristic of countless other bank robberies of the era. They also were all reported on or written about in enough detail to make good stories. I would have loved to include a chapter on the man who stole a hearse as his getaway car, the woman who robbed a bank the day after her wedding, and the Flint bank that opened a branch near Buick Motors in a spare room of a house used as a tailor shop. The hastily opened branch kept their silver in a cigar box. When that branch was robbed and Flint police late that evening traced the robbers to Saginaw and approached the local law for assistance in locating the wrong doers, the out-of-town cops were told to come back in the morning. But, in spite of hours and days of research, that is all I know about each of the above robberies.

Michigan history has never ceased to amaze, surprise, and entertain me. My hope is that this book and the stories in it will shed light on a little known corner of our state's history and give readers as much pleasure, and provoke as much interest and awe in this great state's colorful past as they did in this writer.

1. Letters of Note, www.lettersofnote.com/2009/what-dandy-car-you-make.html

Chapter 1

Angling for Dollars at Farmers State Bank

July 29, 1920

*"The room erupted in gunfire and flying
lead filled the open doorway."*

*W*hen does a fishing trip become a bank robbery? After everything went bad, a man was dead, and the robbers were licking their wounds and looking at the world from behind prison bars, one of the gangsters who stuck up the Farmers State Bank in Grass Lake on Thursday morning told police the group was on a fishing vacation and the notion of robbing a bank didn't even come up until Wednesday afternoon. W. E. Harris' confession would have the police believe a group of six gun-toting fishermen spent nearly two weeks at the Mack Island Hotel on Wolf Lake, known for its plentiful perch and bass and as a playground for the wealthy elite of Jackson County, and the idea of robbing a bank and pulling it off the very next morning was damn near an afterthought to the fishing trip. As a fish story it's a whopper, seeing as three of the six men were ex-cons, at least one had robbed a bank previously, another was a murderer, and nary a one held down a job.

One day the group was mixing with the hoi polloi of Jackson County, or wetting lines in Wolf Lake, and the next morning four of them rowed away from the hotel in a fishing boat filled to the gunnels with fishing paraphernalia. They rowed the boat to a grove of trees edging the shore some distance from the hotel and ditched the boat in favor of the car earlier stashed under the trees. Then, just before 11 AM on July 7, 1920, and six miles away, three of the fishing party entered the Farmers State Bank in the little village of Grass Lake armed with handguns while the fourth waited in the getaway car. The first bandit in the door marched to the cashier's compartment and ordered the two bank employees, Cashier Floyd Mellenkamp and Assistant Cashier Harry Knight, to raise their hands over their heads while the second bandit confronted the bank's two customers and told them to do the same. The four were moved to a back corner of the bank and told to face the wall. Their hands were then tied behind their backs with fishing line, and they were walked into a toilet and the door locked.

With the bank now in their possession, the three robbers made a thorough search of the vault bagging all the currency they could find, adding security bonds to the mix, and then topping it off with $1,300 in gold and silver coins. The three bandits walked out the front door with their loot and into the waiting car. The gangsters left town without anyone but the four tied up and locked in the toilet knowing the bank had just been robbed. The crooks drove a short distance out of town, told the two compatriots waiting there for them they didn't need to change cars, and headed back to Wolf Lake. They again hid the getaway car, stolen the night before in Jackson, in the grove of trees. The four men who pulled the job then jumped into the car holding the other two gang members and drove back to the Mack Island Hotel where they split up the take.

A few minutes after the robbers drove out of town, the bank's president walked into the building and wondered what was going on and why no one, not even his employees, were about. He started searching the bank and quickly discovered the four in the restroom, freed them, and called the sheriff. When word spread around the village, several groups quickly formed, headed off every which way, turned up nothing, and drifted back into the village.

When the call came into Sheriff Ed Larrabee's office in Jackson, he was out on another matter. Undersheriff Harry Worden took the call, and Deputy Sheriffs Verl Kutt and Van Loomis along with a state food inspector and Herman Hauck, a local Essex Motor Car salesman, were also present. Worden immediately told Hauck they needed his fastest Essex, which Hauck volunteered to drive, and as they rushed from the room, the state food inspector mentioned bootleggers had been hanging around the Mack Island Hotel. When the deputies arrived at the bank, they found very few clues, and only a vague description of the robbers could be arrived at. The four in the bank agreed all three gunmen were on the short side and stocky. One was wearing automobile goggles making him even more difficult to describe. And all three looked to be in their forties. Someone volunteered the information that a Buick Six was seen in front of the bank around the time the bank was robbed.

Undersheriff Worden noticed the robbers used green fish cord to tie up the witnesses and found another piece of the line on the floor of the bank. It was significantly different from the fishing line used by locals. The odd line coupled with the mention that a group of strangers had been staying at the Mack Island Hotel sent Worden, Deputy Kutt and a small posse of armed men heading for Wolf Lake a half dozen miles due south of Grass Lake.

When the sheriff's team arrived at the lake, the first person they encountered was Lester Bacon lying in a hammock. Worden knew Bacon's criminal past, exchanged a few words with him and moved on, not knowing Bacon was the gang's lookout while they split the money. The Undersheriff knew something was amiss when Bacon claimed he hadn't been anywhere that day but his car's radiator was still boiling hot to the touch. The deputies walked toward the tenant house when they met W. K. McIntyre, the proprietor of the Mack Island Hotel, and inquired about who might be staying at his resort. After a brief discussion McIntyre led them to the tenant house, which was set back from the hotel a short way, and climbed the stairs with Worden and Kutt to the second floor veranda. McIntyre walked to the last door on the end with the deputies close behind and knocked on the door. The proprietor told the men inside there was somebody here to see them. At this point Worden shoved McIntyre aside and waited.

After some commotion from within the room, a man later identified as W. E. Harris stepped out and shut the door after him and told the lawmen disrobed women were in the room. Worden responded they would wait until the women left before entering the room. Deputy Kutt then spoke up and said, "No, Harry, we won't wait." [1] Harris suddenly turned around, pushed open the door and yelled, "Are you all set." [2] The room erupted in gunfire and flying lead filled the open doorway. Two bullets struck Undersheriff Worden who fell mortally wounded.

Deputy Kutt grabbed Harris and tried to wrestle him to the floor, but neither could get the best of the other and the pair careened around the second-story screened in porch. When they tumbled in front of the open door, another round of fire came from the room and a bullet creased the deputy sheriff's scalp. Like any scalp wound, it bled profusely. Someone else in the room shot through the window and narrowly missed Mr. McIntyre. Still locked in each other's grip, Harris and Kutt rolled down the veranda's staircase. At the foot of the stairs, Deputy Sheriff Loomis waited for an opening then clubbed Harris over the head with the butt of his pistol. Finally subdued, Harris was placed in handcuffs.

In what was beginning to sound like a major gun battle, Deputy Sheriff Van Loomis started up the now bloody veranda stairs toward the room when he was met by a hail of bullets from the gun of Walter Wilson. Loomis ducked for cover and blindly returned fire. Emptying his pistol, he rushed the staircase and found he'd hit Wilson five out of six shots including in the leg and groin. Although badly wounded, Wilson saw the deputy coming, brought his gun to bear, and pulled the trigger, but the revolver misfired. Before Loomis could get to him, Wilson became unconscious.

The two other men in the room, "Doc" Stowe and Dan Rosenberg weren't about to step out on the veranda and into the firestorm that dropped Wilson. They climbed through the room's back window and jumped. Rosenberg landed clean and ran. Stowe wasn't so lucky and broke his leg in the fall but still managed to hobble and crawl to the swamp edging the property where he slithered into the tall grass and hoped he wouldn't be found.

After cuffing Harris, Deputy Kutt disarmed the bandit and marched him toward the hotel when he met Henry Hague of Jackson who was vacationing at the resort. Hague was probably shaken by all the shooting, the blood pouring from the deputy's head wound, and greatly surprised to find the man he had seen around the hotel for the last few days, and in all likelihood spoken with socially, being led his way in handcuffs. He was even more surprised when Deputy Kutt asked him to watch his prisoner while he went into the hotel and called for backup. When Kutt came out of the hotel, he spotted yet another man he immediately assumed to be a gang member because he had a handgun sticking out of his pocket. Already bloodied and battered, Kutt lunged for the man, later identified as George Comfort, and grappled with him before the gangster could get the revolver free from his pants. The fight raged across the yard with neither man getting the advantage. Mr. Hague had taken Harris down to the lake so he could wash his face, and figuring his captive was too hurt to run rushed to help Kutt pin down Comfort. Mr. McIntyre also hurried to Kutt's aid, and the three finally subdued the outlaw and disarmed him.

Dan Rosenberg was flying down the road and away from the hotel like an Olympic sprinter when he met a deputy sheriff racing to the scene and was arrested. Lester Bacon, the 6th member of the gang simply stood on the hotel lawn like an ornament until someone put him in handcuffs and led him away. Left alone when his civilian guard went to help Deputy Kutt, W. E. Harris, still handcuffed, hot-footed it to the swamp, and disappeared into the tangle of watery, dense foliage.

Jackson County Sheriff Larrabee had been out of the office when the call came in announcing the bank robbery. The sheriff, along with Deputy Sheriff Miller and Coroner Harry Mills, drove to the bank and arrived long after Worden and Kutt had left for Wolf Lake. The trio examined the bank and were heading back to Jackson when their car was stopped and they were told someone had been murdered at Wolf Lake. They sped toward Mack Island Hotel and found the place hip deep in police and armed volunteers by the time they arrived. When told Undersheriff Worden was dead, the sheriff nearly broke down, but he put aside his grief when he learned two of the robbers were still at large.

Thinking it a near certainty the remaining robbers were hunkered down in the swamp, the sheriff quickly organized the armed volunteers and deputies and had them combing the edges of the wetlands. When they got to the area where some thought Stowe might be hiding, the sheriff ordered several of the men to aerate that specific section of the swamp with whatever weapon they carried. Stowe immediately turned jack-in-the-box as bullets and buckshot ripped the brush around him. He popped up from his hiding place and surrendered.

In the lull after capturing Stowe, Sheriff Larrabee walked over to the tenant house, mounted the stairs to the second floor veranda and with a face wet with tears knelt next to the body of Undersheriff Worden. After a few moments he rose and the body was carried from the veranda. Neither Walter Wilson, who lay a few feet away and in great pain, nor James Stowe sitting nearby with his leg in a bandage would look at Worden's body as it was lifted up, taken from the veranda, and transported to his home.

Throughout the hunt for Stowe, men from miles around continued to show up at the Mack Island Hotel armed and willing to help. Even the warden of Jackson State Prison arrived with twenty men armed with high power rifles and asked how they could lend assistance. The sheriff had enough men to entirely surround the swamp, which he had them do and then sent groups of volunteers walking through the wetlands hoping to flush Harris. When that didn't work, he cleared the swamp and ordered the posse to empty their guns into the marsh trying to scare Harris into giving up. It didn't.

Captain Percy Taylor, a World War I officer with combat experience offered Sheriff Larrabee a new plan. With the sheriff's permission, Taylor formed the men in a long skirmish line that stretched the entire width of the swamp and ordered them forward. The skirmish line plunged into the swamp fighting their way through dense thickets, sinking up to their waists in water, wading through sucking mud all while keeping in good formation. The line had just taken a few steps past a barbwire fence marking the halfway point when half-a-dozen men spotted Harris in a clump of marsh grass. The fugitive tried to raise his still manacled hands and gave up.

Comfort, Bacon, Rosenberg, Stowe, and Wilson had already been taken to Jackson by the time Harris was corralled, so the sheriff led the last of the culprits to the room where the bank robbers had been staying at hotel. Harris' shirt was blood-stained, he was exhausted, and appeared grateful for the offered cigarette as he was asked and answered questions. After a few questions the sheriff sent Harris to join his fellow bandits in jail. The police circled the jail Thursday night, and one officer was always on duty in the gang's cell block putting a stop to any thoughts of an escape attempt.

Thursday night W. E. Harris confessed to the bank robbery, and once he began talking he couldn't keep his mouth shut. Harris admitted he, Wilson, and Rosenberg had been staying at the Mack Island Hotel for several weeks with Stowe only joining them a few days ago. In fact, when the full story made the papers, there must have been a number of highly embarrassed Jacksonite big wigs. The bank robbers were wined and dined by Jackson County's Upper Crust who regularly vacationed at the hotel. The gangsters had dressed to the nines and passed themselves off as moneyed businessmen, although no one apparently thought to ask what kind of business. Many of the single young women at the resort were quite taken with the 'worldly tycoons,' and Kodak Brownies were busy snapping photos of the local beauties canoeing or sunning on the beach with the 'men of mystery.' The gangsters found that paying any attention to a woman was most often warmly returned and seldom rebuffed.

It seems very questionable that amidst all this fun one of the group had a light bulb go off in his head and thought, "let's rob a bank." He then dangled the idea before the rest of the group, and they gobbled it up hook, line, and sinker. It's even harder to swallow the idea that final plans for the bank job weren't made until the morning of the robbery. It was much easier to believe the mobsters planned on using the hotel for casing the bank, making the plans, and then hiding there in plain sight after the robbery. Later, Harris himself cast doubt on his earlier story when he admitted, "We did not think anyone would look for us at Mack Island. We thought we would be passed up as guests at the hotel. That is the reason we decided to divide the money in the tenant house instead of our rooms in the hotel." [3] It later came to light that Lester Bacon and George Comfort, the local men in the gang, had thoroughly cased the Farmer's State Bank before the rest of the gang arrived, and even convinced the other four bank robbers that the Mack Hotel on Wolf Lake was the perfect place to gather before the robbery and hide afterward. The two had probably written "Doc" Stowe and presented him with the complete plans for the robbery.

With the bank robbers in jail, a thorough investigation into all circumstances concerning the robbery and the death of Undersheriff Worden was undertaken. Early on Friday morning, Jackson State Prison Warden Hulbert showed up with a record clerk and fingerprint expert in tow and sat in on the questioning of the robbers in the county jail. The fingerprints and questioning quickly revealed that three of the gangsters had previously served time. Wilson was known under two aliases and had served terms in Indiana and in Illinois for highway robbery. Comfort had done hard time on four separate sentences, and Stowe had spent eight years in jail and had been free for little more than a year. No one admitted to shooting Worden, but the police believed Rosenberg had been the one to pull the trigger on the undersheriff.

The sheriff asked the public that if anyone found anything pertaining to the robbery to bring it to the jail. All the paper currency and securities had been found at the hotel, but two revolvers belonging to the gangsters were still missing as well as a quantity of gold and silver coins.

On Saturday, Walter Wilson underwent surgery for the removal of several bullets. Stowe also went to the hospital to have the dressing on his broken leg changed and was returned to the jail. There were no new developments in the case other than an incident that perplexed and annoyed the sheriff. Near noon on Saturday, a man from a nearby restaurant delivered six dinners neatly packaged in baskets for the six gangsters. The baskets contained roast beef, mashed potatoes, gravy, fresh tomatoes, onions, bread and butter and coffee. Each basket also contained tobacco and rolling papers. When questioned, the delivery man said a woman had ordered the meals for the prisoners. The sheriff begrudgingly allowed the prisoners to eat the catered dinner but wanted to know who ordered it. The woman was never identified, but in all likelihood it was the wife of Walter Wilson who arrived in Jackson on Friday but was not permitted to see her husband. The sheriff said he would allow it only if her husband were about to die of his wounds.

If the roast beef dinner raised the prisoners' spirits, further developments on Saturday might have had them asking for Pepto-Bismol. The Pennsylvania police identified W. E. Harris as being wanted for bank robbery in their state, for jumping a $10,000 bail for another bank robbery, and running whiskey. Evidently a man of many illegal talents and a multitude of failures, he had been arrested in Lansing for picking pockets and thrown out of town. His rap sheet listed a total of 24 arrests. Dave Rosenberg was wanted in Pennsylvania for murder, and the sheriff was looking into the possibility Rosenberg was also wanted on the same charge in Chicago. Walter Wilson had spent five years in a Missouri penitentiary and had been arrested in Chicago for burglary.

On November 9, 1921 "Doc" Stowe, W. E. Harris, and Galinski (Rosenberg's real name) received double life sentences. Repeated appeals for their parole were denied. A judge on one of the appeal boards observed that Harry Worden was still dead. Harris died a prisoner in 1952 at age 72. Comfort and Bacon were sentenced to 15–30 years and 10–20 years respectively. Comfort died in prison. Bacon was the only robber paroled. When Wilson was well enough to attend court, he too received a double life sentence.

Some $1,500 in gold and silver coins were never recovered, and it is generally agreed the loot was buried somewhere near the tenant house which has since been torn down and obliterated. The lost loot is described on several internet websites that list lost treasures. One can only imagine what the value of all those nearly 100-year-old gold and silver coins would be if a single 1920 U. S. $20 gold piece is worth more than $1,000 on today's market. The two revolvers dropped or thrown away by the robbers were also never found and are either at the bottom of the swamp or were picked up by souvenir hunters.

Undersheriff Harry Worden left behind a wife and three children: a boy 2, and girls 5 and 7. His wife was in poor health, and a committee was formed to raise funds for the family. According to Deputy Sheriff Walter Mayer, a close friend of Worden's, the undersheriff had a premonition of his coming death. About a week before the bank robbery he came to his friend and told him he had a feeling he was going to die suddenly and soon. He asked Mayer that in the event of his death to make sure his leather wallet got to his wife. Worden said it contained important documents he wanted his wife to have. He also told Mayer he had recently tried to buy more life insurance, but the company had turned him down. Funeral services for Worden were held on Sunday at 2 PM in the Worden home under Masonic auspices. The Bankers Association had offered a $5,000 reward for the capture of the Farmers State Bank robbers, and both Deputy Sheriffs Kutt and Loomis were to receive a share of the reward for their heroic work in capturing the six men. They both refused to accept any money and requested that Worden's widow get their shares.

1. Jackson Citizen Patriot 7-29-1920 p1, c1
2. IBID
3. Jackson Citizen Patriot 7-31-1920 p1, c3

Chapter 2

Bay City's Madaj Gang

January 15, 1921

"...an utter disregard for human life."

$\mathcal{B}$ ay City, the boisterous, often dangerous, hell-raising, and awash-in-alcohol lumbering town of the 1870s, where bordellos and shanghaied sailors were almost as common as sugar beet farms in the Thumb a hundred years later, had by World War I become, if not demure, at least more than semi-civilized. The town boasted quiet neighborhoods peopled by retired lumber barons and new money businessmen. And if, like every town, it had cultural and social rough edges, it was assumed by most residents they would soon be sanded smooth. Except for the still unsolved murder of lumber baron Franklin Parker, the town had, like most cities, grown used to the occasional crime. For Bay City that would abruptly change at the end of the First World War when a crime wave rippled through the city starting in the summer of 1919, then hit the town like a tsunami on the night of January 15, 1921. The event was both rooted in the past and presaged more crime and violence.

In 1916 Bay City's Center Avenue was lined with mansions built by the town's wealthiest inhabitants. It was a street where violent crime was as uncommon as a prayer meeting in a speakeasy. Or it was until September 3 when the wealthy Mr. Parker was enjoying his usual evening stroll under the maple-arched street when he was ordered to stick 'em up. The Harvard grad turned to look behind him for the impertinent voice even as he raised his cane to strike out at his assailant. He fell to the street shot twice and died 24 hours later. The only clue to the murder was that Parker was killed by a .32 caliber pistol stolen from a home the night of the shooting. The police chief was convinced it was not the doing of a professional robber. The case remained unsolved.

Parker's murder was not forgotten during the tumult of World War I, but it had become a cold case, especially with the heating up of crime following the war. On August 8, 1919, the Bay City Iron Works safe was cracked and $4,250 in Liberty bonds and saving stamps were taken. Three months later on November 7, 1919, the Breen Hardware Store was robbed of two rifles, eight pistols, and ammunition for the weapons. Just a day after the Breen robbery, two gunmen robbed a Bay City jewelry store. Shots were fired and the jeweler was wounded. In the same month on the nineteenth, four gunman with handkerchiefs pulled up over their faces took $200 from the safe of a Standard Oil service station and pistol whipped the employee before leaving. The beating was savage and unnecessary. As soon as the bandits left, the bludgeoned attendant stumbled from the filling station with blood streaming from several head wounds. He was treated and patched up at a local drug store.

Faced with a string of vicious and unsolved robberies, the police began to look at Steve Madaj and his circle of friends as the culprits behind the crime wave. Steve Madaj was a child of Bay City. Orphaned before he was a teen-ager, he raised himself and learned how to get by, by doing whatever it took to get by. In the war hysteria leading up to America's involvement in World War I, Madaj joined Bay City's 128th Ambulance Company and was shipped to Europe when America joined the fight. He served with the company for eighteen months. Apparently the young man didn't easily adjust to military life and on more than one occasion got crossways with military discipline, procedures, and protocol. He was sent home early while his unit stayed in Europe.

By 1919 the often out of work Steve Madaj was hanging out in a south side pool hall with other unemployed WWI vets. The pool room toughs, usually with Madaj in the lead, would often stop cars on the street and beg, swindle, or "borrow" money from drivers before they let the cars move on. The gang, with Madaj as their undisputed leader, felt the world owed them. And whatever they imagined the debt was, if it wasn't given, they were going to take it. The self-justification let them slip from petty crime to violent crime as easily as chalking a cue.

Claude Leonard, the Standard Oil gas station attendant who was beaten after the robbery, had seen a green Cadillac touring car drive up. He had started for the door, but two men from the big Caddie hurried into the station with guns drawn and left moments later with $200 and Leonard bleeding profusely. Leonard was sure two men stayed in the Cadillac while the other pair came into the station. The car proved to be the only real clue even after it was discovered it had been stolen. With the growing suspicion that Madaj and his friends might be responsible for the ballooning crime rate, two detectives were detailed to check out the WWI veteran. They learned Madaj got occasional work at a local farm, and the day after the Standard Oil robbery the two detectives drove a departmental Ford out to the farm to speak to Madaj only to become hopelessly stuck in a mud-filled track masquerading as a road.

A farm boy took great amusement in watching the two policemen struggle to get the old Ford unglued and delivered his opinion of the Ford with which the cops couldn't argue. The boy then dropped a bombshell when he said, "You ought to have a car like Steve Madaj. He's got a big green Cadillac that goes right through that stuff." [1] The Cadillac had been stolen three days prior to the robbery and found abandoned an hour after the stickup, but here was solid evidence that Madaj had the car for three days.

Later on the same day, a hungry Captain Ripsky of the Bay City police pushed open the door of a restaurant looking for a bite to eat and spotted Madaj having a late dinner. Ripsky walked up to Madaj and told him he would like to be talked to at police headquarters. Steve calmly replied he'd like to finish eating before heading over. At police headquarters Madaj was arrested and left to brood in a cell all night. The next afternoon after lengthy questioning he admitted to stealing the car, but he denied any part in the Standard Oil job. He claimed he was out driving the day of the robbery when a group of hunters hijacked the car. He couldn't be shaken from the story, and on December 9, 1921, he pleaded guilty to auto theft and was sentenced to eighteen months in Jackson State prison.

If police breathed a sigh of relief and Bay City relaxed a little thinking that with Steve Madaj gone the crime wave would subside, they were tragically proved wrong just 15 days into the New Year. The Bay County Savings, Broadway Branch, cashier Mr. Loll described the tragic event 15 years later in the magazine Master Detective. "It was approaching closing time, and my assistant William Grimmer and I were standing behind the cashier's desk. Grimmer was working on the books and I was talking to Mr. DeBats and Mr. [Labra] Persons… when suddenly the door burst open and three masked men, each carrying two revolvers, rushed in and yelled, 'Put 'em up!'

"They didn't wait an instant for us to obey but commenced to fire at once and both DeBats and Persons fell with the first volley. Half turning in their tracks, thinking someone was playing a joke, they both fell to the floor without a single word.

"One man remained on guard near the door and blazed away at everything in sight. The other two jumped over the counter into my office and pointing their guns at Grimmer and me, yelled, 'Get down on the floor, you _____ and don't move.' While one of them kept his gun trained on us, the other gathered up money lying loose upon the counter and the bag of pennies in the safe. While this was going on, I attempted to raise my head to catch a look at the fellows, but one of them fired a bullet into the floor a few inches from my face and growled, 'Keep down and lie still.'[2]

"There was a bandit outside the bank waiting in the car because all the while the three were in the bank I could hear shooting going on outside. As soon as they had gathered up all the money in sight, they told us to, 'stick where you are if you want to go on living,' and then dashed out of the bank."[3] Everyone in the bank heard the getaway car race down the street with the killers still firing from the fast moving car. The cashier called the police as soon as the bandits went out the door with $4,380 in loot.

A fraternal lodge owned or rented club space at the back of the bank building, and eight members were present when the shooting started. They knew immediately the bank was being robbed and poured out of the club running for the front of the building only to be met by the pistol-waving getaway driver who shouted for them to stay away. Two of the club members showed more bravery than discretion and failed to stop, so the driver opened fire with both pistols. A second robber then came out of the bank and began shooting at the lodge members. Miraculously, none of the men caught a bullet. There was a second witness to the attack on the club members from a man who lived next door to the bank. Hearing all the shooting, he looked out his window and saw a man standing beside the getaway car with a pistol in each hand firing down the street. He also saw a second robber emerge from the bank firing wildly and apparently without aiming at anything. Overcome with excitement or a huge adrenalin rush, the second hoodlum jumped up and down as he discharged each round.

The call from the bank to the Bay City Police was logged in at 8:45 PM during the evening shift roll-call. Cashier Loll told the shift captain about the robbery and that two men had been shot. Within minutes several police cars converged on the bank, and the officers had to push their way through the growing throng outside before facing the bloody aftermath of the robbery. The odor of gunpowder permeated the air, and the interior looked like it had been torn apart by gunfire. The focus of everyone in the bank was the two bodies, each in front of a teller's window, lying on the floor in pools of blood.

Physicians who rushed to aid the wounded discovered Mr. Persons had died instantly from a fatal shot to the head and a wound to the stomach. Martin L. DeBats had been hit three times. One round struck his shoulder, a second grazed his arm, and the third struck the left side of his head. The doctors could do nothing for him, and he died shortly after they arrived.

There were few clues or leads to follow. Four men of medium height all wearing ¾ length coats comprised the bank crew, and the getaway vehicle was a seven passenger Buick touring car. One woman remembered seeing two strange men hanging around the bank and the area the previous day. The week before the robbery, a large car had driven up just minutes after closing. Two men had jumped from the car and rattled the locked doors trying to gain entry before giving up, returning to the car, and driving off.

Bay City Police Chief Davis literally tried to cordon off the city and shut every street out of town. A lone automobile carrying unarmed men sped after the getaway car but gave up the chase at 28th and Broadway when the crooks fired at their pursuers. The police could easily follow the tire tracks of the Buick for several blocks until the car hit pavement and the tracks disappeared.

The police station was overrun by volunteers, and within two hours of the robbery, a hundred automobiles manned by armed, angry, and determined men—many of them carrying along a stout rope for the speedy application of justice—were combing the streets and roads in and around Bay City. Police tried to downplay any thoughts of a lynching party by the volunteers, but many of the private cars hunting the killers carried more than enough rope to string up all four robbers. That seemed more than likely for a few frenzied minutes when the Sisters of St. James Convent called the police to report a car had been abandoned on their grounds and four men had been seen fleeing from the car and running south on Jackson. When the police arrived, closely followed by volunteers, the engine was still warm, the car was in gear, and all four doors gaped open. But an intense search of the neighborhood south of the convent turned up nothing. Police quickly learned the car had been stolen earlier that night.

Throughout the night and into the morning, the police monitored every road between Bay City and Saginaw, and police in both Saginaw and Flint were asked to be on the lookout for the car and killers. Suspects were hauled in from gin mills, pool halls, bordellos, and blind pigs. Anyone even looking suspicious was taken to the county jail and questioned. Within hours of the robbery and murders, people began to gather outside police headquarters hoping to hear the criminals were in custody. The crowd continued to grow until it almost engulfed the building.

On Sunday morning the murderers still remained at large, and the police and volunteers who had joined the search were exhausted. They were replaced by more eager volunteers wanting a part in capturing the killers. Yet as Sunday evening slipped into darkness, the police and hundreds of volunteers had not uncovered any new clues. Hundreds of suspects had been questioned, and investigators had come up with nothing.

The police firmly believed the bank crew was from Bay City, or the immediate area, and hadn't left town. Rewards were posted that eventually reached $15,000, and the police again scoured the city in search of the killers. The police were also becoming convinced that the robbery was pulled off by Steve Madaj's gang, but there was no evidence on which to either arrest or hold them.

There might not be any solid evidence or even a promising lead, but there was a whole truck load of cop intuition and gut feeling that kept pointing a finger at Madaj's gang. It became evermore apparent to the entire law enforcement community they needed to bring Steve Madaj back to Bay City to stand trial for the Standard Oil robbery. It was the feeling of both the police and the prosecutor that the trial could lead to breaking open the bank robbery, in part because there were so many little similarities in how the bandits operated in both crimes.

Judge Houghton asked the governor to return Madaj to Bay City to stand trial. The convicted car thief had been a model prisoner at Jackson and told the warden he was eager to help the police capture the bank robbers. Steve Madaj was back in the Bay County jail on January 21, 1921. He was quickly taken to see Judge Houghton who told him law enforcement officials knew he took part in the Standard Oil robbery and asked him who else was on the crew. If he cooperated the law would go easy on him, and if he named names on the bank robbery the judge would make sure he got the $15,000 in reward money.

Steve Madaj's response to the judge's overture was a lengthy concoction of outlandish nonsense and lies about driving around the night of the Standard Oil robbery when he happened to give a lift to three men he didn't know. He couldn't remember their names but admitted that after driving them around one of them suggested they rob the Standard station. Madaj went along with them but didn't know who they were, and he split from the three immediately after the crime. Judge Houghton politely told him he was full of baloney and he wouldn't waste any more time talking to him. He was returned to the county jail where local detectives spent hours questioning him, but he stuck to his story like super glue. Tired of lie after lie, the police were ready to throw in the towel on Madaj and ship him back to Jackson when he surprised everyone. On January 24, 1921, he appeared before Circuit Court Judge Houghton and pleaded guilty to the Standard Oil holdup and complicity in the Breen Hardware robbery but said, in both crimes, he only drove the car and did not know any of his accomplices. The police were at a dead end without Madaj's help.

The big break in the bank robbery case came unexpectedly a day later. The police picked up a young man and took him to a hotel for questioning. The police got nothing from him and asked Assistant Prosecuting Attorney Dell H. Thompson if he wanted a crack at the kid. Thompson jumped at the opportunity but wanted to question the man alone. The Assistant D. A., an imposingly large man who could assume a gruff demeanor, walked into the room and badgered, questioned, threatened, and finally promised both immunity and that the young man's name would never come to light if he came clean. The kid cracked like a raw egg and spilled everything.

As X told it, the bank robbery had been planned before Madaj was sent to prison for stealing the car and postponed. But the gang grew desperate for money and decided to pull the job on the 7th only to arrive at the bank after closing. So the bank robbery was postponed until the fifteenth. The unidentified informant named five robbers and said he had been dropped from the crew at the last minute because Kubiak, who had risen to leader after Madaj's incarceration, thought him a coward. Detectives were dispatched to investigate the five men, and all came back with the news that for out-of-work men they were spending a lot of money on new clothes, watches, and luxury items.

The five men were arrested and, to lessen the threat of a mob lynching, jailed in a variety of locales. Aloysius Nowak and Ramon Olejniczak were locked up in Saginaw; Edward Walkowiak was placed behind bars in Caro, Stanley Delestowicz in the Bay City jail, and Stephen Kubiak in the county jail. It was no accident Kubiak found himself in a cell a floor directly above Madaj and that Assistant D. A. Thompson knew it was possible to communicate between the two cells. As expected, none of the cocky young thieves admitted to anything. Knowing that Kubiak and Madaj would talk to each other and probably in Polish, Thompson hired a stenographer who spoke the language, dressed him like a bum, and put him in a cell next to Madaj's. The two crooks talked endlessly about the stickup, and the stenographer took it all down in shorthand. The Assistant D. A. ended up with all the details of the bank robbery from the robbers themselves.

Confronted by Thompson with the entire story of the bank robbery and gas station stickup from the transcripts of his conversations with Madaj, Kubiak realized he was up to his neck in legal quicksand. He confessed and gave complete details of the bank robbery and the Standard Oil job. Kubiak even told how they were getting out of the car in front of the bank when DeBats, still in his grocer's apron, walked in ahead of the robbers and made the thieves momentarily pause which provoked Nowak to say, "I'll teach DeBats a lesson for hanging around a bank when I want to transact business." [4] Nowak infuriated the police by saying he was justified in killing both men. Madaj, faced with the others' confessions, stuck to his story of the Standard Oil robbery.

Fearing mob violence, the gang's trial was secretly scheduled for 1:30 AM. When the judge gaveled the court to order, there were 200 people packed into the room and standing outside in the court house halls. After the five confessed, Nowak, Olejniczak, and Kubiak received life sentences at hard labor at Marquette State Prison. The sentencing of Walkowiak and Delestowicz were deferred. The three headed for Marquette were immediately shackled and dispatched by a waiting police car to Kawkawlin where they boarded a Michigan Central Railroad train for shipment to the U.P. prison.

The prisoners bound for Marquette, still unaware that a Polish speaking stenographer had been planted in the jail cell next to Madaj, were convinced someone had informed on them. Nowak felt certain Madaj had turned them in for the reward. Before boarding the train at Kawkawlin, Nowak approached a guard and told him he wasn't going to let Madaj get away with anything and said Steve Madaj had killed Franklin Parker on September 9, 1916, and Stanley Delestowicz was with Madaj at the time.

When the guard returned to Bay City, he rushed to tell Sheriff Trudell of Nowak's accusation. The sheriff had Delestowicz in an interview room within two hours, and after three days of relentless questioning, Delestowicz broke, signed a confession, and was escorted to Madaj's cell where he pointed at Madaj as the killer of the lumber baron. Madaj refused to talk, and his trial for first degree murder was set for March 14, 1921. On March 6 guards foiled an escape attempt by Madaj, and just two days later it was discovered the prisoner had nearly sawn through three metal hinges of the cell door. On March 17 both men were found guilty of murder. Madaj was sentenced to two life terms in Marquette, and Delestowicz received 10–20 years.

Madaj hadn't spent a year at Marquette before he escaped and made it to a nearby swamp where he was recaptured. His freedom totaled less than 30 minutes. On being escorted back to his cell, Madaj told his guards no prison could hold him. He backed up his words on April 21, 1923, when he again made it over the prison walls with another convict, Russell Smith, and this time he made good his escape. He and Smith hopped freights across the U.P. and down through Wisconsin and made it to Chicago. There the mob got him a gun and a car. One shudders at what the mob got from Madaj as a return in services. In spite of a determined search by the authorities, when Madaj made his second escape, he simply disappeared without a trace. Months passed and rumors circulated that he had been seen in Bay City but when checked out always proved false.

Then there he was at 2:15 PM on June 18, 1924, fourteen months after escaping from Marquette, walking into the Kosciuszko Branch of the Bay City Savings Bank with another man. Madaj vaulted over the railing to stand in front of cashier Michael Dardas and shouted, "Stick 'em up, and hurry." [5]

The second man had the customers and bank personnel line up facing a wall with their hands in the air while Madaj bound Dardas' wrists with copper wire. Madaj evidently knew Dardas because he asked him by name where the money was kept. When Dardas directed Madaj to the safe, the escaped convict began stuffing his pockets. At this point in the robbery, the second robber became unhappy with a customer who had only raised his hands to shoulder height and yelled at him raise them higher. Madaj paused pocketing the money and told his companion just to shoot the man if he didn't follow orders. The bank captives were convinced Madaj, himself, would have pulled the trigger if any of them didn't reach for the ceiling.

After the two hoodlums emptied the safe, the seven customers and the employees were locked in the vault, and the two robbers ran to a waiting Hudson Touring car. With a getaway driver at the wheel, the car sped away from the bank. Someone must have pushed a silent alarm because the police arrived in time to give chase and followed the highwaymen through town and east into the Thumb area on back roads. The three gangsters finally shook the police near Caro, Michigan. For three months not a trace of Madaj or the other bank robbers could be found.

On September 12, 1924, Henry Nellett and his two young sons were loading hay stored in a barn on a non-working farm near Bay City. While their dad worked, the two boys went exploring the deserted farm. When they happened to look in the garage window, they saw a car and ran to tell their dad. Henry went to investigate, and as he neared the garage, an armed man stepped from the house and told Mr. Nellett not to come any closer. Nellett recognized Steve Madaj and asked what he was doing there. Madaj, in front of the father's two boys, answered with his gun. He fired twice; both rounds hit Nellett, and he died as he fell to the ground. The terrified boys ran for the barn and hid in the hay. After an hour passed, they crawled out from under the hay and ran to the nearest phone where they called police who rushed to the scene of Madaj's second known murder.

Again the killer vanished. Tips flooded in that placed him in Flint, Detroit, Kalamazoo, and Chicago, but the man was always gone. Well not always. The day Madaj's crew drove into Chicago, the police made it so hot he left that night and hitch-hiked back to Bay City. The Chicago police had confiscated his car and even his gun. Madaj happened to be sitting on the porch of his rooming house in the Windy City, on the day of his arrival, when the police walked up on the porch looking for Madaj and didn't recognize him. The killer kept up a running conversation as the large police detail filed into the house then crept away as the cops went through every room looking for him.

Then on October 15, 1924, a Bay City resident tipped off Sheriff Trudell that Madaj was staying at a the home of an old school friend. Trudell gathered a posse, surrounded the house, and charged through the front door to find the tired, hungry killer at the kitchen table eating. He went peacefully to jail denying he'd killed Nellett. Madaj said his partners, Eugene Isaacson and Al Demock of Flint were the killers. Nellett's boys looked through the bars of Madaj's cell and identified him as their father's killer.

With the news of his capture, huge crowds jammed the hallways of the jail, and a long line snaked out of the building and down the street. Madaj asked the sheriff to permit the public to walk by his cell and take a look. In the three days he spent confined in the Bay County jail, an estimated 2,000 people passed by his cell, and it couldn't help but be noted that many young women had left work early to ogle the famous killer.

What do you do with an escaped killer serving two life sentences who killed again in cold blood? Send him back to prison is all—it's as if he had been given a free pass for murder. When he did get back to Marquette, he spent long periods in solitary confinement. And in what seems, from this distance, to be a complete miscarriage of justice, three of the four men who robbed the Bay County Savings in which two customers were killed in cold blood were released from prison within ten years. Only Nowak, who proved to be anything but a model prisoner, remained in Marquette State Prison.

In 1924 it was taken for granted by the law enforcement community that if Madaj were ever pardoned for the killing of Parker in 1916 he would face trial for Nellett's murder. In 1931 Madaj's third attempt at a prison escape was foiled when homemade guns, bombs, and a rope ladder were discovered in his cell. The cell's bars had been sawed through when guards put an end to the attempt.

Madaj was transferred to Jackson on July 1, 1944. He was fifty years old and worked as an electrician. He tried repeatedly for parole and was repeatedly turned down. In the early 1960s World War I veterans began circulating petitions in Bay City supporting his parole. In 1962 Governor John B. Swainson surprisingly commuted Madaj's sentence, and the two-time killer walked free. Some have said it was a political move by the governor, who was up for re-election, to gain votes in the Bay City area.

Not everyone was pleased to see Madaj gain his freedom. Circuit Court Judge Leon R. Dardas wrote the governor saying, "…he had serious and strenuous objections to the release of this man." [6] Judge Dardas, whose father had his hands bound in wire by Madaj during the June 1924 robbery, further noted Madaj had killed Henry Nellett in front of his sons, and Dardas' father had died with the still livid scars from the wire used on his wrists. He concluded, "The prisoner's entire record both in and out of prison shows a definite inclination to violence and an utter disregard for human lives." [7] Nellett's sons were so upset they went to prosecutor Marty Legatz's office after Madaj's release and demanded he be tried for their father's murder. Legatz said he couldn't because no witnesses were still alive. When the boys said they would kill Madaj, the prosecutor threatened he would then have to try them for murder.

Many of the young woman who filed by Steve Madaj in the county jail after his capture for bank robbery and the killing of Nellett looked upon the killer as a romantic figure. One such star-struck girl was 14-year-old hair dresser Violet Eichhorn. She wrote Madaj while he was in prison and married him upon his release. They lived a peaceful life and were married for 15 years. Violet died in 1977, and Madaj followed her to the grave in 1979. They are buried side-by-side in Bay City's Elm Lawn Cemetery.

1. Master Detective V14, #6 8-1936 p34 "Cobra's of Crime" By Theodore Trudell
2. IBID p73
3. IBID
4. Master Detective V 15, #1 9-1936 p66 "Cobra's of Crime" By Theodore Trudell
5. Master Detective V 15, #2 10-1936 p52 "Cobra's of Crime" By Theodore Trudell
6. Rogers, D. Lawrence Ghosts, Crimes & Urban Legends p57
7. IBID

Chapter 3

The Bungalow on Weaver Street

December 7, 1921

"There was just something hinky about the whole situation."

*D*ecember 7, 1941, will always carry a train load of emotional and historical baggage for the American people. President Roosevelt called it, "A date that will live in infamy." Twenty-one years earlier on the very same date, the City of Grand Rapids also came under attack, and although the losses were significantly smaller, they were no less emotionally devastating and heartlessly cruel.

At 2:10 PM on December 7, 1921, a gang of armed men stepped out of an automobile and into the Michigan Exchange Branch of the Grand Rapids Savings Bank and walked out a few minutes later with $14,817.71. The bank robbery went off without a hitch; one local man sitting in a car outside the bank waiting for a friend didn't even realize a robbery had taken place. The mayhem, the tragedy, and the grief spawned by the bank robbery were just waiting down the road. And closure? It's still someplace out there in southern Michigan and given up hope that the last act in this tragedy will ever be played out.

The heist went off like it was a model of how a bank was supposed to be held up. If one of the thugs had brought a motion picture camera and recorded the robbery, it could have been used as a training film. Four bandits walked into the bank on Wednesday afternoon and immediately took control. Neither the bank manager, R. A. Westrate, nor the teller, Cornelius DeMaagd, knew their place of business was being robbed until one of the thugs walked into Westrate's office and said, "Put 'em up." [1]

The bandits ordered the teller, manager and the bookkeeper, Abel VanderWoude, to the back of the bank at gun point and made them face a wall. Two bank customers were invited to join the employees at the back of the bank while the robbers cleaned out the teller's cage. When two customers wandered in to conduct business, they too ended up studying the wall at the back of the bank with the original five.

Once the cage was empty, the bandits ordered the manager to open the safe. They then marched the bankers and their customers into the small 8 x 10 open vault which didn't hold any money, just the bank records. With the safe empty, the thugs tried to close the vault door with the seven men inside but couldn't get the door to shut tight. After a couple of tries, they gave up on subtlety and repeatedly tried to slam it shut. They finally got it to lock, but the door remained slightly ajar. Those inside couldn't open it, but the crack permitted fresh air to flow into the cramped quarters and made it much easier to call for help as soon as the crooks left—which they didn't do immediately. Throughout, the bandits seemed to be highly professional and models of efficiency. They didn't work as if rushed but went about looting the bank without raising a sweat and disappeared as quietly and unobtrusively as they arrived.

Mr. Nicholas Veenkamp watched the bandits leave the bank but didn't realize it had been robbed until his brother-in-law ran out of the bank with the news. A Grand Rapids fireman was even sitting in a car in front of the bank during the robbery without knowing what was going on inside until it was over.

By the time the men in the vault were let out, which was only minutes, the crooks were blocks away speeding for their hideout. Police flooded the area around the bank; every detective on the force was at the bank, and all patrolmen were told to be on the lookout for suspicious characters. The county sheriff telephoned neighboring towns asking them to watch for the bandits or a car carrying them. In spite of all this police activity, the law wasn't even close to catching up with the gangsters.

The bandits had made a clean getaway with no one in pursuit and were barreling through Grand Rapids in a Buick when the getaway driver took an unnecessary chance, rolled the dice, and lost. The man behind the wheel of the Buick bet he could beat a Michigan Central freight train to a railroad crossing. At 2:20 PM, just ten minutes after robbing the bank, the Buick collided with the freight train at the Hall St. crossing and was crumpled up and tossed aside like an empty pack of cigarettes. Miraculously, none of the bandits were killed on impact, and the most grievously injured only suffered a deep facial wound. Onlookers rushed to help pull the men from the mangled Buick and were surprised when the passengers began to extract themselves from the automobile. Those who came to help included Mr. A. J. Gerard who helped pull men from the wreck and even offered to drive the worst hurt passenger to the hospital. Mr. Henry J. Gelger also stopped to help, and surprise turned into utter amazement when the Buick's occupants drew pistols, hijacked Mr. Gelger's automobile, and disappeared driving down the street.

When the police arrived, they looked through the Buick and found three hats and an overcoat. When they checked the license plate number with the state, they discovered the car had been stolen two weeks earlier in Grand Rapids.

The hijacked auto was a Cadillac touring car, and police expected the bandits were making tracks for the city limits and meant to put as many miles as possible between them and Grand Rapids. Instead, the gang headed to a safe house they had rented in Grand Rapids where they planned to lay low until the heat of the hunt cooled down.

The trouble with laying low began well before they robbed the bank. The gang moved into the Weaver Street bungalow a week before the robbery and immediately stuck out like Mae West at a convent. The men never left the house together. They stayed up very late and slept until noon. When they did emerge from the house, it was in ones or twos. None of them seemed to have a job, and although everyone in the neighborhood was nearly positive four men lived in the house, the four were never seen together. Then there was the car that arrived at the house every evening and left about midnight. The occupants also didn't have the electricity turned on and lit the house at night with a kerosene lamp or two.

The owner of the house, Mrs. Edna Horner had asked Charles Williams, a local salesman, to handle the business side of renting her little bungalow on Weaver St. which he did to a pretty blonde woman in the last week of November. On paper it was rented to a Mr. & Mrs. Charles E. Walker of Flint. Then on the very day of the bank robbery, Mrs. Horner asked Mr. Williams to go over to the house and retrieve a few things she'd left behind. Little did Williams know he was tempting fate and putting his life at risk when, barely three hours after the robbery, he went to the Weaver Street house at 5:30 PM. It was dark when he arrived and the house showed only one dim light inside. He was on the little front porch and fumbling for the key to the front door when it was thrown open by big, ornery looking yahoo who yelled, "What in the hell do you want?" [2]

Williams with more courage than common sense explained he'd come to pick up some things for the owner, and in spite of being sworn at again, he slipped past the ill-tempered hulk and into the house. Williams headed for the dining room, lit by a kerosene lamp, but the man at the door quickly stepped in front of him and said, "Stay where you are kid, if you know what's good for you."[3]

Williams asked why the electricity wasn't turned on and tried to head for the back room when he saw a hand reach out from inside the dining room and shut the door. Still not spooked, Williams managed to get his hands on a couple of the owner's belongings and then headed for the basement saying he'd left a wrench down there. Mr. Intimidation finally got through to Williams when he told the salesman to forget about the wrench and more or less get the hell out of the house—now. Williams was lucky to leave the house with his shoes kicking up dust motes rather than pointing skyward from the end of a gurney. He never connected the suspicious activity to the bank robbery but thought they might be bootleggers.

Mr. A. J. Gerard was late getting home that night and understandably so. He was one of the men who witnessed the car/train collision and the extraordinary events that followed. And in one of the richest ironic twists of fate in the history of Michigan bank robberies, he lived across the street from the bungalow at 355 Weaver Street where all the strange goings on had kept neighbors guessing and enthralled for the past week.

When he finally reached home a little before eight, his mother-in-law filled him in on the latest activities across the street which included watching two men walk to the house that afternoon by cutting through a field while carrying a large satchel. Then a few minutes later a third man came to the house by riding a street car. Mr. Gerard felt there was just something hinky about the whole situation, and with the bank robbery in mind he called the police and reported the suspicious activity. The police, over the last few hours, had been inundated with tips and leads that hadn't paid off and their investigation had gone nowhere, but this tip—like all the rest—had to be checked out.

Detective Samuel Slater was handed the job of following up on Gerard's call. The detective was an experienced cop and had been shot at more than once. The most recent had occurred only two years previously when he answered a domestic dispute call. When walking up to the house, a shot was fired that passed through the closed front door and fortunately missed him. Slater was convinced the tip would come to nothing, but as per procedures took along Special Officer George Brandsma as back up. Slater left the police station with a smile creasing his face as he told fellow officers, "Well, we'll go over and look her over. There's nothing to be gained, I know, but that's our business." [4] When the pair arrived on Weaver Street, they talked to Gerard, watched the house for a few minutes (which appeared completely dark), then decided to cross the street and knock on the door.

Detective Slater was climbing the porch steps when someone in the house fired twice. The bullets passed through the closed front door and tore through Slater's body. As Slater staggered backward from the impact of the bullets, Officer Brandsma, without drawing his side arm, charged past his partner, crashed through the still-closed front door, and was met with a hail of gunfire. Two bullets struck Brandsma's heart and a third pierced his skull. Any one of the three would have killed him instantly. When Gerard heard the gunshots, he immediately called the police.

Officer Slater somehow managed to stumble back across the street, and Gerard met him at the door of his house and helped him into a chair. As blood poured from two abdominal wounds and lacerated intestines, Slater murmured, "They got me. We didn't have a chance. I'm afraid I'm done for." [5] When reinforcements arrived, along with an ambulance, Slater was rushed to the hospital. His wife was already there when the ambulance crew wheeled Slater in on a gurney, and she stood at his side as a priest administered last rights. The critically wounded man was then rushed into surgery.

Immediately after the shooting, neighbors watched three men and a blonde woman run from the bungalow, in which Officer Brandsma lay dead, to the detached garage. The foursome pushed a large touring car from the building, cranked it to life, and sped west down Weaver. Moments after the touring car roared away, a fourth man was observed leaving the house, jumping in a small, closed car hidden in back of the bungalow, and racing after the touring car.

The police arrived at the now empty house en masse and were soon joined by carloads of volunteers looking to help. Police discovered a partially eaten and obviously interrupted meal on the dining room table with bonds, traveler's checks, and some cash sharing the table with the food. Like a few hours before, when Williams barraged into the house, a lone kerosene lamp on the dining room table provided the only light. Close the dining room door, and it would look from the outside like the house was completely dark.

The civilians wanting to help were directed to police headquarters where more than fifty were armed with Springfield rifles and sent to hunt the robbers. The armed bands blanketed the surrounding countryside during the night and failed to find the killers or any trace of them. By 8 AM on Thursday morning, all members of the impromptu posse had returned to the police station and handed in the rifles and ammunition. The police also worked through the night running down every new tip and lead.

The Grand Rapids Superintendent of Police contacted every town within 200 miles asking them to be on the lookout for the bandits. Sheriffs in adjoining counties conducted extensive patrols, and a couple of suspects, including a blonde woman, were briefly questioned and released. The hundreds of man hours and hundreds of miles of patrols went for naught. It was as if the killers had disappeared into thin air.

That didn't stop the wildest of rumors from circulating through the city and from appearing in out-of-town newspapers. Stories were printed across the state that the bandits were seen here, there, and everywhere. It was reported the robbers were involved in a running shootout before being captured. The United Press even ran a story the gang was headed to Detroit when it was met by an Ingham County posse and three people were killed. Bradley, Plainwell, and Pine Lake all claimed to be where a battle was fought between the gang and the law. All were unfounded and false. Things got even more confused when the police thought they caught the mysterious blonde, then within a couple of days announced they had abandoned the whole idea there was ever a blonde involved in the robbery or its planning.

Throughout Thursday Detective Slater clung to life. On Thursday afternoon it was reported that Slater had only minutes to live, yet on Friday morning he still drew breath. Friday December 9, 1921, Samuel Slater turned fifty-three; he died that afternoon at 2:30 PM in Grand Rapids' St. Mary's Hospital. Slater had three daughters. The oldest had been in the act of buying her dad a Christmas present when she was informed he'd been shot.

George Brandsma was 38 and the father of five, the youngest only 15 months old, and had said good night to his family just two hours before his murder. The dedicated cop and family man had been promoted to Special Officer of the Night Squad only a month before. Brandsma had a $500 life insurance policy, and both his and Slater's wife would receive $50 a month in compensation from the city. The Grand Rapids Savings Bank paid off the mortgage on the Brandsma house and paid all funeral expenses for both officers. A $2,000 gift was also given to both slain officer's families.

Samuel Slater and George Brandsma are both on the internet's "Officer Down Memorial Page" which honors law enforcement officers killed in the line of duty. Only one of the armed robbers has ever been identified. Odds are better than good that the killers continued to rob banks, and like most bank robbers were eventually caught and served time. Still, after almost a hundred years, the murders of these two public servants begs for justice and closure.

The one man captured and convicted of the robbery was Leo Bolger, the driver of the getaway car. He was sentenced to life imprisonment in Jackson State Prison, but that is not the end of his story. He was later transferred to Marquette State Prison where he became the inmate assistant nurse and was an innocent witness, victim, and hero of the bloodiest day in the history of the U.P. prison.

Andrew Germano, Martin Duver, and Charles Rosbury, three Detroit criminal hard cases serving long-term sentences at Marquette, worked out an escape plan that involved smuggling revolvers into the prison in cans of precooked chicken and gravy. On August 27, 1931, the trio faked medical complaints and received passes to the inmate infirmary. Germano, who complained of a sore stomach, was the first to see Dr. A. W. Hornbogen, who for years had provided free medical services to the inmates. Germano had a revolver hidden in his waist band, and when Dr. Hornbogen asked him to take off his shirt to be examined, the convict shot him dead. Also in the examining room with the doctor were inmate nurse Frank Oligschlager and inmate assistant Leo Bolger. When the fatal shot was fired, Oligschlager swatted the gun out of Germano's hand. Martin Duver was in the waiting room. Upon hearing the shot, Martin burst into the room, pulled his gun, and shot Oligschlager in the abdomen. Bolger then entered the fray by picking up a medical instrument and throwing it at Germano, Duver then turned and put a bullet in the inmate assistant. Oligschlager would take sixteen hours to die. The unaccountably lucky Bolger quickly recovered.

The three convicts left the blood-splattered examination room and its victims and wreaked havoc for the next hour or so as they ran through the prison, shooting at guards, the warden, and taking hostages. Unable to shoot their way out of the prison, the three finally barricaded themselves on the third floor of an industrial building. They battled prison guards, the state police, and Marquette city police until the warden had tear gas fired into the floor. Knowing escape was hopeless, the three convicts committed suicide.

Michigan governor William Brucker, in recognition of their brave and selfless efforts to protect Dr. Hornbogen and contain the escape, posthumously commuted the sentence of Frank Oligschlager and commuted Leo Bolger's sentence to immediate release with the condition that he find employment. Unfortunately, it is not known what Leo Bolger did with his unexpected second chance to make a life for himself.

1. Grand Rapids Press 12-7-1921 p1, c8
2. Grand Rapids Press 12-8-1921 p2, c3
3. IBID
4. IBID
5. IBID

Chapter 4

An Eau Claire Welcome: Come for a Day Spend a Lifetime

April 4, 1922

"The big car tore down the dusty main drag under a barrage of small arms fire..."

*M*ike Frankovitz of Gary, Indiana, regularly traveled to the quiet, peaceful, southwestern Michigan town of Eau Claire to visit with relatives. On what would turn out to be his last visit to the small town, which was and is rarely the talk of the state or even the county, all hell broke loose. Eau Claire made headlines and front page news in papers across the Midwest. Mike Frankovitz, 35, was not only at the epicenter of what would be one of the most exciting and memorable chapters in the town's history; he was the one responsible for the whole hullabaloo.

On his many visits to Eau Claire, Frankovitz became taken with the idea of robbing the Eau Claire State Bank. Back in Gary he sold the idea of hitting the bank to three fellow employees at the factory where he worked.

The quartet traveled to Elkhart, Indiana, and stole a Pratt, 6-cylinder touring car and drove to Eau Claire where they cased the bank and explored the local roads to plan their getaway. On April 4, 1922, at 9:15 AM, the big Pratt pulled up and stopped in front of the Eau Claire State Bank.

Frankovitz and another man got out and entered the bank. That left two men sitting in the car, in front of the bank, with the motor running while they stared intently at the bank door, all of which instantly raised suspicion and alertness among neighboring shop owners.

When the two robbers walked into the bank, they yelled for everybody to raise their hands—which included the bank president Homer Hess, cashier Kenneth Talman, an assistant cashier, and a bank clerk. Mr. Hess showed some hesitation or confusion in complying with the order and was rewarded with two pistols jammed in his face. That quickly got his attention and cleared up any confusion, and his hands went for the ceiling. Hess was ordered to walk over to where the other bank employees stood, and as he made his way toward them, he slightly stumbled. The lurch produced a reflex reaction in one of the bandit's trigger fingers, the revolver fired, and Hess suffered a slight flesh wound to the stomach.

The shot sent everyone in the bank into a semi panic, but someone among the employees kept their head enough to step on a floor alarm as the two bandits began furiously grabbing money from the tellers' windows and stuffing it in a large leather satchel. The take in the mad rush for cash came to $1,185 with more than $3,000 in cash left sitting in plain sight and overlooked the by the crooks.

The crack of the gunshot from inside the bank left the locals in no doubt that their bank was being robbed, and within moments the Pratt came under fire. The two men in the car drew their pistols and returned fire even as additional townsfolk picked up shotguns or hunting rifles and began plunking holes in the big touring car. As the firefight heated to a fever pitch, the two inside men ran from the bank and piled into the Pratt. Whoever was at the wheel had the car moving before the last of the two landed in the backseat. The big car tore down the dusty main drag under a barrage of small arms fire and made it out of the city with none of the four bandits buying a bullet or even being nicked.

The Pratt was still in sight as the men of Eau Claire climbed into a dozen automobiles and gave chase. The posse's lead car was soon close enough that a running gun battle broke out between the dogged pursuers and the robbers. The rifleman in the posse's lead car holed the Pratt repeatedly and kicked up road dust as he unsuccessfully tried to shoot out the Pratt's tires.

If the ire of the Eau Claire populous quickly boiled over and led to immediate action, it was matched by the inspired and lightning response of Mrs. Jack Claxton who happened to be on duty at the local telephone switchboard. With shots ringing out in her town, she knew the bank was being robbed and, like everyone else in Eau Claire, had no idea in which direction the thieves were headed. That missing piece of information was of no concern to Mrs. Claxton, she simply opened every telephone line at her disposal and shouted to the world, "The Eau Claire bank has been robbed and the bandits are headed your way."[1] It was like calling out the Minute Men. All over the county, men dropped everything they were doing, picked up the nearest gun, and rushed to throw up road blocks at critical junctions.

The bandits had headed south for Berrien Center on M-140. They were probably on their way to Niles and then the state line, but as the Pratt roared into little Berrien Center with bandits hanging out the windows and brandishing pistols, they discovered the handiwork of Mrs. Claxton. The townspeople had erected a barricade that would have made the set designer of Les Miserables proud. Wagons, crates, boxes, and lumber piled several feet high closed off M-140, and crouching behind a nearby fence, a line of armed men checked their ammunition and made ready to complete the job of turning the Pratt and its passengers into a colander on four wheels. The crooks might not have employed the best judgment when it came to deciding to rob a bank, but it didn't take any decision making skills to realize they had to get the hell out of Berrien Center PDQ. The

Pratt skidded into a 180-degree turn and headed back out of town toward Eau Claire and a well-armed posse hurdling their way.

Half way back to Eau Claire, the fleeing outlaws turned onto a side road they hoped would take them around the town. They didn't get very far down the road before the Pratt hit a mud hole you could lose a mule in and became hopelessly stuck as it sank past the axles. The robbers knew the car was of no further use and abandoned it, but only after trying to burn it by dropping lighted matches into the gas tank and passenger compartment. The ad hoc posse arrived at the scene before the car was fully aflame and, at no little risk to themselves, put the fire out.

While the posse was busy with the burning car, the four bank robbers took off across country, heading for deep cover in a Tamarack swamp. The Eau Claire posse stood around the smoldering Pratt trying to figure out in which direction the outlaws had fled when a local farmer climbed his windmill, took a long look around and spotted the bandit quartet making their way through the swamp. A shout and an outstretched arm ending in a pointing finger had the 50-man posse off and running toward the swamp.

The bandits must have known their situation was beginning to look hopeless because it wasn't long before Henry Griffin, 24, either volunteered—or picked the short straw—and became the gang's rear guard, saddled with slowing down their pursuers. Not long after leaving Griffin behind, the other three outlaws discovered they had run up against a river and were cornered.

When Henry Griffin dropped back and looked for a well concealed hiding place from which to snipe at the approaching posse, he didn't know until it was over that he had set himself up for a personal duel with Earl Wymer, widely acknowledged as an expert marksman. To make it even worse, Griffin had a revolver while Wymer carried a high-powered hunting rifle.

While Griffin ducked and weaved from cover to cover and fired his revolver with virtually no hope of even coming close enough to make Wymer seek cover, the marksman hammered half a dozen rounds at the elusive robber. When Wymer blew a chuck out of Griffin's arm, the outlaw threw down his gun and surrendered.

With Griffin down and on his way to a doctor and jail, the posse drew the knot even tighter around the three remaining crooks. When the trio wouldn't surrender, the 50 men in the posse rose up and laced the woods where it was thought the three were hiding with withering fire. The fusillade thoroughly chewed up the scenery and convinced the bank robbers they didn't stand a chance. They threw down their guns and walked out of the swamp with hands above their heads. The men were taken to the county jail while a search was conducted for the stolen money. It was thought the robbers had buried their loot in the swamp, but it couldn't be found. When questioned, the prisoners said they had left the money in the Pratt. The police found the leather satchel used to carry the money out of the bank but no money. If the crooks had buried the money in the swamp in hopes of retrieving it at a later date, it would be a long wait.

When the police and prosecuting attorney checked into the men's backgrounds in Gary, they were convinced the four were professional bank robbers who used their factory jobs as cover for their real careers. Three weeks shy a day of the robbery, on April 24, Mike Frankovitz, George Ellis, Elmo Evans, and Henry Griffin pleaded guilty to bank robbery, and each received a 30–35 year sentence in a state prison. What was supposed to be a short trip to Michigan turned into a very long stay.

1. Myers, Robert C., Historical Sketches of Berrien County. Berrien County Historical Assoc. 2009. Berrien Springs, MI p156.

Chapter 5

The Metamora Job

June 1, 1922

"...the two weapons unleashed 1,000 rounds into the thicket..."

O mar Potter, assistant cashier of the Metamora State Bank, thought it was just going to be another normal transaction as he reached for the piece of paper that was handed to him through the teller's window on June 1, 1922. He picked up the slip of paper and read, "Throw up your hands, don't move or reach for anything or you are a dead man."[1] The Lapeer County Press thought the note was a novel start to a bank robbery. Who would have guessed that in 50 years or so a note to the teller would become a tiresomely typical MO for solo bank robbers. And there was hardly anything typical about the subsequent events that unfolded following the stickup of the Metamora State Bank in the little village of the same name in Lapeer County.

Novel or not, the words on the note had the desired effect. Potter stood rooted to the floor like a 100-year-old oak and was motionless as a statue after he put up his hands. Ward Peck, the bank's cashier, walked over to check out Omar's strange behavior, read the note, also raised his hands and became just as immovable as his co-worker. The pair were walked, at gun point, into the vault, and the two robbers began sweeping up the cash like a shop vac. Little did the stickup artists know that the bank robbery would trigger a deadly chain of events leading through Hadley, Lapeer, Flint, and Detroit and would ultimately destroy a criminal outfit spanning much of southeastern Michigan.

After stuffing a gunny sack with silver and cash totaling $6,500 the two crooks walked out of the bank and headed for the getaway car and its two occupants. The car had been parked a block south of the bank in hopes it wouldn't draw attention to what was going on inside the bank. The car failed to raise any eyebrows, but the two gunmen walking out of the bank didn't go unnoticed. Don Gleason's meat market sat near the bank, and when the butcher saw the two armed men leave the bank carrying a gunny sack, he knew with absolute certainty he was watching the conclusion of bank robbery. Gleason grabbed a gun, stepped out on the sidewalk, and opened fire. He hit one bandit in the leg but the wound hardly seemed to slow the crook down at all as he began running for the dark green Columbia and threw himself in the back seat. The robbers quickly returned fire, nicking Gleason in the arm before speeding south out of town. Gleason, in spite of his wound, wasn't ready to quit the fight and joined the assistant cashier Omar Pratt and three other Metamora men who armed themselves and gave chase.

Metamora's Minutemen caught up with the bandits about six miles south of town near the village of Thomas. The not entirely reliable Columbia had become cranky, and the crooks had to stop and baby the automobile back into good humor. Shots were exchanged with neither side doing the other any damage. Urged on by the gunfire, the crooks soon had the Columbia running smoothly and once again the chase was on. The bandits quickly outran their pursuers and swung west into Hadley Township and a whole new world of trouble.

Mrs. Ivy Mundie, Metamora's central switchboard operator, had quickly learned of the robbery and immediately took it upon herself to call the police and sheriffs in surrounding communities to inform them bandits could be heading their way. She also called numerous farmers and asked them to keep an eye out for the robbers. She also encouraged them to spread the word, and, informally and unofficially, invited them to join the hunt. Within minutes of the robbery, Mrs. Mundie's self-anointed mounties-for-a-day, as well as duly elected and appointed lawmen, were converging on Metamora in the hundreds.

Near the old German cemetery south of Hadley, several carloads of well-armed civilians, sheriff deputies from three counties, police from Pontiac and Flint, and even a Pere Marquette Railroad detective convinced the outlaws escape by car was no longer an option. Desperate to shake the growing pursuit, the crooks abandoned the Columbia and took off on foot. In an area now known for its horse ranches, equestrian trials, and boarding stables, the chase became an old fashioned fox hunt with the bandit quartet running for their lives across two to three miles of woods and fields with the law figuratively baying at their heels. Two posse members spotted the gang crossing a road into an area known as Coleman Woods. The estimated 500 vigilantes and lawmen quickly surrounded the woods and sent a skirmish line into the trees to flush out the desperadoes. Leo Cummings, all of 18 years old from Goodrich, and George Witley spied the four in the wooded undergrowth and were immediately shot at by the outlaws. Cummings shot back striking Mike Kolski in the side. Witley took advantage of the distraction caused by Kolski's wounding to slide through the brush and jump Jerry Skopency and over-power him. The other two bandits, one of which was wounded in the hand, just up and ran. Kolski, 30 of Flint, and Skopency, 35 of Detroit, were taken to the police by a group of vigilantes. It was an unpleasant walk through the woods for the two captives, who were roughly treated by the civilians and threatened with a beating for supposedly firing on farmers working their fields. The police put a stop to the threats and ill treatment and took the two to the Lapeer County jail. There it was learned that the Flint Police had been hunting Kolski for three weeks on prohibition charges after running from a car the police had stopped for transporting liquor.

The gunfire brought police and posse members running, and the two remaining robbers were chased into a dense thicket. The police closed in with William Buckler, a former Flint cop turned railroad detective, near the front. He had been visiting friends in the Flint Police Department when the call came in from Mrs. Mundie, and he decided to join his buddies in the hunt.

To get a better look at the thicket, Detective Buckler broke cover to step over a fence and was shot in the head by bandits. When he fell to the ground, he reached out an arm and pointed to where he could see two men hiding in the densest part of the thicket. Detective Shirley Johnson of Flint and Patrolman Roy Reynolds of Pontiac unlimbered their BARs and yelled for the robbers to surrender. The desperadoes answered with a salvo of pistol fire. Reynolds and Johnson leveled their high-powered automatic rifles where Buckler was pointing and let their guns rip on full automatic. It was later estimated the two weapons unleashed 1,000 rounds into the thicket and turned it into mulch. When the two guns quit chattering, the police, with ears still ringing, advanced on the former thicket and found the lifeless bodies of both robbers. A search of their clothes failed to reveal their identity. The bodies were taken to the Lapeer County morgue.

William Buckler was rushed to the Goodrich Hospital where it was reported he had a deep scalp wound and a fractured skull. He was considered in good condition, but the hospital wasn't a fount of optimism when it came to the detective's ultimate fate. The hospital reported, "…he would probably recover."[2]

The two captive bank robbers still weren't saying anything, and the investigation was spinning its wheels when a tip phoned in to the Flint Police sent a team of officers on Friday to a house on Fenton Road's 1600 block. Detective Shirley Johnson headed up the raid, and even a cursory look around the place led police to conclude they had uncovered a large criminal network that, like an investment broker, believed and practiced diversification. In the gangsters' case, it was diversification of illegal activities.

Yes, bank robbing proved to be a significant part of the criminal portfolio, but the two large stills in the house's second floor made it obvious the gang was multi-talented when it came to crime. The house, it turned out, was owned by Mike Kolski who had been wounded and captured the previous day and spent the night in jail. And who should be tending the stills but Mrs. Kolski. Here was a woman who besides keeping house, raising three kids, and cooking for whoever might show up at what was beginning to look like the headquarters for a band of gangsters, also knew her way around sour mash and stills.

When Detective Lt. Schewe asked if Mrs. Kolski was aware that her husband had been shot, captured, and jailed in the last 24 hours, it became readily apparent she could have taught a Civil War muleskinner (men truly gifted in the art of profanity) a thing or two about swearing. Then the rage turned to tears, and she asked if indeed her husband had been shot because she had not seen him since early yesterday morning.

A thorough search of the house turned up 20 gallons of moonshine, and the pockets of various men's pants found throughout the house were stuffed with ammunition. In the garage police found a nearly new Paige touring car. Mrs. Kolski claimed the car belonged to an unknown person who rented the garage. Not believing Mrs. Kolski for a second, the police drove the Paige to the police station where it was dusted for prints and checked against a list of stolen Paiges. Not long after the car was taken to the police station, another officer came across a complete set of specialized steel dies car thieves used to alter the VIN numbers of stolen vehicles. It didn't help Mrs. Kolski's reliability when she was found to have a key to the garage on her person. On questioning neighbors police were told the house, over the past few weeks, always seemed to be filled with men. Neighbors also remarked about the constant flow of expensive automobiles into and out of the place.

The police had hit a law enforcement trifecta taking down a high volume bootlegging operation, a sizable auto theft ring, and a crew of bank robbers. Now if they could just round up the rest of gang. An envelope with the name Stanley Slenkiewiez at 3375 E. Warren, Detroit, was also found in the house, and it was hoped this would lead to a Detroit connection.

Back in Lapeer, the two dead robbers stubbornly refused to give up their identities even though from Thursday night through Friday morning 4,000 people lined up and viewed the bodies of the two men and not a one could positively ID either corpse. One man thought he might have seen one of the dead robbers working some time ago in a Flint pool room. Jerry Skopency, who had refused to answer any questions since his capture, broke his silence on Friday and said Mestke was the other dead man's name and he was from Detroit. He got the city right but the man's name slightly wrong. Skopency also told Lapeer County Sheriff Ray Baker he had been shanghaied in Detroit by the other three men and forced to drive the trio to Metamora where one of the men said he wanted to withdraw money from a bank. This might have been somewhat difficult for the sheriff to swallow because after abandoning the getaway car and running through the countryside he never tried to escape.

Police in Flint were of the opinion the outlaw gang was much larger than the four who hit the Metamora bank. They didn't have long to wait before their theory was proved correct and also showed the gang members were capable of extraordinarily dumb behavior. The proof of both came Friday afternoon when four men, who were so poorly dressed they looked like road-weary hoboes, drove into town, took a brief tour of Metamora, and then parked directly in front of the Metamora State Bank and gave it the evil eye. With the recent past still in everybody's mind, the four suspicious looking men raised red flags all over town. And if they didn't make themselves obvious enough, one of the four loudly cursed out the bank employees and before the car sped off yelled, "Never mind, we'll get you yet." [3]

The car wasn't out of town before telephones were ringing in every nearby police department. In minutes every lawman within 50 miles of Metamora was looking for the shabbily dressed quartet. Sheriff Joe Butler of Pontiac and Motorcycle Officer Harold Tinker crossed paths with the four in Oxford, Michigan, and after several rounds of rough and tumble persuasion, the lawmen subdued, handcuffed, and delivered the quartet to the Lapeer County jail. Four hacksaw blades were found in the men's car, and it was later learned the car had been seen near the county jail. The four were questioned by the Lapeer County Prosecuting Attorney who got nothing out of them but their names, and that proved to be a mouthful. They were Anthony Crzusklinzek, 43, Alexander Zylowski, 25, Joe Sabinski, and Joe Urban, all Detroiters. It was discovered Joe Urban's father had a farm four miles north of Lapeer which led police to think the robbers may have visited the farm before robbing the bank.

Mike Kolski, which turned out to be an alias for Mike Koyalsky, on Friday told the police the two dead bank robbers were the gang's leaders but swore he didn't know their names. The four gangsters who tried to intimidate Metamora and the village's bank employees said they couldn't, but more probably wouldn't, identify the two corpses, but seeing the bodies sparked an animated and excited discussion among the four in a foreign language no one knew or even recognized.

Late Friday, experts arrived in Lapeer to fingerprint the two dead robbers as well as the four recently arrested gang members. Lapeer County Sheriff Baker reached out to Wayne County law enforcement because he had become convinced the gang, comprised of at least a dozen members, was headquartered in Detroit. Kolski let it be known the gang was even larger than Sheriff Baker surmised when he told the lawman there were at least twelve members still at large. It seemed every new piece of information indicated the police were on the trail of an ever larger and more dangerous gang that operated throughout southern Michigan from bases in Detroit and Flint.

In yet the strangest twist to this story, Joe August, a former merchant in both Lapeer and Flint, seemingly came out of nowhere and visited the "I-didn't-do-it," bank robber Jerry Skopency and had a long talk with him on Friday. On Saturday Mr. August drove to Detroit and returned the same day with several Detroiters (their names were not made known) who visited the morgue and positively identified the dead robbers as Alexander Yuschkevitz and Miske Kowalsky, both of Detroit. So you have a man—Jerry—who, although driving the getaway car and fleeing on foot from a pursuing posse, steadfastly claims his innocence yet sends a man he has no known history with to Detroit and that man returns with unnamed men who identify, by name, the two dead men who were the supposed leaders of the gang. Now there is as convoluted a turn in the case as the above sentence. How a retired Flint merchant with no known connections to the Detroit criminal community could do in a day what law enforcement couldn't do in three will always remain a mystery. As will the Detroiters who identified Yuschkevitz and Kowalsky. And August wasn't yet done sticking his toe in these bewildering waters.

On Saturday, the citizens of Metamora asked the Michigan State Police to guard their town against any further threats or acts of violence from the gang that robbed their bank and threatened their citizens. Two troopers were sent to the village to guard it until further notice. The village wouldn't have to worry about the four men who prompted the request for guards because the Detroit police announced the foursome were wanted in the Motor City on burglary charges and sent a paddy wagon to bring them back and stand trial.

Also on Saturday, Mrs. Kolski or Koyalsky came from Flint with her three children to visit her husband in his cell. The crook broke down and wept when his kids stood outside the bars and stared at their father. On Monday, the ever reserved and bad-news-might-just-be-around-the-corner Goodrich Hospital reported Detective Buckler was resting comfortably and, "Unless complication set in, the officer has a good chance to recover." [4]

Alexander Yuschkevitz and Miske Kowalsky were buried Tuesday in Lapeer's Mt. Hope cemetery even as new surprises and incongruities kept coming. Joe August stepped on stage again on Monday when he and Lapeer undertaker George McDonald took it upon themselves to head for Detroit and conduct their own investigation. As preposterous as this sounds, the merchant and the mortician proved they might have missed their calling. They learned Yuschkevitz had enlisted in the Canadian army under the name Alex U. Ansley, served four years, was honorably discharged, and received $18.75 a month from the British government as a pension for his war service. He had $300 in the bank and was known in Detroit under yet another name—Boris Savis. Miske Kowalsky was said to have no friends at all, if being seen for the past several weeks in the constant company of Savis/Ansley/Yuschkevitz, or whatever his name was, didn't count as a possible friend. The two amateur sleuths also reported Jerry Skopency had held a job for the past five months, had a good reputation, and his boss vouched for his fine work habits.

Jerry Skopency continued to proclaim his innocence. He never wavered from his story that three strangers had approached him in Detroit and said they were going to meet some girls and asked him along. He never said if or where they met any girls but once again told how that Mike said he had money in an account at the Metamora bank and asked him to drive to that town so he could make a withdrawal. When they got to the bank, Kowalsky, according to Skopency, held him at gun point in the car while the other two men robbed the bank. If Jerry Skopency was not guilty of bank robbery and if gullibility were a crime the man would have served a life sentence for the latter. Skopency hired an attorney and stood before a preliminary hearing on June 15. Nine witnesses were examined by the judge before he was bound over to the circuit court to stand trial at the September term. Mike Koyalsky or Kolski (even the newspapers of the day were undecided on his name) was also at the preliminary hearing and bound over for trial. Since neither one had any chance of raising the $15,000 bail, they were returned to the Lapeer County jail to await trial. After numerous delays by Skopency's attorney, the two surviving, accused bank robbers' trials were finally held. Kolski was found guilty and shipped to a state prison for a lengthy stay. The jury found Jerry Skopency innocent, and he walked out of court a free man.

Then there was the final surprise. The Flint Clearing House Association (a group of five banks) volunteered to pay Detective Buckler's hospital bills. The decision to step forward and support the wounded railroad detective was made after the Metamora State Bank announced it would not contribute one thin dime to help cover any of Buckler's hospital costs. When asked what the bank would do in helping Buckler, the response was, "…they could see no obligation on their part, since their loss would have been covered by insurance, even if the money taken by the robbers had not been recovered."[5]

There is one final piece of irony. While the police across southeast Michigan were working overtime to put a gang guilty of bank robbery, auto theft, and bootlegging in jail, Mayor Swanton of Traverse City was hell bent on arresting another serious threat to society. Reported in the same newspapers as the account of the Metamora bank robbery and virtually in an adjoining column, the mayor ordered a ban on women wearing knickers and commanded his chief of police to arrest any woman wearing the offending garment in public. Mayor Swanton imposed the ban out of the belief that knickers directly led to a disturbingly large share of the corruption and downfall seen in the youth of Traverse City. It is interesting to note the city's Chamber of Commerce evidently felt that the corruption and downfall of its city's youth was OK with them because the organization thought women should be allowed to wear knickers.

It is unknown if any accused criminal anywhere, at any time, ever used the "knicker defense."

1. Lapeer County Record 6-7-1922 p1, c3
2. Flint Daily Journal 6-8-1922 p1, c7
3. Flint Daily Journal 6-3-1922 p7, c3
4. Flint Daily Journal 6-5-1922 p1, c7
5. Flint Daily Journal 6-12-22 p15, c3

Chapter 6

Peoples National Bank of Hamtramck

March 4, 1924

"...crooks either owned the little city...or were given free passes to do as they pleased."

Located directly across the street on Joseph Campau from the Hamtramck Police Department one would think the Peoples National Bank of Hamtramck would be looked upon by professional bank robbers as an apple that they should never try to pick. It was not so much forbidden fruit as fruit on a tree to which an ill-tempered pit bull has been chained. Yet there are always perceived mitigating circumstances, no matter how dumb or illogical they may look in retrospect, that cause even professionals to overlook the obvious. The mitigating circumstance in the case of the Peoples National Bank robbery was the city in which it did business—Hamtramck, Michigan.

In the 1920s it seemed the crooks either owned the little city that was entirely surrounded by Detroit, or were given free passes to do as they pleased. It was 2.1 square-miles of graft, corruption, and a veritable petri dish in which criminal microorganisms flourished. It used to be a quiet little residential enclave, a donut hole surrounded by Detroit, until the Dodge Brothers opened a huge plant in the city in 1914 and people poured in to take jobs building Dodge motor cars. Whatever bastion of respectability remained in the over-crowded streets and burgeoning tax base, little remained after Prohibition became law.

By the early 1920s, ordinary folks had simply lost control of their town. The city government became so corrupt and the town so overrun with gangs and crooks the citizens asked the governor to take over Hamtramck and declare martial law. Alcohol was sold openly at restaurants, pool halls, and even candy stores. Soft drink parlors sold the hard stuff instead of pop. Blind pigs and gambling dens flourished, and within the little city could be found over 100 houses of ill repute that turned tricks 24/7 with the precision and speed of the assembly line just up the road.

In 1923 Governor Groesbeck ordered in the state police. The governor removed the mayor from office and put the town under martial law. The state police and Wayne County Sheriff's Office raided 75 stills and broke up two breweries. The raids destroyed 20,000 gallons of hooch. The town's 400 speakeasies were closed as well as most if not all the bordellos. The last whorehouse in the city didn't close its doors until the 1950s. The Wayne County Sheriff's Office also took over the policing and administration of the Hamtramck Police Department. The good Hamtramck cops stayed, and like cops everywhere put their lives on the line to continue the uphill battle to make their community safe. Although city government was cleaned up, the gangs continued to flourish in the two-square-mile city. The Green Sedan Gang, the Shotgun Gang, and many others continued to operate out of Hamtramck, including the infamous Lamon Mob which specialized in kidnapping and extorting speakeasy owners and other crooks not associated with the Purple Gang.

In a warped kind of way, one can almost understand the mindset of the robbers who decided to take down Peoples National Bank. So what if the bank was across the street from police headquarters, they would just take that into their planning. And when it came right down to the nitty-gritty, bank robbers, killers, and strong-arm crooks considered Hamtramck their town. It wouldn't be surprising if they thought they could rob the bank if it had been on the floor above the police station.

The gang planned on diverting the police and sending them to the north end of town just before the robbery by having a cohort on the north end pull a fire alarm. The alarm sent firemen and equipment flying out of the building next to the police station. Most of the police accompanied the fire apparatus which left just a skeleton crew at police headquarters. A large crowd was still lingering on Joseph Campau, in front of the police station and fire house, when shots could be heard coming from the bank across the street.

Almost as soon as the firemen and firefighting vehicles disappeared up the street, three bank robbers entered the bank. One remained on guard at the front door while the other two confronted the four tellers manning their stations behind high steel cages. One of the two robbers asked a teller to make change for a $5 bill, and while the teller was concentrating on the task, the two men pulled guns and one of them told everyone in the bank to "Stick 'em up." [1]

Teller Stanley Przybyiski initially obeyed the order then dropped to the floor and pushed the alarm that was connected to the police station. With a curse one of the gunmen began climbing over the tall wire cage, hindered by a gun in one hand and further slowed by stopping to take pot shots at Przybyiski. Finally reaching the top of the cage, the gunman threw a leg over the enclosure and dropped to the floor. As he rose to his feet, he discovered he was looking straight down the barrels of pistols held by both Przybyiski and Cashier Carl Luczynski. Whether it was instinct or sheer bravado, the outlaw started to raise his own gun. The movement was answered simultaneously as both bank employees shot the gunman who crumpled to the floor mortally wounded.

When the alarm sounded in police headquarters, Officers Frank Boza and John Sikoraki drew their pistols and ran toward the bank. As they crossed Joseph Campau, lead started scouring the pavement around their feet and whirring by their ears as the robber stationed at the bank's front door opened fire. The pair of cops fired back as they sprinted for the bank. All this mayhem unfolded in front of a large crowd of spectators who had stood and watched the fire equipment roll into action, and then before they even began to disperse, gun shots rippled from the bank. The crowd stood as if frozen in spot as the two policemen charged the bank with guns blazing. Incredibly, no one was reported running for cover, and no mention was made of any panic sweeping through the spectators. They stood there as if they couldn't believe what they were witnessing.

Then one officer went down. Frank Boza, a five-and-a-half-year veteran, had the look of a cop who'd seen it all and could handle anything that came his way. He was built like a middle linebacker with broad, sloping shoulders; he had a lantern jaw, piercing eyes, and a mouth that was firm and serious but looked only a tick away from an easy smile. A photograph in full uniform gave the unmistakable impression that here was a cop's cop. He was a few steps ahead of Sikoraki and firing at the robber guarding the bank's front door when a bullet tore into his neck. He staggered a few steps before falling to the pavement.

Officer Sikoraki kept advancing and firing at the bank robber as he crossed the street. As can happen in the chaos of battle, neither Sikoraki nor the gunman, who was later identified as John Seminara, scored a hit in their deadly dual. Sikoraki and Seminara were both still standing and unhurt when the former arrived at the bank door and simply pushed Seminara out of the way. Sikoraki stepped into bank and found the third bank robber aiming his piece at the doorway. Sikoraki quickly back pedaled out the door only to run into

Seminara who shoved a pistol into the cop's side. Sikoraki instinctively brushed the gun aside and shot the robber.

The transfixed crowd on the street saw Seminara stagger out the bank and run up an alley. The sight of the fleeing robber broke the crowd's paralysis, and some of the spectators ran after the wounded man and caught up with him when he collapsed from his wounds. The last gunman still standing raced out of the bank right behind Sikoraki and ran toward the Michigan Central Railroad yards with Sikoraki and officers just arriving at the scene in hot pursuit and trying to bring him down with pistol fire. The police were followed by a large crowd hoping to see justice done. The crowd included the mayor of the city and a justice of the peace. The gunman made it into the vast labyrinth of tracks and railroad cars lined up on sidings and lost his pursuers. A major search of the railroad yards was immediately initiated. Somehow during all this chaos, the gang's getaway driver escaped notice, and when he belatedly realized the plan had gone in the tank, he vamoosed.

Frank Boza had regained his feet in all the pandemonium and staggered back to police headquarters. A doctor there attended the wounded officer and reported the gunshot looked like a flesh wound and was probably more painful than serious. Boza was taken to Grace Hospital. The robber wounded inside the teller's cage was brought across the street and laid on the police headquarters floor next to the other wounded robber man who had shot Frank Boza and been wounded by Officer Sikoraki. Neither felon was looked at by a physician although an ambulance had been called to pick them up. Frank Boza's shooter was slowly bleeding out and spent what strength he had left denouncing the police while his partner in crime died before the ambulance arrived.

Luczynski and Przybyiski took their shooting of the bank robber in stride. Neither man acted like they were particularly shook up after surviving a duel with a killer.

Przybyiski stated matter-of-factly, "We were lucky and got the drop on him; otherwise we might be dead." [2] Luczynski, a veteran of WWI, told police he was almost obsessive about gauging the distance from his teller's window to the alarm button. He confessed he often thought about what he would do if an armed robbery occurred during his shift. Now he knew.

The third man in the crew, the only one of the three hoodlums who entered the bank and wasn't shot and who lost the police in the railroad yard, was arrested by Hamtramck police soon after the robbery. One would think a bank robber who escaped a botched job in which two of his gang and a police officer were shot would possess enough innate survival instincts or just plain common sense to lie low or get out of town. Apparently not this bank robber, because he went to a pool hall. Just the kind of place to be noticed when the police are furiously searching the city for the accomplices of the man who shot a cop. He was arrested in the pool hall and was positively identified by bank employees as one of the three bandits who robbed the Peoples National Bank.

At Grace Hospital it quickly became apparent that Officer Boza's neck wound was anything but superficial. It remains unclear what exactly went wrong, but whatever it was, his condition worsened rapidly, and without anyone ever notifying his family he was hurt or in the hospital, Frank Boza died of a wound received while running to the aid of the citizens he was worn to protect.

Exhibiting a complete absence of tact and with the empathy of a hyena, a Hamtramck detective drove to the Boza household, and when Mrs. Boza answered his knock on the door, the detective said, "Well, Boza's dead." [3] The new widow couldn't believe the news, and when it did register, she fainted. After Mrs. Boza came to grips with harsh reality, she lamented, "I wanted him to be brave and fine, I wanted him to give his best but we need him so, the children and me… He worked so hard to earn what we have. We saved and saved, and we were just beginning to see where it was all worthwhile, for the children's sake, and now we are alone." [4] Mrs. Boza was nearly blind and indeed couldn't see a thing without her glasses. There was still a mortgage on the house, and three children were left fatherless, the youngest a toddler.

Hamtramck Justice of the Peace Walter Phillips noted a day after the robbery that the Peoples National Bank was the fifth bank robbery to occur in the geographically minute city since the Commissioner of Public Safety Max A. Wosinski abolished the bank squad seven months ago. In the crooked and boisterous Hamtramck, one man did his job, paid with his life, and left his family bereft. Meanwhile politicians elected and appointed took bribes, received payoffs, and used the public trust to fleece the people who elected them. It may not still be happening in Hamtramck, but it's a process and an outrage that persists to this day.

It is an age-old story. One man gives his life for his city, another takes the city for all it's worth.

1. Detroit Free Press March 3, 1924 p2, c1
2. Detroit News March 7, 1924 p1, c3
3. Detroit Free Press March 5, 1924 p2, c1
4. IBID p2, c3

Chapter 7

The Paul Jaworski Crime Wave

1923—January 21, 1929

"It's suicide to fight back..."

*B*aby Face Nelson, Pretty Boy Floyd, Alvin Karpis, Machine Gun Kelly, and Bonnie and Clyde have become woven into the fabric of the culture and mythology of Depression Era America. Yet Paul Jaworski and his Flathead Gang have remained in obscurity even though they were deadly, remorseless killers who were as close to zero on the moral compass scales as any of the above outlaws. Whether as a cold-blooded killer, an accomplished and habitual bank robber, or simply an audacious armed robber who pulled off some of the era's most daring and often bloody armed robberies, Paul Jaworski is simply not given his due. Unless, of course, one considers dying in the electric chair his due.

Jaworski was born in 1900 in Poland as Paul Poluzynski. The family came to America five years later and settled briefly in Pennsylvania, first in Butler then in Pittsburgh. It was in Butler the young boy had his first brush with the law when, it could hardly be more symbolic, he was arrested for stealing apples. At around the age of 15, Paul and family moved to Hamtramck, the bustling, two-square-mile city that nestled inside Detroit like a Russian doll. It was home to a rapidly expanding influx of Polish immigrants who came to work in the Dodge plant. The postage-stamp-sized city, as noted in the last chapter, was awash in political corruption, and if trickle-down economics didn't work, trickle-down corruption proved wildly successful. It was a spawning ground for youth gangs and a place where teen hoodlums graduated to major crimes. The young Paul Jaworski took to it like a Hooded Merganser to water.

The young hoodlum left home at 19 and cut all ties with his family. When he walked out of his house for the last time, Jaworski probably wouldn't have done a single thing differently even if he knew that a decade in the future he would be strapped to an electric chair. He filled his last decade with countless robberies, the death of several men in three different states (including police officers), and a handful of jaw-dropping, countrywide-grabbing-headline robberies.

It's likely the deciding factor in Jaworski's leaving home was the growing association with Hamtramck's Shotgun Gang who introduced Paul to heavy-weight crime. The Shotgun Gang were prolific bank robbers, and their weapon of choice was the sawed-off shotgun—hence their name. For Paul, being around the gang was like receiving an internship in bank robbery. The crew's trademarks were the ruthless use of violence or the utterly convincing promise of violence if anyone in the bank stepped out of line. They were also known for the swiftness with which they pulled off a job. The gang struck like a bolt of lightning. Paul probably wasn't in on many—if any—bank jobs, but just being around the Shotgun Gang was like brushing up against wet paint—a lot rubbed off.

The Shotgun Gang had a good run for about a year before their karma took a sudden, disastrous turn for the worse. Two of the gang's top men were shot dead by the law. A third lead member was captured, tried, and awarded a poorly appointed cell with three bad meals a day behind barbed-wire-capped walls.

Jaworski was running a gang that committed small-time robberies when the Shotgun Gang fell apart for lack of leadership. But the end of the Shotgunners paid big dividends for Jaworski because two of its former members, Mike Komieczka, also known as "Mike the Pug," and Stanley "Big Stack" Podolski attached themselves to Jaworski's crew. Under "Big Stack's" mentorship, Paul and his Flathead Gang became major players in bank robberies and armed payroll robberies in Ohio, Pennsylvania, and Michigan.

Stanley "Big Stack" Podolski stood 6'2" and pushed the scales past 200 pounds. "Mike the Pug" Komieczka got his nickname because of his limited stature. They made a strikingly mismatched pair of crooks and often pulled off robberies together while in the Jaworski gang. They quickly became the Mutt and Jeff (an equally mismatched pair of popular cartoon characters) of Detroit crime. Membership in the Flatheads appears to have fluctuated widely. A few, like "Mike the Pug," "Big Stack," and Frank "Whitey" Kraft, were close-held confidants of Paul and were nearly always involved in any caper while others came and went with regularity and some apparently were gang members only for as long as it took to pull off one job.

The first major bank job by the newly reconfigured Jaworski gang was the Detroit Savings Bank Branch in 1923. It went off without a hitch and the gang walked away with $30,000. Later, in December of the same year, the gang hit the Pittsburgh Terminal Coal Company branch at Beadling, Pennsylvania. The company's paymaster delivered the $23,000 payroll, alone, without guards, on a motorcycle. The gang simply waited in hiding with a shotgun until the paymaster rode down an isolated stretch of road, which he always took, and blew the man off his bike with a round of buckshot. The killers then emerged from hiding, shot the badly wounded and unarmed man when he reached for something in his pocket, and drove away with the loot.

Over the next few years, the gang preyed repeatedly on Detroit-area banks. When the law got too close, often prompted by civic leaders and businesses who badgered the police to put more heat on suspected bank robbers, the gang shifted operations to Pittsburgh, where they specialized in payroll robbery. When the heat cooled off in the Motor City, the gang drifted back and picked up where they had left off. In Detroit, the members of the gang often operated independently of Jaworski, and it has never been established exactly how many banks they robbed in the Detroit area. Best estimates hold the Jaworski mob responsible for at least fourteen major robberies along with several murders and many other lesser jobs.

$ $ $

The robbery of the Carpenter Street Branch of the Liberty State Bank in Hamtramck on April 2, 1924, typified the gang's professionalism, bravado, and wagon load of chutzpah. It was not only the second time the gang robbed the same bank but the second time they robbed it in the same month. The first robbery netted the robbers $3,000, and on the second score they walked away with a $3,600 pay day. As in the first robbery, the getaway driver stayed in a large touring car while three goons with guns drawn entered the bank and announced a stickup. No customers were present as the armed bandits ordered the manager and bookkeeper to raise their hands and stand against a wall. Two of the crew leaped into the tellers' cages and shoveled money into bags while the gang leader turned to the manager and said, "Perhaps you remember me. I'm the guy that was here before. My name's Stanley."[1] Dykowski, the bank's manager, recognized the speaker from the previous robbery but not the other two men. He might have recognized the getaway driver because it is very likely "Mike the Pug" was behind the wheel.

The men fled in the touring car and disappeared. In a brazen act of one-upmanship, the getaway car was found abandoned with the motor still running at 10 PM the same night. It was parked just 60 feet from a Hamtramck police station. It had been stolen the day before from a dealer's lot and was graced by stolen license plates.

$ $ $

The following month the Fort Street Branch of the Bank of Detroit paid off to the tune of five figures to two armed bank robbers in a well planned and executed robbery on May 17, 1924. Harold K. Taggart, the bank's bookkeeper, arrived at the bank on Saturday morning 20 minutes before its 9 AM opening. He was the first employee to arrive at the bank and had inserted his key in the front door lock when two men came up behind him, hit him over the head, and knocked him senseless. The two thugs finished unlocking the bank door, dragged Taggart inside, and locked the book-keeper in a restroom.

The robbers then hid behind a counter and waited for the rest of the employees to arrive for work. The robbers knew exactly what they were doing and had fully scouted out the bank's employees. They even knew the bank's customers almost as well as the employees. On week days the bank didn't open until 10 AM, but it opened an hour earlier on Saturdays because several nearby businesses paid their people by check on Saturday mornings. Due to the heavy demand for cash by check cashers, this branch always had more cash on hand on Saturdays, and the robbers knew it.

The next man in the door was teller Joseph Kania. He failed to notice the hiding robbers and, as usual, went directly to the small vault at the back of the bank, in which the time lock turned off at 8:30 AM, and began to open it. The last two employees arrived just moments later. When they entered the building, the two bandits leaped up with guns drawn and took control of the bank.

The four employees, even while facing loaded weapons, were immediately aware of what an odd pair the two crooks made. They were Mutt and Jeff personified. One looked a good inch or two over 6-feet and looked like he could make a bathroom scale squeal in pain. The other could possibly push the scales to 120 pounds if he was sopping wet and his pockets were full of pennies. He might have reached 5-feet, but only if he stood on his tip toes. Both were dressed in suits and caps. They were distinctly memorable, and this wasn't the first or last bank they would rob together.

The smaller robber brandished two pistols while "Big Stack" made do with one. They order Kania to continue to open the safe. While the man was dialing the combination, the outsized bandit told the teller they had been casing the bank and planning the job for the past two months. None of the four employees could remember ever seeing either robber before. Once the safe was opened, the robbers transferred the money to sacks they had brought with them. The bank's employees all told police they were impressed with the precision, economy of movement, the thorough professionalism of the pair, and the constant stream of profanity that accompanied every order.

When the vault had been emptied, the smaller of the two men grabbed the bank keys to let himself out the front door and said he was going to get the car. On the way out, he turned to Miss Moore, the only female employee, and thanked her for not screaming and apologized for the colorful, blue language used by himself and his partner. By way of explanation he said, "You know we have to be emphatic." [2] The man hadn't been out the door for more than a moment or two when an automobile pulled up in front and its horn sounded. The big guy sprinted for the car, and it took off down Fort and was lost to view.

The pair took the bank for $30,000, the second biggest robbery to date in Detroit history. It was the fourteenth bank robbery in Detroit since January 1, 1924.

$ $ $

Things didn't go quite so smoothly a year later when the gang robbed Branch Y of the American State Bank on Epworth Boulevard. On Tuesday afternoon of April 14, 1925 (which also happened to be the home opener for the Tigers at what was then called Navin Field), the Y Branch was robbed for the second time in three weeks, unfortunately with the same tragic results.

Only branch manager W.P. Guenshe and teller Charles Taggart Jr. were working when three stickup artists entered the bank. A fourth remained behind the wheel of a maroon touring car parked out front with the motor running. The three gun-toting thugs ordered Taggart and Guenshe to raise their hands and let them into the tellers' cages. As one of the bandits entered Taggart's cage, the teller made a move for the burglar alarm. Without hesitation the gunman pulled the trigger and fired a single round into Taggart's head. Guenshe heard the shot but didn't see Taggart fall to the cage's floor. The manager was ordered to the front of the room and made to sit on the floor. A customer entered the bank and was ordered on the floor with Guenshe. While one gunman watched the two victims on the floor, the other bandits grabbed several stacks of bills and all three fled out the door to the getaway car.

A man who was sitting in his car near the bank saw the three armed men come out the front door and threaten shopkeepers on either side of the bank before jumping in the big car and speeding off. The witness, acting as a lone posse of one, keyed his ignition and set off after the bandits but couldn't keep up with the bigger car.

Taggart was rushed to Providence Hospital where he was pronounced dead on arrival. Taggart had been present three weeks earlier when a gang attempted to rob his bank and killed a customer when the robbery went bad. At the time Taggart had made the comment he would raise his hands and keep them up if he ever found himself looking down the barrel of an outlaw's gun. He said, "It is suicide to fight back…" [3]

The bank's manager was nearly positive the day's bandits were not the same gang that had hit the bank three weeks before. The manager described the most recent robbers as clean shaven Americans ranging in age from 25 to 39. Especially notable was one of the trio, "Big Stack," who stood head and shoulders above the two other thugs. Once again "Mike the Pug" was probably the getaway driver.

The police were near apoplectic. Police Commissioner Croul announced he had directed his department to round up every thug in the city and bring them in for questioning. Then he doubled down by declaring the roundup would only be the first step in driving the thugs out of Detroit. Deputy Commissioner James Sprott called the murder of Taggart one of the worst cold-bloodied shootings in his experience. Sprott then called out the bankers for not staffing their places of business with guards. He said, "Bank officials are in a measure responsible for a large number of deaths occurring in these raids. The countless number of banks and branches are not properly guarded. Every institution should have turrets containing armed guards." [4] The question not asked was whether banks could afford to turn themselves into armed fortresses.

$ $ $

Evidently the commissioner's vow to pick up every thug in town on Tuesday had either not gotten underway yet or the roundup missed a couple, in fact a couple of familiar ones. Just minutes before the 3 PM closing on the day after the American State Bank robbery and murder of teller Charles Taggart Jr., two men, one very short and the other quite tall, walked into the Northwestern State Bank on Grand River and walked out with $7,000.

On entering the bank, the shorter of the two crooks walked up to the bank manager, jabbed him with a gun and told him to put his hands up. The bandit then added the warning if he tried to trip an alarm he would, "...get what Taggart got yesterday." [5] While the taller gunman began cleaning out the teller's cash drawers, the short one got the key from the manager, locked the front door, and kept his gun trained on the manager and the other two bank workers. With the tellers' cages empty, the manager was marched to the vault and told to open the safe, which he did on the second try. The thugs then told the three employees they could light up cigarettes while they finished bagging the money. Just before leaving, the two robbers walked everyone into the vault and closed the door. Witnesses outside the bank later told police the pair drove off in a large touring car.

After all the big promises just the day before by the police commissioner, this robbery was the equivalent of having humble pie jammed down his throat. Commissioner Croul figuratively threw up his hands in surrender and admitted it was impossible for police to guard all the banks. "If we were to furnish police guards for all the banks and branches in the city, it would require so many men that the gangsters would find citizens easy prey." [6] Which one would likely observe was already the case. James Sprott, the deputy commissioner, also felt compelled to wet his oar by stating it appeared banks were unconcerned, even apathetic, to armed robberies because their stolen funds were insured against loss and, "do not seem to be awake to the risk which their employees are forced to take." [7]

The police were at their wit's end, and Jaworski's Flathead Gang plus several other Detroit-area gangs seemed able to rob banks and businesses with impunity. They were failing to enforce Prohibition, and the thousands of man hours that went into that losing fight were also lost combating Detroit's armed robbers and numerous gangs. When Prohibition became law in May of 1918, a year earlier than the rest of the country, Detroit had 1,800 licensed saloons. By 1925 25,000 illegal blind pigs operated in the city and six million cases of Canadian whiskey came across the Detroit River each year. Additionally, more beer and booze was made in the city than came across the river. Detroit was awash in illegal hooch and all the crime that came with it. The Purple Gang would take over control of nearly all the illegal alcohol in the city. Utterly ruthless and deadly as a pit viper, it is thought the Purple Gang accounted for at least 500 murders in Detroit. When Al Capone sent representatives to the Motor City to tell the Purple Gang he was taking over their operation, the Chicago men were killed. The Purple Gang allowed other gangs a free pass in the city as long as they didn't try to hone in on their booze monopoly. Gangs thrived. The Detroit police were outnumbered, often outgunned, and simply couldn't keep up with the murders, robberies, violence, and crime spawned by illegal booze. A robbery crew or a gang that specialized in kidnapping was often tripped up by fate or plain bad luck rather than the over-worked and understaffed police.

$ $ $

Fate came close to dealing the gang a bad hand on June 5, 1925. The Jaworski Gang's reliance on intimidation, penchant for employing strong arm tactics, and their cool, nonchalant attitude toward violence didn't pay any dividends when they attempted to rob the Peninsula State Bank on the corner of Chene and Ferry Avenue.

While the fourth member of the holdup crew waited outside behind the wheel of a touring car, three members entered the bank behind drawn pistols. One gunman walked to L. J. Wiersbicki's teller window in a threatening manner. The second thug covered the bank manager and three women with his pistol. The third man walked up to the bank's only male customer, Maurice Markowski, and for no apparent reason, clubbed him over the head with his pistol butt.

Markowski dropped like a sack of coal and drew the momentary attention of the gunman guarding Wiersbicki. When the thug turned his head to watch the customer succumb to gravity, Wiersbicki, who was also an armed special deputy sheriff, dropped to the floor and tripped the bank's alarm system. The moment the alarm went off, the gunman turned back to where Wiersbicki had been standing a moment ago and began emptying his pistol into the teller's cage. One bullet grazed Wiersbicki, who pulled his revolver and began firing back at the bandits. This ignited a furious gun battle as the other two bandits began squeezing off rounds at Wiersbicki, who was hugging the floor of his teller's cage and returning fire by shooting through the wooden partition. The thieves also turned their guns on the employees and customers, who all had dived for shelter behind counters and tables. Police later estimated thirty shots had been exchanged in a matter of seconds with only L. J. Wiersbicki receiving a superficial wound.

As the brief flurry of shots slowed, the leader of the gang yelled, "Get out, boys, the police have an alarm and a crowd is forming." [8] The bandits retreated through the front door all the while firing rounds into the bank. They jumped in the waiting touring car and it sped from the curb. A passing motorist saw the armed men exit the bank and dive into the getaway car and gave chase but eventually lost them on Woodward Avenue.

There were no clues as to the gunmen's identity, no one was ever brought in or questioned, and if the teller Wiersbicki hadn't dropped to the floor and ignited a firefight, the trigger happy Jaworski gang would have easily made off with $5,000.

$ $ $

For armed robbers, every bank job was a roll of the dice. On June 13, 1925, the dice came up snake eyes and the Flatheads crapped out. Four bank robbers were caught after a running gun battle, a twelve year child was seriously wounded, and a Detroit cop paid the ultimate price for trying to keep his city safe. Three of the robbers were new to the gang and had only arrived in Detroit from Chicago a week earlier to meet Stanley "Big Stack" Podolski. Stanley had decided what bank to rob, personally cased it, laid out the plans for pulling the job, and recruited three Chicago hoodlums to fill out the crew. The very superstitious Paul Jaworski wouldn't take part in this heist because it fell on Friday the 13th.

At 10:10 AM on the unlucky Friday, three robbers strolled through the doors of Central Saving Bank waving guns and ordered the three visible employees and one customer to lie down on the floor. What the crooks didn't know was that the bank manager was in a restroom. He heard the robbers giving commands and pressed a silent alarm. One can only wonder if present day banks have burglar alarms in staff toilets.

Oblivious to the fact that the police were on their way, the bandits made a teller open the vault and quickly began cramming money and silver into a hand grip. Two customers entered the bank while the robbery was underway, and they were invited to lay on the floor with the others but not before they were relieved of any cash they had. R. S. Knapp later identified John Podolski, no relation to "Big Stack," as the man who robbed him of $40. With the vault cleared out, the gang fled the bank only to be met and cutoff from the getaway auto by an arriving police car. The trio took off down an alley with Officer Kaliszewski in hot pursuit. Another half-dozen policeman and a mob of thrill seekers, many of the latter were children, followed Kaliszewski into the alley. A fusillade of shots from the robbers turned the narrow alley into a kill zone, and Officer K went down. The police following behind him returned fire, and the alley became a shooting gallery. Incredibly, the firefight did not dampen nor deter the public's enthusiasm for the chase as they continued to trail the police as rounds whizzed by low overhead. One stray bullet struck a 12-year-old boy in the neck as he walked by the mouth of the alley with his mother. He remained in the hospital in serious condition for several days.

The trio of gunmen broke out of the alley and tried to scatter, but the cops and the crowd were so close behind the robbers couldn't shake them. One hid under a porch on Joseph Campau until tear gas forced him out and into the arms of the law. Another was captured in a Grandy Street garage. The last of the three was arrested after he left his bullet-riddled coat at a tailor's shop for repairs. The police were there when he came to pick it up.

The fourth crook, the getaway driver, had leaped from his car onto the running board of a passing automobile. The surprised driver of the commandeered vehicle needed no more urging to take his passenger wherever he wanted to go than the pistol pointed at his head. A policeman spotted the man and emptied his service revolver at the bank robber-turned-carjacker but failed to hit him, but the gunshots alerted a police car arriving on the scene. The cop driving the car spotted the fleeing robber, who was still perched on the running board, and forced the car to the curb and arrested the man.

The course of the running gun battle could be followed down the alley and through the neighborhood by the trail of money left on the ground by the fleeing robbers. Long after the men were in custody, the public appeared at police head-quarters to turn in the money they had picked up. One little girl walked into the bank with $1,200 she'd found scattered on the ground. Other locals looked upon the money strewn here and there across several blocks as a giant Easter egg hunt and it was finders' keepers. Of the $23,000 that went out the bank door with the thieves, $18,000 was recovered. Officer Kaliszewski died in the alley from his wounds. He had been married six months and had been on the police force for less than a year.

All four bandits were charged with murder, and 20 eyewitnesses either identified them in person or picked them out from mug shots. Three of the crew pleaded guilty to the robbery and the murder of Officer Kaliszewski. They all received life sentences at Marquette State Prison. "Big Stack" was also arrested but was sprung on a solid alibi. The arrest and publicity brought him to the attention of a teller who was present at the 1923 Detroit Savings Branch Bank robbery and identified the big guy as one of the robbers. The gang offered the teller $1,000 if he would testify he was mis-taken, but the teller wouldn't budge and Podolski got 20–40 in Marquette's cold, stone walls.

The gang's ranks were considerable thinned by all the arrests and police attention, but they were far from forced out of action. On November 20, 1925, the gang hit a Brink's armored car at Dubois and Franklin and got away with $18,000. They left behind a murdered guard and another who made it to the hospital in serious condition. The rob-bery further thinned the Jaworski organization when "Mike the Pug" Komieczka and Walter Markowski were convicted of murdering the Brink's guard. They both received life sentences and were sent to join their fellow gang members on the shores of Lake Superior.

After the Brink's robbery, what was left of the gang decamped for Pittsburgh where they could escape from the intense manhunt generated by the Detroit police. They kept a low profile or at least didn't do anything of note that provoked Pennsylvania law enforcement to loose the dogs on them for better than a year.

The low profile came to an abrupt halt on March 11, 1927, when the gang buried a prodigious quantity of dynamite in the middle of a Pennsylvania road and touched it off as an armored car passed over the massive charge. The blast flipped the vehicle on its back and nearly tore it in two. By some miracle, neither of the guards died from the explosion, but when one of the obviously shell-shocked guards was slow to respond to orders, one of the thugs shot and killed him. The gang of killers had a $104,000 payday, but the robbery and brutal killing unleashed a furious police manhunt. Within days, a tip led police to a Pennsylvania farm where they arrested Paul Jaworski.

It was at the Pennsylvania farmhouse that the man born as Paul Poluzynski, and known by one alias after another, acquired the name by which he has been known ever since. When the arresting Pennsylvania cop asked Paul his name, he answered Smith. Of course no one believed that was his name and another officer happened to spot a magazine on the floor with the name Jaworski written in pencil on the cover. The cop jumped to the wrong conclusion, called Paul a liar, and said his name was Jaworski. Paul replied that name was as good as any and henceforth he was and is today known as Paul Jaworski.

In the city lockup, Paul was handed a fake telegram supposedly sent by a fellow gang member that named him as taking part in a previous robbery. After reading the counterfeit telegram, Jaworski admitted his involvement in that robbery and came clean on two other Pennsylvania payroll robberies in which guards were killed. In court he was also tried for murder in a December 1925 stickup in which yet another man was killed. He was found guilty on all counts, which included three murders, on March 18, 1927, and sentenced to death in the electric chair. The killer didn't stick around waiting to be lit up like the Rockefeller Center Christmas Tree.

He found a guard who, for the right amount of money, looked the other way when a visitor smuggled four pistols into the prison. Jaworski took two; the smuggler, who turned out to be his brother, kept two. The brothers then turned the guns on the guards and shot their way out of the prison. Two guards were hit in the wild shootout and one died of his wounds.

$ $ $

Although rumored in Detroit, Jaworski remained free and out of sight for more than a year until June 6, 1928, when he masterminded and pulled off one of the most audacious robberies in Detroit's and Michigan's history. On the morning of the June 6 with a light rain glistening the streets and making the passing cars on Detroit's main drags shush and swish through shallow puddles, a large sedan pulled up to the Detroit News offices on West Lafayette and dropped off five dapper, dressed-to-kill men with fedoras pulled down over their faces as if to keep off the rain. One of the five carried a large package wrapped in red paper.

The group walked into the building's lobby and up the stairs to the second floor where the wrapping paper came off the package and out came three sawed-off shotguns. The two men who didn't get the murderous shotguns pulled pistols from their pockets and walked to the entrance to the editorial offices and flashed the guns. The three with room-sweeping shotguns entered the newspaper's business office. Two of them climbed on a long counter running the length of the room and then walked the counter to and climbed over a 10-foot-high glass partition enclosing the cashier's cage. The two in the cage began emptying cash and payroll envelopes into a bag while the third gunman stood on the counter and kept his eye on the fifty or so women sitting behind typewriters. When he spied a woman quietly and slowly moving toward a silent alarm, he fired his gun into the floor and yelled at the woman to get back to her desk. The shot sent the room into shrieking pandemonium, but no one left their seat.

Just across the hall, the two men guarding the editorial room heard the ding of an elevator announcing its imminent arrival on their floor. One of thugs ran for the elevator and tried to grab the elevator operator when the door opened but she somehow fought him off, closed the door, and took her car to the lobby where she yelled to one and all the Detroit News was being robbed. Two men who heard her instantly ran for the nearest policeman, which just happened to be outside at the corner of Lafayette directing traffic.

Moments after the elevator doors closed and headed down, the three men emerged from the business office and the five-man crew ran down the stairs to the lobby and got to the front door just ahead of an attendant who would have locked the crooks in the building by closing an iron gate. The bandits were heading out of the building just as Officer George Barstad opened the vestibule door and came face to face with the crooks. One of the crew carrying a sawed-off shotgun leveled it at Barstad and shot him point blank. He went down in a heap, and as the five desperadoes fled the building, at least one of them pumped two more rounds into the helpless and wounded man. Officer Barstad had been shot in the right eye, stomach, and right arm. He was taken to Detroit Receiving Hospital where doctors were not hopeful.

Officer Guyot Craig was just leaving a pool hall across and down the street when he saw the gunmen pour from the Detroit News and head for their getaway car. Craig immediately opened fire, and before the officer got off a couple of shots, the five hoodlums began firing at him. The lawman thought he wounded one of the gunmen who he saw fall and then was helped into the car. In return Craig was wounded in the foot. It was later estimated that at least a hundred people on the street witnessed the uneven gun fight.

As the robbers' touring car sped away from the scene of the crime, a police cruiser driven by Officer James Moffet arrived and gave chase. Moffet remained on the killers' tail even after the hoods broke out the back window of the getaway car and started shooting at him. The cop lost the car full of gangsters when it turned off Vernon Avenue onto a side street. Moffet reported he believed one of the bandits was seriously wounded.

The Jaworski gang immediately sat atop the police list of suspects for the deadly robbery. An anonymous tip that the gang was back in Detroit bolstered their suspicions, but when mug shots were passed among the witnesses, no one picked Jaworski out of the photo lineup as one of the robbers. When a witness recalled one of the crew was wearing a mustache and glasses, a police artist drew them on the Jaworski's photo and a trio of witnesses identified him as the man who appeared to be in charge of the gang.

The audacious and deadly robbery solidified Paul Jaworski's credentials as one of the country's most dangerous and wanted men. But except as a possible suspect in another robbery, Jaworski vanished. Nothing was seen or heard of the wanted outlaw through the summer of 1928. Then on September 13, 1928, in Cleveland, Ohio, a grocery clerk walked past a downtown diner, looked in the window and saw a familiar face from the past. He stared a minute before realizing he was looking at a member of his childhood choir in a Butler, Pennsylvania, Ukranian church. He hadn't seen the man since he was a boy, but there was no doubt it was Paul Jaworski, whose career he had followed in newspapers. The man also knew of the several thousand dollar reward on Jaworski and promptly called the Cleveland police.

Officers Wieczorek and Effinger arrived at the diner to check out the tip and when they approached the two men Jaworski opened fire killing Officer Wieczorek and wounding Effinger. Paul and the second man—longtime associate "Whitey" Kraft—ran out the restaurant's back door and split up. Kraft got away but two Cleveland police spotted Jaworski and followed him into an apartment building. Police surrounded the building, and a furious shootout ensued that was watched by an estimated 500 people. Jaworski had barricaded himself in the kitchen of a first-floor apartment. When the police couldn't flush Paul with guns, they lobbed tear gas into the suite. As the tear gas billowed from the apartment Jaworski charged from the building with a pistol in each hand firing as he came. A shotgun blast of buckshot to the side of his head put Jaworski down. He had also taken two pistol wounds to the chest, and it was first thought he would die from the wounds. He recovered but would suffer partial paralysis on the right side from brain damage and couldn't walk without assistance. He was indicted for the death of Officer Anthony Wieczorek while still in the hospital under 24-hour guard.

Jaworski admitted to the Detroit News robbery and said he shot Officer Barstad. He also confessed he lost his share of the take in a poker game on the night of the robbery. On October 20, 1928, Jaworski was extradited to Pennsylvania and his overdue date with the electric chair. Cleveland prosecutors wanted to try him for the murder of Officer Wieczorek but had bumped up against some legal hiccups in their case. Also, someone must have asked the question: why spend the money and time for a conviction and execution when Pennsylvania was ready to carry out its sentence?

Jaworski's lawyers filed a motion for a new trial and tried to get a commutation of the death penalty. Both attempts failed. The only thing that delayed his January 2 execution to January 21 was a requirement that a sanity evaluation be completed. He evidently passed that test with flying colors. In the hours before his execution, he was asked if he would like to see a priest. He replied, "I preached atheism since the day I quit singing in the choir. A man is yellow if he spends his life believing in nothing and then comes crawling to church because he is afraid his death is near." [9] Just before his execution, he mailed postcards to friends that listed his future address as, "45 Hellfire Road." [10]

Because of the wound to the head and the resulting brain damage, it took the help of two guards for Jaworski to walk the 'last mile' to the death chamber. He had a cigar in his mouth for the walk and joked it better last a lifetime. When he entered the execution room, the cigar was taken away and again he declined priestly assistance to meet his end. At 7:02 AM at the Rockview Penitentiary at Bellefonte, Pennsylvania, the condemned was strapped into the electric chair at the wrists, waist, and ankles with electrodes attached to his head and one leg. The switch was thrown and Paul Jaworski rode 2,000 volts into the hereafter. Jaworski boasted of killing 26 men but in reality probably only killed six—as if that wasn't enough for a psychopathic killer to brag about. The family never claimed Jaworski's body, and he was buried in a potter's field.

The last member of the Jaworski gang, Frank "Whitey" Kraft remained at large until January 22, 1931. Kraft had been a boyhood friend of Paul, and they had grown up together in Hamtramck. They were partners in crime since childhood. After the Detroit News robbery, area police were ordered to shoot to kill Kraft if he offered any resistance if found and his mug shot was given to every police recruit when he received his badge.

On January 22, 1931, Kraft was spotted, fittingly enough, in Hamtramck by two of that city's patrolmen. When they tried to arrest Kraft, he drew a gun and fired. Both officers returned fire and put a permanent end to the last of Jaworski's gang.

1. Detroit Free Press April 3, 1924 p1, c8
2. Detroit News 5-17-1924 p1, c1
3. Detroit Free Press 4-15-1925 p1, c1
4. IBID
5. Detroit Free Press 4-16-1925 p1, c4
6. IBID
7. IBID
8. Detroit Free Press 6-6-1925 p3, c6
9. Murderpedia.org/male.J/j/Jaworski-paul-html
10. IBID

Chapter 8

The First Battle of Hogan's Alley

March 31, 1924

*"...the denizens of Hogan's Alley rushed to fill
their pockets like it was raining money."*

*W*ith apologies to Meredith Wilson who wrote the music and lyrics to Music Man;
Well, you got trouble in a downriver city.
I say trouble, my friend, right there in Ecorse.
Friends, let me tell ya what I mean.
They got hidden boat basins, and rum-runnin' boats
With a capitol "B."
And that rhymes with "P" and that stands for Prohibition.
On January 16, 1920, when prohibition became law in the United States, Ecorse, Michigan, and other small communities downriver from Detroit became, in short order, criminal boomtowns. By the mid-1920s a half-million cases of Canadian whiskey a month were smuggled across the Detroit River. Seventy-five percent of all the liquor that found its way into the U.S. during Prohibition did so by crossing either the St. Clair or Detroit rivers. Within five years of the country going dry, illegal liquor was Detroit's second biggest business. Smuggling was especially prolific in downriver Detroit because the river was often less than a mile wide. There were an abundance small coves and islands

where smugglers could either hide from or avoid authorities, and the towns' small police forces couldn't cope with the tidal wave of liquor. Among all the downriver communities, Ecorse soon became the country's number one port of entry for Canadian booze.

Canadian breweries and distilleries built export docks across the river from Ecorse. Geography further conspired to make Ecorse a smugglers paradise by placing Canada's Fighting Island between the American town and the export dock. It acted like a curtain hiding the arrival, loading, and departure of the rum runners. Ecorse's city fathers even built a tall wooden wall along the city's shoreline to make it more difficult for Federal agents to monitor the coming and going of smugglers. As a result the little town on the Detroit River became a mecca for bootleggers, smugglers, and infamous nightclubs. Criminals of every stripe and those in the general public who got a thrill out of hobnobbing with the dangerous, seamy underside of American society crowded its streets and drank many a bottle of Canadian whiskey dry within minutes of it coming off a boat.

Ecorse was generally recognized as one of the toughest small towns in America, and Hogan's Alley held the blue ribbon for being the most dangerous, crime-ridden pocket of hell within the town. The alley was a typical outgrowth of rum running, gangs, and criminal expansion. It was a side street off Jefferson Avenue that ended at the Detroit River. Lining the dimly lit alley was a row of decrepit shanties that catered to smugglers, low-lifes, and common criminals. Admittance to the alley and any of the wretched, dark, and dirty buildings—all of which operated as blind pigs—was by password. Here, and in other spots in small downriver communities, boat slips and old channels were roofed over so smugglers could slip into a virtual underground waterway and motor nearly a block inland before docking and unloading their boats while completely hidden from view and well away from the river. This is where the story ended; it began a few blocks away.

Shortly before noon on March 31, 1924, four well-dressed men—bank robbers in Detroit generally dressed in suits and ties to conduct their business—entered the Commonwealth Federal Savings Branch Bank on Fort and Military and yelled for the three employees and seven to ten customers to raise their hands. The four-member bank crew pulled off the robbery with the expertise and speed of seasoned professional bandits. While one armed robber watched the employees and customers, the three other highwaymen thoroughly rifled the tellers' cages and grabbed every available buck, but one. George James, a customer, was holding a $20 bill in his hand when the crooks burst in the bank, and when he made as if to give it to the robbers, he was told to put it in his pocket; they didn't want his money.

In what seemed like the blink of an eye, the bank robbers had appeared, cleaned out the tellers' cages to the tune of $17,000+, and disappeared out the door. As the quartet exited the bank and piled into their getaway car, a Detroit police cruiser happened to pass the bank and immediately recognized a bank robbery was going down. As the robbers sped away, the police gave chase. And here is a classic example of why a getaway driver has to be as good at handling a car at full speed as a NASCAR driver and know the local streets and alleys better than a cop who has driven the same streets for ten years. Within minutes the cops lost the getaway car, and the robbers simply disappeared in spite of an intensive search.

Downriver in Ecorse, the police were probably aware of the Commonwealth bank robbery, but it was out of their jurisdiction and quite likely long out of their minds by late afternoon. It wasn't as if Ecorse Chief of Police Albert M. Jaeger didn't already have enough on his plate. In 1920 Jaeger was the town's fire chief and had a force of three firemen under his command when the village president gave him a second hat to wear, chief of police.

On the afternoon of March 31, 1924, Jaeger received a call that would have him wearing his police chief's hat. He was asked to escort two sheriff deputies to the Robbers Roost in Hogan's Alley on the off chance that four men who had recently made off with a safe from an Ecorse dry goods store might be hanging out there. Yes, where else would robbers go to hide from the law than an illegal blind pig named the Robbers Roost on a street infamous for its criminal element. At times the total absence of subtly is wondrous to behold. To even up the sides, Chief Jaeger brought along Benjamin Montie, a fireman and an auxiliary policeman.

The four lawmen arrived at Hogan's Alley and walked directly to the Robbers Roost. They didn't knock on the door and wait for someone to ask for the password, they simply kicked it in. When the door burst open and slammed against the shack's wall, two very startled men leaped from a money-covered table, raced across the room, dove through a window, and landed in the Detroit River. The pair started swimming for the Canadian side of the river like Olympic hopefuls until the cops got to the window with drawn guns and threatened to shoot the two if they didn't turn back and surrender. When the two sopping wet and cold men pulled themselves from the river, they were handcuffed together and carted off to the county jail by the two deputy sheriffs. A brief search revealed that each of the men had more than $1,000 in large bills in their possession. The pair didn't have any guns, but there were cartridges in both their pockets so the police knew they had probably thrown them away before climbing out of the river.

Chief Jaeger and Ben Montie remained in the Robbers Roost as the deputies took off with the two wet fugitives. The table where the arrested men had sat was covered in money, and it looked like they had been counting it. The two curious

Ecorse policemen began exploring their surroundings and found that all the shacks were connected by tunnels and each ramshackle building had a boat well, trap doors, and false walls. It became abundantly obvious the area must be a major smuggling depot.

Within minutes of the deputies' departure with the prisoners, an auto drove up to the shack and two well-dressed men walked into the Roost. The two officers drew their guns and shouted for the men to raise their hands. Montie walked over and handcuffed a man who would later be identified as Leo Corbett. Despite the handcuffs and before Montie could conduct a thorough search, the man somehow drew a gun and fired a bullet through Montie's heart. The auxiliary policeman fell into a boat well, dead before he hit the water.

Montie's killer, still in handcuffs, started to run for freedom. Jaeger turned his attention from the second man and opened fire on the fleeing crook. The police chief hit him once, but the man continued to stagger away when Jaeger fired again and dropped him. He was the shootout's second fatality. The second man—it would later be learned his name was Eliza Meade—made it to the car while Jaeger was engaged with Montie's killer and sped away. As Meade barreled out of the alley, he threw money from the car into the street resulting in a mad dash for cash as the denizens of Hogan's Alley rushed to fill their pockets like it was raining money. Sheriff deputies, who'd been dispatched from the jail, arrived just as Meade was leaving the alley and took off after him. Meade couldn't lose his pursuers and in desperation drove into a swamp, abandoned the car, and fled on foot into the wetland.

More deputies were called to search the swamp while others returned to Robbers Roost. Montie's body was raised from the boat well and taken to his house where his unsuspecting wife learned of the tragedy when her husband's body was carried into their home.

The dead thug was taken to a funeral parlor where Detroit police identified the man as Leo Corbett, the leader of a Toledo gang that had descended on Detroit three months earlier and raised hell, robbed banks, and held up pay agents and businesses throughout the area. Detroit police had hunted them relentlessly and fruitlessly. Corbett and the two men taken into custody were also identified as the morning robbers of the Detroit Commonwealth Savings Bank.

In a careful search of the Robbers Roost, the police found thousands of dollars from several recent bank and armed robberies. They also found evidence linking the gang to the shooting of two Detroit policemen on Gratiot Avenue a week earlier. Eliza Meade was later nabbed in Arizona, brought back to Michigan to stand trial, and like the other two members of the gang was sentenced to 20–40 years in Marquette State Prison.

There was a second Battle of Hogan's Alley in 1928 when thirty Customs Border Patrol Officers staked out the alley, both by car and in three boats in the Detroit River, waiting to spring a trap on rum runners. When the smugglers pulled into an alley pier, the customs agents rushed in and arrested seven men. The smugglers yelled for help and over 200 people poured out of Hogan Alley's illegal bars and attacked the agents. The mob slashed the lawmen's car tires, smashed windshields, barricaded the end of the alley, and sent volleys of bricks, bottles, and rocks into the agents' ranks. The customs officials soon had enough, and they tightened ranks into a compact group, charged the end of the alley, broke through the barricade and escaped with their lives if not with their dignity intact.

The end of Hogan's Alley came before the end of Prohibition when Jefferson Avenue was widened in 1929. During the construction work, the shanties were torn down and the boat wells and slips were filled in. Prohibition couldn't shut down Hogan's Alley, but it didn't stand a chance against eminent domain.

Chapter 9

The Demise of the Shotgun Gang

August 5, 1924

"You got me this time."

*F*rank Parmentye and the Shotgun Gang were like Fourth of July fireworks. They had a meteoric rise, lit up the town and the sky with a lot of noise and excitement, and in the end were over just as quickly. But they did go out with a bang. As described in chapter six, the Shotgun Gang weaned Paul Jaworski from a life in petty crime in Hamtramck and their fall from criminal grace propelled Jaworski's rise to one of the top Midwest Prohibition Era outlaws. As criminal wet nurses, the sawed-off shotgun wielding crew were ruthless, stone-cold killers, and their brief tenure as one of Detroit's premier bank robbery outfits came to an end just as one would expect—violently.

Frank Parmentye, the heart and soul of the gang cut his teeth on crime as a kid in Hamtramck. His first brush with the law came in 1916 when he was seventeen and arrested for simple larceny and fined $25. In hardly more time than it takes to hot wire a car, he was back in court for "unlawfully driving away automobiles" [1] which leaves one wondering if there is a difference between the above and simple auto theft? Parmentye got a pair of six-month sentences for joy riding or car theft. He didn't serve out the sentence and was let out on parole which he quickly violated. Eventually, his almost obsessive criminal activities resulted in a trip north to Marquette and a stretch in the state prison.

He was released from Marquette on September 1, 1923, and placed on two years' parole. They might as well have told him he couldn't cross his legs when he sat down because crime seemed just as natural and inevitable as the former. Within months of his release, Parmentye and his gang were robbing banks with the regularity of a Swiss watch. His top lieutenants were Stanley Gawlick and Vance Hardy. Gawlick would often enter a bank with a sawed-off shotgun pointing the way like a leader dog for the blind and shout, "Well here's Stanley, back again." [2]

Within less than a year, Parmentye killed a police officer, wounded a bank teller, and became involved in a running gun battle with police through the streets of Detroit in which a bystander was shot and killed. The gang leader was reliably connected to numerous bank robberies, armed robberies, and was wanted for the murder of Louis Lambert, in which he once again proved he could kill with the thoughtless ease of swatting a mosquito. Lambert, the proprietor of a near-beer saloon was returning to his place of business from a neighborhood bank when he was pulled into Parmentye's automobile, robbed of $4,000 in cash, then shot dead and his body thrown in a ditch.

All that came to an end on August 5, 1924, when the gang tried to rob the Continental Savings Bank. Employees at the bank had become suspicious, and probably more than a little apprehensive when their bank was visited twice by two men who conducted no business while there but appeared more than casually observant. They seemed to make special note of the tellers' cages placement, the location of the doors and offices, and even paid attention to the attitude and demeanor of the tellers. It was unnerving to be watched so closely and openly, and all the employees became absolutely certain the bank was being cased by professional bank robbers. Bank officials went to the police and convinced them to temporarily assign two officers to guard the bank.

On Monday August 5, a touring car carrying four men pulled to a stop in front of the bank. Three overcoat and straw hat clad men briskly climbed out of the car and made for the bank's front door. As soon as the trio entered the bank, the man later identified as Parmentye noticed Officer Ashworth and without a moment's hesitation pulled his revolver and shot the policeman at point blank range. Ashworth took the bullet in his heart and died instantly. The shooting didn't stop the crew from pulling the gangs' trademark sawed-off shotguns from under their coats, looting the teller's cages, and fleeing with $2,400. As the three left the bank with their swag, Parmentye fired into the bank and hit a teller in the arm. In return, bank employees opened fire at the bandits as they dashed for the getaway car. Left lying on the sidewalk as the crooks pulled away was a straw hat with a bullet hole in the back indicating at least one of the rounds found its mark.

Police were of the opinion that this was the same gang that failed in an attempted robbery of the Commercial Bank on East Forest the previous Friday. That robbery was aborted not by the arrival of the police, a pushed burglar alarm, or armed guards, but by a woman who saw the shotguns, panicked, and loosed a scream that rippled the whiskey in the Canadian distilleries across the river. Subjected to a sound that could be heard three counties away, the robbers turned and fled.

The law enforcement community was also pretty comfortable with the theory the gang was led by Frank Parmentye who, along with Martin O. Shea, escaped fifteen days earlier from the Detroit Receiving Hospital prison ward. Two weeks before the Continental robbery, Frank was arrested in the company of several ex-cons and suspected stickup artists. Because of some unspecified illness, he was taken to the prisoner's ward at the Detroit Receiving Hospital. He and Shea, who had a bullet wound in the groin, were examined by a doctor who declared they were too ill to escape. The doctor left, and the pair promptly climbed down a rope ladder from the hospital's second floor, were picked up by a waiting car, and again on the loose and headed for mayhem.

It soon became apparent to officers investigating the Continental robbery that the four gangsters split into two groups shortly after leaving the bank. George Robertson reported to police he had started his car in the garage when two men—who fit the description of the bank robbers—walked up, dragged him from the car, knocked him unconscious, and then locked him in his own bathroom. They then drove off in Robertson's car.

Late Monday afternoon, the gang's touring car was found. Inside, a cap and a couple of blood-spattered straw hats attested to the bloody shootout at the bank. Two shotguns were found a few yards from the car hidden in shrubbery. The vehicle's license plates had, of course, been stolen the day before. The gray touring car had been seen at both the Continental Bank robbery and the attempted robbery three days earlier at the Commercial Bank. Employees at the Continental Bank positively identified Fred Parmentye as one of the robbers and named him as the killer of Officer Ashworth.

On Monday evening, about five blocks from where the gangs' getaway car was found, blood stains smearing the alley behind a house on 5937 Harding Avenue led police to the discovery of a body in the garage at the above address. The male corpse had been shot once in the head. Signs indicated the body had been dragged along the alley and into the garage. Police were convinced the dead man was one of the four gangsters who robbed the Continental Bank that morning. Identification papers on the body said the man was Joe Musky of Toledo, but Hamtramck detectives were sure that was an alias and they were looking at the recently departed

Stanley Gawlick who was wanted for numerous bank robberies. A further search of the pockets produced shotgun shells, a revolver, and a snapshot of a man and woman.

The body in the garage led police to search the house where two recently fired pistols, a .45 and a .22 caliber Colt, were discovered. On the second floor the police found fresh blood stained sheets on one of the beds. All of which led police to conclude they had found the bank robbing crew's hideout. A canvas of the nearby homes revealed the Harding Avenue residents had utterly no curiosity concerning their new neighbors or were ardent followers of the three monkeys whose mantra was hear, see, or speak no evil.

Although an extensive manhunt combed the area looking for Parmentye, it was a tip to police that pointed them to where the killer was holed up. The fugitive had grown a mustache, dyed his hair, taken a second story room in clapboard house on Russell Street, and laid low. Fully aware the man was armed and wouldn't be taken without a fight, fifteen cops answered the call. Eight police surrounded the house, and seven entered the building and made their way to the killer's room.

The door was unlocked so the lead officers, Detective Lt. Patrick O'Grady and Lt. Frank Holland, threw it open and were the first into the room. Parmentye must have heard them coming because he was already at the window tearing the screen off when the door flew open. The killer glanced down at the street and was greeted with the unwelcome sight of shotgun-armed cops looking up at him. Parmentye turned and lunged for a .38 caliber revolver he left in a chair. When he reached for the pistol, both officers fired and Parmentye went down. When the detectives reached him, he whispered, "You got me this time." [3] He died en route to the hospital. He was 25 years old and had spent almost half his life as a criminal.

In addition to the .38 and a shotgun, a Mrs. Max Turnow was also found in Parmentye's room. She was the wife of the man who rented the room to the killer after his escape from the hospital. Mr. Turnow was taken into custody and had even more explaining to do than his wife.

At the news of Parmentye's death, Martin Shea, still in hiding after his escape from the hospital, sent a note via an underworld contact vowing to kill the two officers who shot his friend. A frantic manhunt ensued and failed to turn up Shea. O'Grady and Holland's homes were put under 24-hour watch in spite of both cops stating they could take care of themselves. Police headquarters issued a terse order, "Get Shea, dead or alive." [4]

A tip from another underworld informant sent police rushing to an alleged gambling joint on Woodward Avenue on Thursday night in search of Martin Shea. Unfortunately, tips work both ways, and only minutes before the police arrived the gambling hall got a tip the police were on the way. When twenty officers arrived they were met by a crowd of seventy gamblers frantically trying to make it out the building even as the police came in the same door. The proprietor neither knew Martin Shea nor could say if he had been in his establishment that night. It was later determined by corralling and interviewing some of the stampeding gamblers that Shea left the place about five minutes before the raid.

Making every effort to rout out and shut down the Shotgun Gang, the police, earlier on Thursday, arrested a man and 'his supposed wife' for operating a blind pig on Cass Avenue that Parmentye and his criminal confederates used as their hangout and watering hole. Police also brought in a taxi driver thought to have driven Shea and Parmentye away from the hospital after they escaped from the prison ward.

The photo of the guy and gal found in Gawlick's pocket was circulated throughout southeastern Michigan and among Toledo police because the girl in the snapshot was thought to be from there. The longshot effort paid off like a lottery ticket and the couple were spotted on a Toledo street by police and held for the Detroit police. The woman, Helen Hudson, alias Helen Woods, refused to answer any questions, and the man gave his name as William Robenski and claimed to be a saltwater sailor from Port Huron. The police didn't buy it and soon identified the man as Joseph Parisi, 21, and charged him with murder in an earlier bank robbery and as the getaway driver in the Continental bank job. Also put under arrest was Parisi's brother, brother-in-law, and sister, all believed to be members of the gang. On Saturday, August 9, the police arrested Fred "Puggy" Hamilton and named him as one of two people who helped Martin Shea escape Detroit and the shoot-to-kill pronouncement by police headquarters. There is no record of Martin Shea ever being arrested or named in association with any criminal activity after fleeing Detroit.

The deadly Shotgun Gang had a brief and violent run that didn't last quite a year before two of the top men were killed and a third went to jail. A lot of effort by over-worked police, a little luck, and an over-abundance of criminal arrogance led to their downfall. Unfortunately, there was a long line of desperate and amoral men ready to step into their shoes and walk the same bloody path that led to either an early and violent death or a decades-long spell in a cold, hard cell that could rot the soul. So it should not be surprising that even with the demise of the Shotgun Gang there was hardly a pause in the ongoing, violent bank robberies that plagued metro Detroit.

Officer William Ashworth was 27 years old when he was killed protecting a Detroit bank. He was single and had been a policeman for barely two months.

1. Detroit Free Press August 8, 1924 p2, c4
2. Kavieff, Paul R. The Violent Years: Prohibition and the Detroit Mobs. Barricade Books, 2001, Fort Lee NJ. p140.
3. Detroit Free Press August 7, 1924 p3, c4
4. IBID p1, c8

Chapter 10

The 40-Mile Shoot Out

February 21, 1925

*"In the end the bandits simply couldn't
out run Mrs. Foresman..."*

*I*t was a car that bespoke money and influence when
it pulled up to the front door of the Millburg Bank a
few miles west of Benton Harbor on February 21, 1925. They
probably didn't see many cars like this in the roughly three-
block-by-three-block unincorporated village after which the
bank was named. The Cadillac Phaeton touring car sported a
V-8 that pumped out 79-horsepower and sent the behemoth
with the 11-foot-long wheelbase hurtling down bad roads at
speeds that could send passengers off to the sweet hereafter in
a heartbeat. It had seating for seven on English long-grained,
hand-buffed, plaited black leather. All open Cadillac touring cars rolled off the assembly line with a black chassis and
a paint job that appeared deep enough to drown in. It also
came with a black convertible top and side curtains which,
when lowered, made it nearly impossible to tell how many
passengers were in the back of the car. This particular top-end
touring car also came equipped with wind screens on either
side of the windshield, tilting headlamps, twelve spoke artil-
lery wheels painted to match the body, a spare tire strapped to
the trunk, and a crew of well-dressed bank robbers.

Cashier Ben Kral and teller Miss Elizabeth Kreitner were a half-hour into a normal business day at the bank when the touring car, with back curtains down, parked near the front door and two youngish, well-attired men jumped from the automobile and hurried inside as if late for a meeting. Both men vaulted the bank railing and before either Kral or Kreitner could fully register what had happened they were each staring into the business end of loaded pistols. The two criminals' first words were unnecessary even if delivered as a duet. They said, "Hands up, and don't touch any buttons." [1]

As the two stunned employees raised their hands, two more well-dressed men exited the Cadillac and entered the bank. Kreitner and Kral were marched at gun point into the small coat room and the door was locked. This was all too much for Miss Kreitner who gave every indication she was about to swoon until one of the bandits reassured her with, "That's all right, little girl. We wouldn't hurt you." [2] With the employees out of the way, the robbery crew went to the vault where they quickly and professionally bagged $2,900 in cash—which, by the way, only amounted to about half the price of the Cadillac—and some $52,000 worth of negotiable securities. Within minutes of hitting the front door, the crooks had stashed the loot in the back in the Cadillac and sped out of town in the direction of Benton Harbor. Little did the bank robbers know they had ignited a chain of events that would unroll like an updated stock film scene found in every Grade B western gracing that era's silent silver screens. It was the classic "posse chases the outlaws with guns blazing" scene but done here with a significant twist. A good part of the posse consisted of telephone operators who never left their switchboards.

The bandits hadn't gone three blocks before Kreitner and Kral broke out of the coat closet and sounded the alarm. Mrs. Earl K. Foresman, chief operator of the local telephone exchange, and her assistants were literally the first to take up the chase. When the alarm came into the switchboard, Mrs. Foresman responded like a calm, cool professional. No wasted words, no missteps in the heat of the moment as she made assignments and divvied up the workload. Within moments, switchboard operators were quickly and efficiently notifying every town, village, and local law enforcement office in the surrounding area of the robbery and describing the getaway car. The operators even called isolated farms asking them to be on the lookout for the crooks.

Within minutes the gangsters' detailed and pre-planned getaway route was kaput. At one town the fleeing robbers found the main street, their intended escape route, blocked by a box car and locomotive parked where the railroad tracks crossed the street. Barricades made from wagons, carts, and lumber sprang up at the main crossroads in many towns in the southwest corner of the state. The town's citizenry loaded their shotguns and deer rifles, manned the do-it-yourself roadblocks, then waited to see if trouble was bound their way. Police in South Bend and Michigan City, Indiana, were also informed of the bank robbery and warned the armed thieves might be trying to elude capture by crossing into their state. Police from several cities on either side of the Indiana/Michigan state line sent out patrols to run back roads and hunt the crooks.

In retrospect, the old switchboard and its operators did as effective a job of spreading the news as all the present day hype about social media. And the work of the operators didn't stop there. Every time the Cadillac was sighted or shots were traded, the women would quickly call and update everyone on their call list which drew the net ever tighter around the fleeing desperadoes. In the end the bandits simply couldn't out run Mrs. Foresman and her roomful of operators.

The Benton Harbor police were warned the Cadillac was headed their way, and while that city's police department set up roadblocks, St. Joseph County Sheriff Franz and Undersheriff Paget rushed to Millburg and organized a posse—who had armed themselves with shotguns, sawed-off shotguns, and hunting rifles—and sent teams out to set up country roadblocks or bird dog the getaway car.

The first official sighting of the getaway car occurred when the Cadillac flew through Stevensville at 60 miles per hour and just beat the erection of a roadblock that would have cut off its escape. Farther south in Galien, Michigan, Deputy Sheriff Con Allen and his friend Floyd Lintner, a onetime deputy sheriff and current auto mechanic, heard the news that the bank robbers were on the run. The pair armed themselves, jumped into a Buick, and sped north. They had gone only a few miles when a distant cloud of dust turned into a fast approaching Cadillac Phaeton getting bigger by the second. Deputy Allen slammed on the brakes and slewed the car around so it stood broadside to the oncoming Cadillac.

Details became somewhat confused in the adrenaline rush of the next few moments. Lintner and Allen used the Buick as a shield as the bandits' car approached their impromptu roadblock, and Allen either did or didn't demand the robbers surrender before the gangsters piled out of the big touring car and unleashed a hail of gunfire at the Buick. The two-man posse gave as good as they got, riddling the Cadillac with buckshot. Lintner and Allen were certain they wounded at least one of the bandits before Lintner was hit. A round from one of the crooks passed under the Buick and tore into the former deputy's right heel and cut a tendon. Even with one of the two posse members down, their fire didn't slacken, and the bank robbers decided they'd had enough. The bandits reluctantly agreed they couldn't get by the Buick, so they climbed back into the Cadillac, backtracked to a minor dirt road, and sped off in the direction of Three Oaks. In spite of Linter's wound, he was still game to give chase, but the Buick had a tire shot out, so Allen drove the hobbled car back to Galien where Lintner received medical attention.

A few minutes after the dust up with Lintner and Allen, the now bullet-scarred getaway car blew through Three Oaks and two miles later crossed into Indiana. Still staying to back roads and driving in any direction but straight for very long—in case the law was still on their tail—the Cadillac raced through New Carlisle, Indiana about noon. They didn't get out of town unnoticed. One of Mrs. Foresman's operators had already phoned town constable Stine Ackley with the news the bandits might be headed his way. In response, Ackley holstered one pistol in his pants pocket, stuffed two more in jacket pockets, and enlisted local farmer and civilian Oscar Smith to ride shotgun. Oscar armed himself with the weapon de jour, an automatic shotgun loaded with buckshot. The two were setting in a Chevy coupe in New Carlisle waiting for trouble on four wheels to make an appearance when it sped right past. Without a moment's hesitation and once again outnumbered, outgunned, and certainly in this case, out-mounted, a new two-man posse took off in pursuit.

The powerful touring car quickly outpaced the coupe, but the problem for the crooks soon became where were they, and where were they headed? The first casualty of the hectic forty-mile chase, numerous road blocks, and one shoot out was the getaway plan. In the 1920s country roads could go bad faster than unrefrigerated milk on a hot day, and the road they took out of New Carlisle proved to be no exception. It soon turned into a muddy, rutted country road seemingly bound for nowhere. The desperadoes must have felt some relief when Jed Dollinger's farm came into view. The Cadillac pulled up beside the barn, which set closest to the road of any of the farm buildings, and a bandit jumped out and headed for the open barn door seeking directions.

In what had become a tortoise and hare race, the dogged little Chevy kept plugging away even when hopelessly behind, only to catch up with the Cadillac as it sat beside the barn. Smith and Ackley passed the Cadillac, stopped near the Dollinger house, and as they stepped from the car Ackley told Smith, "We'll shoot if we have to." [3]

Then with enough grit to fill a gravel pit, Constable Stine Ackley walked up to the touring car, opened its back door and asked, "What do you want?" [4] The occupants weren't in a talkative mood, but the three rifles on the floor of the back seat and a pistol filling at least one hand of every man in the car was answer enough, and the lawman, with a revolver in both hands, emptied them into the car. The gangster's guns replied to Ackley's opening volley, and as he was reaching for his third handgun, the constable was felled by a bullet in the groin.

When the shooting started Smith stepped to the front of the Cadillac, brought the shotgun to his shoulder, and began pulling the trigger. He sent round after round of buckshot through the Caddy's windshield flaying the bank robbers with bits of flying glass, lead pellets, and shredded upholstery. Unable to withstand Smith's furious barrage, the bloodied gangsters dove from the car and ran for shelter in the nearby farm buildings. Smith spotted one of the bandits breaking from the group headed for the barn, and like shooting clay pigeons, he coolly swung the shotgun to the new target, adjusted his lead, pulled the trigger, and saw the man drop. Only later did Smith realize the man he shot was not accounted for.

The five gangsters were in terrible shape. They bled from numerous facial wounds, and two of them suffered from serious leg wounds, but the situation was growing even more desperate for Ackley and Smith. Constable Ackley was on the ground with a bullet in his groin and out of ammunition leaving Smith as the only thing standing in the way of the gang's getaway. If the crooks could only temporarily disregard their wounds or galvanize their mettle, so to speak, and charge the volunteer lawman before help arrived, freedom lay just steps away, if the pulverized Cadillac was still drivable. The window of opportunity was there, but it closed before the robbers could find the will to act. Alerted by switchboard operators, several carloads of police had been driving roads in the area looking for the fleeing Cadillac. Indiana's South Bend chief of police and several of his officers happened to be less than a mile from the Dollinger farm when Ackley and Smith shot it out with the gangsters. Hearing the crack of pistols and the closely fired blasts from a shotgun, the lawmen raced toward the sound of the trouble, arrived when needed most, and charged into the fight. The bank robbers recognized the inevitable and reluctantly surrendered when the South Bend police joined the fray.

Ackley was rushed to a South Bend hospital while the five crooks—all suffering from various wounds—were transported to the South Bend police station and locked in a cell. Four of the gangsters suffered from multiple facial wounds from flying glass and pellets that temporarily blinded one of them. The two gun battles had left 32-year-old Mishawaka, Indiana, Eddie Sommers' entire body peppered with buckshot. Burt Murray and James Long, 42, both from Chicago, had facial wounds. Thirty-one-year-old Frank King of Toledo was gored by a bullet in his leg that left a 5" long, 2" wide, and 1" deep furrow that permanently damaged his knee. The worst injured was John Marshall, 32, of Hamilton, Ontario, whose left leg had been shattered by a bullet. Compounding his misery was a face acned by bits of windshield and buckshot.

The news of the arrests spread so fast a crowd, hoping for a glimpse of the desperadoes, awaited their arrival outside the South Bend police station. On Saturday evening three of the robbers were chauffeured to St. Joseph in a sheriff's car while ambulances delivered the two with serious leg wounds back to the state they had so desperately tried to flee earlier in the day. And again, in Michigan, a crowd gathered in front of the jail waiting patiently for a look at the now infamous bank robbers.

As soon as the prisoners arrived, and before he asked them any questions, the sheriff sent for a doctor who examined and treated their wounds. When Sheriff Franz did get his chance at the bank robbers all five refused to talk, but their fingerprints spoke volumes. Every one of them had served time, some were on parole, others were wanted for various crimes, and each had a handful of aliases.

Sam Kruger of Benton Harbor had more than just a passing interest in how much of the stolen money and securities were recovered when the bandits were arrested because he was the insurance agent carrying the robbery policy on the Millburg bank. On Sunday morning he traveled to Indiana to take possession of the recovered loot only to discover it amounted to chump change—literally. Found in the Cadillac, wrapped in a sack was $200 in dimes, $18 in nickels, $19.50 in pennies, a $500 Liberty bond, and a variety of mortgages.

Disappointed, Kruger led a group to the Dollinger farm and nosed around. Not far from where the Cadillac had been shot to pieces, Kruger found a sawed-off shotgun covered in blood and a trail of blood that led to a fence from which hung a tattered piece of scarf. On the other side of the fence the blood-dappled trail led to an abandoned farmhouse where it was temporarily lost then rediscovered in a nearby field. This had to be the man Oscar Smith winged as the bandits fled the Cadillac. The group with Kruger spread out over the countryside in the general direction pointed by the bloody trail and turned up a farmer who told them he had gone outside last night to see why his dogs were barking and found a stranger who asked if he could spend the night in his barn. When told no the man wandered off. Despite further searching, Kruger's group couldn't find another trace of what they were certain was a sixth robber. They promptly notified the police who began a search for the sixth man who probably had walked off with close to $3,000 in cash.

There was still some initial skepticism concerning the existence of a sixth bank robber, but Oscar Smith added his weight to the argument claiming he was sure this was the man he shot running from the car. Then a La Porte, Indiana, man came forward on December 23 to tell police a stranger with his arm in a homemade sling approached him a day after the robbery and not far from the Dollinger farm claiming he'd been in a car accident. He then offered the La Porte man $20 for a ride into South Bend. It may have taken some time for the dim bulb to flicker and light up in the cerebral cortex of the man with the $20 threshold for becoming a Good Samaritan, but when it did, he went to the police with a complete description of the man with the badly injured arm. A wide ranging manhunt turned up nothing.

Bank robbers, once captured, provoked the same curiosity as a two-headed calf or some other oddity found in a carnival midway freak show. Only in this case, the 500 visitors who shuffled through the jail on Monday to ogle the gunmen didn't have to be talked into it by a barker or pay an entry fee. The five robbers were arraigned Monday and a $100,000 bail was set for each. The police were convinced they would plead innocent.

Every day the five remained in jail, their legal situation grew worse. Edward Sommers and Frank King were suspected of committing several other bank robberies including the Grand Rapid Savings job in December of 1921 in which two lawmen were killed. John Marshall's fingerprints identified him as the accused murderer of Chicago policeman Sgt. Edward Marpool on October 26, 1920. Edward Gilmore was a convicted burglar, and he and James Long were positively eye-balled by witnesses as participants in a Springfield bank robbery near Jackson. Strangely enough, the identification of Gilmore and James as part of the Springfield gang freed two local men who, in the county's rush to justice, had (although innocent) been convicted of being two of the three men who robbed the Springfield Bank. The Cadillac also matched the car used in the Springfield job, right down to the curtained windows and identical tire tracks, all of which led police to believe the five men in the St. Joseph jail all took part in the Springfield heist and maybe several more.

Plaudits came from around the state for the way Sheriff Franz stayed at his desk and directed the search for the bank robbers and how with the cooperation of the switchboard operators directed and coordinated various police units into an ever tightening noose around the fleeing criminals. Sheriff Franz was very aware of the part the telephone operators played in catching the bank robbers and by way of thank you sent them a box of candy.

In a classic case of you can't keep a good man down, Constable Stine Ackley, regardless of being wounded in the groin on Saturday, was back on the job in New Carlisle the following Monday.

In 1929 James Kane was arrested and later convicted of being the bank robber who got away. He received a life sentence.

1.   Benton Harbor News-Palladium 2-21-1925 p1, c1
2.   IBID
3.   Benton Harbor News-Palladium 2-23-1925 p1, c5
4.   IBID

Chapter 11

Cassopolis and the Third Approach

November 24, 1925

"...the repeated explosions blew out the bank's windows and those in adjacent buildings and completely wrecked the inside of the bank."

It's a matter of style. Some bank robbers were all finesse and stealth. They broke into banks at night, cracked the safe without blowing it up, and quietly disappeared into the dark. There were those who counted on a brazen show of force, thorough planning, a fast car, and used the often undeclared promise of violence to rob banks in broad daylight. And then there was the third approach. A gang of gun-wielding thugs simply drove into a small town late at night, took over the sleeping village, isolated it from the rest of the world, blew the safe in the town's bank, and rode off into the night like a wandering band of marauding barbarians.

On Tuesday, November 24, 1925 Cassopolis, Michigan became the little town in the path of the marauding barbarians. State Highway 60, in the 1920s, was a heavily used truck route connecting Chicago and Detroit. It passed through innumerable little towns most Michiganders couldn't even point to on the palm of their hands like Mendon, Leonidas, Jones, Fabius, Vandalia, and yes, Cassopolis. Truck traffic kept coffee pots perking and short-order cooks on their feet in Cassopolis at two all-night restaurants, and when the bank robbers drove into town at 2:30 AM, the restaurants were the first places they hit.

Pat Wallace was alone in his eatery when three gun-toting thugs entered and instead of ordering off the menu tied Wallace's hands behind his back. They then walked him across the highway to Parney's, the town's other all-night diner, where the gangsters found three customers and the restaurant's owner. One of the three customers was Cass County Deputy Sheriff Clyde Benham. Like Wallace, they all had their hands tied behind their backs. The five trussed captives were ordered across the street and made to huddle under a stairway of the local hospital while the bank crew tried to break into the bank's back door.

At this point, if the gang put any stock in omens, they might have begun to rethink this caper because the back door beat them. They couldn't get it open. So they ran to the front of the bank and smashed through the front door. The captives were marched into the bank, pushed into a coat room, and told to keep their heads down.

No one at the time was sure how many men were in the bank crew because they seemed to be everywhere at once. Either before they rounded up all the insomniacs from the two diners or nearly at the same time, another gang member went to the telephone exchange and sawed through all of the telephone wires coming out of the building; at least, whoever did it thought they did. The bandits somehow missed a single wire going to the town of Dowagiac and another going to Dr. Kelsey's house, the president of the village.

Mrs. Josephine August, the night duty telephone operator, knew something was wrong with the phone lines almost immediately, and when the shooting and explosions started to rock her small town, she tried desperately to contact the outside world and call for help. She eventually made it through to Dowagiac on the one out-of-town line the robbers failed to cut. The Dowagiac operators then sent word to the surrounding area that Cassopolis was literally under attack. Mrs. August also reached Dr. Kelsey on the uncut line to his home.

Thinking they now had the town to themselves, the gangsters got a little noisy. One of the highwaymen systematically shot out all the street lights near the bank as well as shooting out the red telephone light that indicated a direct line to the sheriff's office. Any citizen found on the streets near the bank had warning shots fired over their heads that usually sent them running for cover or back from where they came. Gunmen took up positions around the bank to repel any rescue attempts while inside the men set to work with sledge hammers on the brick wall surrounding the safe. When the face of the vault was clear of bricks, the crew's explosive expert rubbed bar soap into the edges of the vault door so when he poured nitroglycerine into the door seams it didn't just run out onto the floor. It took three separate blasts to blow off the vault door, and the repeated explosions blew out the bank's windows, those in adjacent buildings, and completely wrecked the inside of the bank. And, needless to say, the blasts woke everybody in town except the dead. What the crooks didn't know and luckily never found out was that the bank was equipped with a device that set off tear gas bombs if the vault was tampered with. Discounting the notion that multiple nitroglycerine explosions does not fall within the definition of tampering, obviously something went very wrong with the safe-cracking deterrent.

Outside, the intensity of the gunfire rose as lawmen and armed citizens edged toward the bank and exchanged fire with the gangsters. From hiding they took potshots at the gangsters when one could be spotted and a war of snipers slowly built into a pitched battle. Dr. James Kelsey lived above his office and directly across the street from the bank.

He didn't need a phone call to know a bank robbery was underway and walked out of his building and turned toward the county jail when one of the gangsters shouted for him to stop. He kept on walking, found cover behind a building, and watched a man shooting out street lights. The town president had come prepared. He took out his German Lugar, pointed it at the bank, and fired. The response was like mistaking a hornet's nest for a piñata. A swarm of rifle and pistol fire filled the air, and Dr. Kelsey made a hasty and prudent retreat. That's when he stumbled across Cass County Sheriff Earl Still and Undersheriff Arthur Nixon who were watching the proceedings from a dark corner. Armed with only .38 revolvers, they were out manned and outgunned.

George Jones lived near the bank, and hearing the shooting and blasts, he ran toward the bank until he was knocked down by a shotgun slug that grazed his neck. Not seriously hurt, Jones was on the ground for only a moment before he was again on his feet and running back the way he came. The fracas at the bank drew the president of the establishment to see what was going on. He drove to the bank and stopped in front to have a look, but not for long because shotgun blasts tore into his car and he raced for home. Dr. George Bonine also encountered the unexpected when he returned from a late night house call and turned onto Main Street unaware he was entering a war zone. That quickly became apparent when half a dozen shotgun blasts came his way, and he floored the car's accelerator. Reaching the outskirts of town, he warned everyone he met of the ongoing shootout at the bank. As in every town and community, there has to be a person who knows everything and must also be the first person to tell everyone else. That person in Cassopolis went from house to house in her car letting people know there was a bank robbery in progress, as if they couldn't guess.

Inside the bank with the vault door finally giving way after three nitroglycerine-powered explosions, the safecracker had to be both frustrated and disappointed to discover an unexpected inner door standing in the way of their loot. With the intensity of the gunfire growing in volume outside, the nitro man soaped the joints of the inner door, gingerly poured in the nitro, set the fuse, and let her rip. When the dust and debris cleared and the safecracker took a look, he found the inner door unmoved by his efforts. Once again he blew the door which shook the building, shattered any windows that were still whole, and in the end got the same result. Either out of nitro, patience, or figuring they were about out of time, the gang escaped through a back window of the bank and disappeared. In desperation to get something for their efforts, or out of simple, ill-tempered vexation, they took $400 in U.S. postage stamps. Ironically, the postage stamps were at the bank because the post office had recently been robbed and the postmaster thought the stamps would be safer at the bank.

The five shell-shocked men locked in the coat room freed themselves and stumbled out into a wrecked bank. Windows were blown into gravel-sized pieces of glass, walls were cracked or shattered, and debris lay everywhere underfoot. Outside more than 150 bullet holes dimpled buildings and automobiles. Windows in nearby buildings had been either shattered by the five explosions or shot out. Even doors had been blown off their hinges. Yet in this torrent of rifle, pistol, and shotgun fire, only one citizen hand been wounded and then only lightly. Many later credited the bandits with purposely shooting wide with the intent of frightening everyone away from the bank and not wanting to wound or kill residents.

Within minutes of the gangsters retreating from the bank and Cassopolis, police began arriving from many of the nearby towns. Patrols were organized, and police crisscrossed the surrounding area hoping to flush the robbers. Police also set up roadblocks on major travel arteries but neither roadblocks nor patrols turned up a clue, a sighting, or a gangster.

The assault on Cassopolis left the citizens and even the police momentarily stunned. One patrol car full of out-of-town police mistook another carload of police as the robbers and opened fire on them. The few clues left in the bank by the robbers during their hasty withdrawal amounted to a pick-axe, crow-bar, a pair of pliers, a hacksaw, a gas can, and a bottle that probably held the nitro. It was thought the gangsters might have headed for South Bend, but that was mere speculation. In the light of a new November day it looked like the robbers had disappeared down a rabbit hole. In reality the Cassopolis raid would be the last hurrah of the Kozak/Carson gang, one of the Michigan's most notorious and successful robbery crews.

Phillip Kozak was born in Russia and immigrated to the U.S. in 1914. When honest labor couldn't turn a buck fast enough to suit him, crime and specifically armed robbery became his career choice. He quickly established a reputation in Detroit for his penchant for brutality and hair-trigger temper. James "Jimmy" Carson was not first-time lucky when, as a teenager, he robbed an Ohio bank. The result was a four year stretch in a Buckeye state prison. After serving his time, he came to Detroit and briefly worked as a Great Lakes seaman before following his true calling as a stickup artist.

Carson started out slowly, holding up the occasional gas station or grocery store. He also had charisma and brains that attracted a coterie of gunman, robbers, and safecrackers. The police believed Carson was the brains of the gang and Kozak supplied the muscle. That doesn't mean Carson didn't still thirst for the adrenaline rush of pulling a job. He once boasted he robbed eight gas stations in one night while driving from Detroit to Ann Arbor. The Detroit police were fairly certain that in one year alone more than 100 armed robberies could be laid at the feet of the Kozak/Carson Gang. Although banks were high on their preferred list, they weren't picky about what they robbed, and the list also included grocery stores, gas stations, drug stores, and even the Detroit trolley system. The gang's main hideout lay 60 miles southwest of Detroit on a farm near Ridgeway in Lenawee County. From there the thugs rampaged throughout southeastern Michigan.

The Michigan State Police and the Detroit Police hurried to Cassopolis to help identify and track down the gangsters. Among the few clues they had to go on was that the robbers didn't wear masks, and a couple sets of fingerprints turned up on both the gas can and the bottle left behind by the robbers. From the first, the state cops and Detroit lawmen suspected the Cassopolis heist was the work of the Kozak/Carson gang, and a state police detective showed the five men held in the bank a book of mug shots hoping for a hit. Clarence Madden, an ex con and a known gunman with the Kozak/Carson gang was quickly identified from a photo. A Lansing resident, Madden was picked up for questioning and released, but the Detroit police were notified of Madden's possible connection with the Cassopolis job.

The Detroit the police, on a tip, were watching a house suspected of being used by the gang. The day after Madden was questioned and released in Lansing, he and another known gang member, James Allen, were observed entering the Detroit house. The two were then seen leaving with Steven Raczkowski, Chester Tutha, Sam Bokosky, and Joe Konon, all known members of the gang. They all were arrested, found to be armed, and all suspected of taking part in the Cassopolis raid.

Clyde Benham, the Cass County deputy sheriff, positively identified Allen, Madden, and Raczkowski as members of the bank robbing crew. A lady living above the bank (what a night she must have endured) identified Chester Tutha and Joe Konon as two of the bank robbers because the pair had come to her apartment door the night of the robbery to check out who was living above the bank.

On February 8, 1926, Tutha, Konon, Madden, and Allen were bound over for trial by the Circuit Court. Raczkowski was turned over to Detroit police on another armed robbery charge. But the two gang leaders remained at large. With most of the gang in jail and no money from the Cassopolis job, Carson and Kozak felt the pinch of a cash flow shortage and decided they would rob a bank. The first requirement of which is to steal a getaway car. Why a jitney cab would be the vehicle of choice is unclear, but that's what they attempted to steal on January 11, 1926. They boarded the jitney in front of the Ford Motor Company in Highland Park and found one other passenger onboard. They rode the jitney to Woodward and Six Mile where the other rider got out. Empty now except for Kozak and Carson, the pair drew their pistols and told the driver to hand over his money and get out of the vehicle. The driver declined to do either and began to struggle with the two crooks. Kozak and Carson pistol whipped the driver and shoved him out onto the street. The fight with the driver caught the eye of Detroit Police Officer Andrew Rusinko who rushed to the driver's aide. It was the officer's first day on the job. It would also be his last as Kozak and Carson both fired at the approaching policeman and killed him.

The murder of Officer Rusinko sparked an intense manhunt for the killers, and a tip to the Detroit police pointed the finger at Kozak and Carson. On January 16, 1926, a Hamtramck cop spotted the two leaving a restaurant. The officer knew Kozak and walked toward him as he reached for his service pistol, but before it cleared the cop's holster, Kozak grabbed his gun hand and Carson shot him multiple times in the back. Only a few hours later they shot another police officer who they suspected of following them. Both men recovered from their wounds, but once again Kozak and Carson were off the radar.

Yet another tip, late on January 16 to the Detroit police put Carson in Ridgeway, Michigan. County, city, and state police descended on the village the next morning, and after asking around and flashing Carson's mug shot, by 9 AM they learned of the gang's hideout on the Barlow farm. The police task force raided the farm and somehow missed Kozak and Carson, who were hiding in the barn. A police presence remained in Ridgeway, and Kozak was captured there the next day. Kozak denied shooting Officer Rusinko but later owned up to being in Cassopolis. On January 19 he admitted to killing Rusinko but refused to name the other shooter. He also later confessed to yet another armed robbery and was sent to Marquette State Prison to serve a 15–30 year sentence.

James Carson remained free until the police persuaded his girlfriend to reach out to Carson and set up a date for February 9, 1926. She stood him up, but the police didn't. He was surrounded and gave up without a fight. Carson confessed to being Rusinko's other shooter on the day of his arrest.

Kozak had originally been sent to Marquette but was later transferred to Ionia State Hospital and on December 14, 1928, was deported to Poland. James Carson was sentenced to life imprisonment at Marquette State Prison.

Only James Allen and Clarence Madden were tried for the Cassopolis robbery, and in spite of being identified by a police officer as taking part in the robbery were found not guilty. Joe Konon, Steven Raczkowski, and Frank Dion were all tried on previous charges and found guilty. Konon got 5–15 years at the state prison in Jackson, the other three were sentenced to 15–30 years at the state prison in Marquette or, as it was known to inmates, "Hardrock." Oddly enough not one person was ever found guilty of the mayhem, attempted bank robbery, and unlawful imprisonment that took place in Cassopolis on November 24, 1925.

Chapter 12

The Hadley Shootout

January 13, 1926

"...this isn't a healthy section of the county to stage bank robberies."

*T*he Citizens Bank of Hadley, on the face of it, hardly seemed worth the trouble of robbing. In 1926 Hadley boasted a population of about 300 and was little more than four corners set among lovely rolling hills some eleven miles southwest of Lapeer. It was a quiet little farming community that generated just enough economic activity to support a small concrete-built bank. Never mind the impression there was unlikely to be enough cash on hand, at any one time, to finance a present-day family of four's weekend at Disneyland. On the other hand, let's not forget the talk about the crazy old lady who became convinced Germany was going to win WWI and took her $50,000 in gold coins to Citizen's Bank because, she believed, the little bank would somehow keep her nest egg safe from the Hun. Word was, according to some, the gold coins were still there. Whether it was or wasn't, the bank and the little village gave every likelihood of being easy pickins.

When the four Toledo bank robbers, filled with liquid courage, cruised into town in a new Jewett sedan, they were convinced knocking over the bank would be as easy as knocking over an outhouse on Halloween. One wonders if the four Toledo gunmen ever heard or read about the famous 1876 Northfield, Minnesota, Raid in which the town folks cut the Dalton Gang and the James brothers to pieces when the famous outlaws tried to rob their bank. It was within months of the 50th anniversary of that famous shootout, and it was about to be déjà vu all over again.

The four young Toledo hoodlums cut the village's telephone lines to the outside world before they rolled into town. The driver of the Jewett stopped the car a block from the bank and three men got out and walked past the post office and telephone exchange as they made for the town's seat of commerce. One stranger in town might cause a head to turn, but three strangers arriving together and walking down the street was not an everyday occurrence in Hadley. They immediately fueled the curiosity of the Hadley's, the husband and wife team who ran the post office and the village's telephone exchange. Both of them watched the trio walk into the bank.

Inside, the three men found Newman Barber, a former bank employee and carrier of a white cane, visiting with cashier Edward H. Potter. The cashier walked over to a teller's window where one of the men asked him for change for a $10 bill. This asking for change happened so often back then one wonders if it was somehow thought of by criminals as a necessary preamble to announcing the bank is being robbed, or was it nothing more than a bank robber's nervous twitch? Maybe it gave a robber a moment to gird his loins before the point of no return. Whatever the purpose, Potter took the ten spot, made change, and when he next looked back at the three men, they were all pointing automatic pistols his way. One motioned with his pistol for Potter to raise his hands. This was all lost on Barber because he was blind. He had no idea, as yet, that a robbery was taking place, and one of the three men who entered the bank had even lit Barber's cigar. Potter was bound, and when Barber reached out with his cane to draw one of the men nearer, the trio bound and gagged him and put him on the floor.

With the bank securely in their hands, one of the robbers pulled the shades on the windows. They grabbed what money they could find, but it didn't amount to much so one of them pulled a knife, went to Potter, who had joined Barber on the floor, and demanded to know where the money was kept. When Potter refused to answer, the knife wielder began jabbing the cashier with the point and threatened to run him through if he didn't loosen his tongue. After a couple of more pokes and with blood running down Potter's leg, he sent the robbers to the back of the vault. In their search for more money, the crooks emptied desk drawers, turned over files, and left the bank looking like it had been pillaged.

The bank's drawn shades were as good as a bank alarm to the Hadley's who were watching from the post office. They could not remember ever seeing them drawn before. Mr. Hadley went to the switchboard and called Leslie Barstensleder who owned a garage that sat across a narrow alley from the bank. He described what he had seen, gave voice to his suspicions, and asked Leslie to carefully see if anything was amiss. Deputy Sheriff Owen Earhart and Ira Jones were also in the garage when Hadley called. Hadley next called Charles Morton at the village hardware who started breaking out ammunition and his stock of shotguns and deer rifles.

After dropping the three gunmen off a block short of the bank, the driver of the Jewett eased the sedan down the road and parked in front of the bank. The car had only stopped a few moments when Deputy Sheriff Earhart walked out of the alley directly to the Jewett and asked the driver what he was doing. The driver hemmed and hawed while playing around with the gear shift lever as if something was wrong with it. The deputy left the driver still searching for a coherent answer, strolled to the back of the car, kicked ice from the Ohio license plate, and noted the number. Earhart then walked back up to the driver and ordered him to, "get out of town right away." [1] The driver didn't need to be told twice and sped out of town.

Ira Jones, a 47-year-old farmer living north of town, who had also been in the garage when Hadley called let curiosity get the best of him. He crossed the alley and tried to look in the bank window, but the pulled shade blocked his view. He then tried to eavesdrop but only heard a cough, so he walked down the alley to the street with curiosity nipping at his heels the whole way. With his first step onto the street, he was drawn to the bank's front door. He just had to have a look.

When Jones walked up to the door, he didn't even get a chance to get a good look inside. One of the thugs saw him approach the bank, and with a gun in each hand, he beat Jones to the door and used his pistols like directional indicators ordering Jones inside. "No thank you," [2] replied Jones. The two-gun bank robber re-invited Jones into the bank with, "You come in here or I'll shoot the hell out of you." [3]

Ira Jones RSVP'ed by turning and running like his life depended on it. The gunman stepped outside and fired three rounds at the fleeing man. One bullet buried itself in Jones right thigh and another creased his chest opening a five-inch-long gash. Jones managed to stay on his feet until he came to the end of the block and dove for cover.

The robber was so intent on stopping Jones he failed to see villagers had gathered in front of the bank and that they were heavily armed with rifles and shotguns. The crowd quickly had his full attention when they opened fire. The initial barrage miraculously missed the gunman who ducked back into the bank as the fusillade pock-marked the building and holed the bank's plate-glass windows. The bank soon became a shooting gallery as rounds from outside poured through windows, the front door, and either chewed up tables and chairs, or ricocheted wildly around the room. Even under the judgment-impairing influence of moonshine, the three robbers knew it was time to cut and run. They fled through a side door and into the alley where all three opened fire on their tormentors. Shots flew everywhere as the townspeople returned fire. Windows, gas pumps, doors, and buildings were all hit, but none of the robbers were even nicked in the furious gunfight. The intense fire drove the thieves down the alley where they tried to hide behind some buildings. Except Mrs. Hadley, at the telephone switchboard, saw where they went to ground. She told Sam Rahm, who happened to be in the telephone office, the robbers had slipped behind a barn. Rahm grabbed his double-barrel shotgun, slipped through Hadley's barn, and out-flanked the bandits. The three Toledo men spotted Rahm just before he opened fire and fled north. They ran behind several buildings and then turned to come out on the main drag out of town looking for the getaway car.

The robbers hardly had time to cuss out the absent driver and car before the armed town folks, still in front of the bank, spotted them and gave chase. Clutching a couple of bags of loot, the bandits ran north with the mob in hot pursuit. When the crooks turned and fired hoping to discourage further pursuit, they made a near fatal mistake. The impromptu posse had dived for cover when the robbers turned and fired, but the citizenry discovered the hoodlums had opened up so much distance between themselves and people from Hadley that the robbers' pistols were out of range. But the robbers were not out of range of their pursuers' hunting rifles. The Hadley posse calmly walked out on the highway, leveled their rifles at the three running targets, and one after another dropped all three. The Toledo gunmen lay on the highway bleeding as they threw away their guns as a sign of surrender. The people of Hadley walked up, collected the guns, and waited for the law to arrive.

When Mrs. Hadley, at the telephone exchange, tried to call the state police post in Flint and the Lapeer County Sheriff she discovered the lines had been cut. But there was an old, long-unused line to Goodrich that she managed to patch through to the village. The Goodrich operator quickly spread the word of the robbery and shootout to the sheriff in Lapeer, the Oakland County Sheriff, and the state police. All three agencies raced to the scene, and Sheriff Conley of Lapeer County arrived shortly after the gunfight ended and transported the three wounded gangsters to Lapeer.

Ira Jones was taken to Dr. W. J. Wall where he was stitched back together. The farmer had lost a dangerous amount of blood, but instead of a hospital, he was sent home to mend. Ralph Green, 22 of Hadley, had a small piece of his ear shot off, and he was also locally attended to.

Word of the Hadley holdup and shootout swept through the country-side like a drought-fueled brush fire, and when farmers learned one of the robbers was still on the loose, they picked up a gun and began quartering the nearby area or rushed to Hadley.

The getaway driver made it only four miles out of town before he lost control of the car on a snowy road and rammed the Jewett into a pile of logs where it stuck. As fate would have it, the wreck happened in front of Ira Jones' farmhouse. The driver went up to the house and knocked on the door. Mrs. Jones, not yet aware of the robbery or her husband's wounding, opened the door and asked who the man was. She didn't wait for an answer because the man smelled like he'd fallen in a vat of moonshine and she slammed the door in his face. The lone desperado trudged down the road stopping at several other farms with the same result. When he spotted a schoolhouse, he asked directions to Metamora and plodded on.

State troopers from the Flint post found the Jewett with the Ohio plates and began following the foot tracks in the snow. Four miles down the road, the troopers found a lone man stumbling through the snow. When ordered to stop, the outlaw pulled a pistol from his pocket, but a state cop beat him to the draw and fired a round that passed between the man's legs and kicked up snow behind him. That was enough to make the culprit drop his gun, and the three officers rushed the man and overpowered him. In addition to the revolver, the bandit carried a one-third full—if you're an optimist—quart jar of moonshine. The police knew where the absent booze had gone because the would-be robber was so sloshed it's a wonder he could follow the road; thankfully it was neither straight nor narrow. The three troopers took the getaway driver into Hadley where the growing crowd all wanted a look at the desperado before he was delivered to the Lapeer County jail.

The bandits were gone and the guns were silent, but the crowd remained. Everyone had to inspect the bullet holes, take a peek at the bank, and if you were an eyewitness to the extraordinary event you repeated what you saw and did over and over. Everyone from the little town was proud to the point of bursting. As one woman from the village put it, "Maybe these bandits will come to know some day that this isn't a healthy section of the county to stage bank robberies. Our men folks know how to shoot. They aren't afraid of anything and we are mighty proud of them." [4]

At the Lapeer County jail, the bandits said they lived in Toledo and identified themselves. The driver of the getaway car was William Willard, 35, and the only one of the four to escape wounding. The others were Franklin Todd, 32, Benton Ford, 24, and Andrew Berry, 26. Berry was shot in the right hip which broke two bones and would keep him bed bound for weeks. Todd received wounds to his head and knee, and Ford took a round through his left thigh. The sheriff and doctors deemed none of them so badly wounded as to need hospital care. The three wounded men were chained to their beds in separate cells under special guard.

On Thursday morning, the wives of the four jailed men arrived in Lapeer and professed profound shock that their husbands would, "…stoop to crime."[5] The four women reported their husbands had dropped them off at a Pontiac hotel while the four men went hunting. A check with the Pontiac hotel named by the women showed their names did not appear on the register. The women hired a lawyer and announced they would stay in Lapeer to be near their men.

After hearing from the Lapeer sheriff, the Toledo police searched the homes of the four robbers and turned up almost $1,000 stolen from the Toledo Commercial Savings Bank and Trust on December 31, 1925. They also found money taken from an armed robbery of the Toledo street car company. The money was variously hidden in walls, floors, and the attic. So maybe the wives weren't quite as appalled as they claimed. Their husbands had pretty much gone whole hog when it came to stooping to crime, and the wives had become quite artful at stooping to lying.

On Saturday, in a surprise announcement, Sheriff Conley said he had learned the bandits stayed with Thomas and James Hayden, bachelor brothers, at their Lapeer County farm on the night before the robbery. During the sheriff's questioning of Benton Ford, the robber admitted the four of them had stayed with relatives of William Willard. When the sheriff confronted Willard about their stay at the Hayden place, the getaway driver let slip that the day before the robbery the Toledo gang used a car owned by Francis Hayden, a nephew of the Hayden brothers, to motor into Hadley, case the bank, and learn the lay of the land. If all that wasn't of enough interest, the bachelor brothers had been arrested some months back for making moonshine, had a case before the state Supreme Court, and up until two years ago Thomas Hayden had, for a decade, served as the director of the local school district.

Justice of the Peace N.C. Karr on Saturday afternoon arraigned the four bank robbers in their cells. The three wounded bandits were still confined to their beds. A reading of the complaint was waved by their lawyers. Examination of the men was set for January 30, and bail was set at $50,000 each. If it had not been waived, the complaint in part would have read, "…entering a bank with intent to rob and intimidating and putting in fear and confining the bank employees." [6]

If they didn't already know, the four Toledo men found out Saturday they were also being pursued by a representative of an automobile finance company. The finance officer arrived in Lapeer for the purpose of repossessing two cars the bandits had bought, or rather made low down payments on and thereafter neglected to make any payments. The Jewett was used in the bank robbery, and the four wives had driven into town in the other car. The sheriff had impounded both, and it would be a long wait before the finance company got either car.

On Sunday there was more bad news for three of the bank robbers. All but William Willard were identified as robbers of a Toledo bank, the perpetrators of a home invasion in which $16,000 worth of jewelry was stolen, and positively identified as the men who stole $3,700 from the Toledo trolley company.

On Monday morning, Michigan's Assistant Attorney General O. I. Smith along with the commander of the Flint State Police post, and a state police captain from Lansing arrived in Lapeer to further question the Ohio men and the three Hayden men, Thomas, 56, his brother James, 54, and their nephew Francis, 26, who were arrested the previous night and housed in the Genesee County jail. The latter was married and the father of two. The arrests of the Hayden men stemmed from interviews on Sunday by the state police.

Benton Ford was the first of the Toledo men, on Sunday, to directly connect the Haydens with active participation in the bank robbery. Ford's mother may have been the catalyst for her son's implicating the Hayden family. She and Ford's two sisters visited Benton on Sunday, and the mother begged her son to make a full statement. A short while later while being questioned by the state police, he made a statement that fully involved the Hayden brothers in the robbery. All four Toledo men were interviewed separately, and they were soon singing in complete harmony with Ford about the Hayden trio.

According to the suddenly cooperative Toledo boys, Thomas Hayden had planned the robbery, recruited them to do the job, and all of the Hayden men had, in various ways, actively assisted in the robbery. Specifically, the Toledo crew's stories, though told separately, all agreed that two weeks prior to the robbery the Hayden brothers wrote William Willard suggesting the bank robbery and urging him to put together a crew. Willard contacted the other three Toledo gangsters who agreed to pull the job because the Haydens claimed it would be easy. A week later Willard got a second letter from the Haydens telling him the roads weren't in good enough condition. The four men and their wives drove to the Hayden farm on Monday after yet another letter said the roads had improved. Throughout the planning and the robbery, the four wives stayed at the farm. Monday the group went over plans for the robbery which was supposed to take place on Tuesday. The group decided to delay the job one day because the roads were not in good enough shape for a fast getaway, but the Toledo men did travel to Hadley and even walked into the bank and looked around. The cashier would later remember seeing the men in the bank the day before the robbery.

The Haydens, according to the men from Toledo, were the ones who suggested pulling the bank's shades. The Lapeer brothers also gave the robbers clothes to wear during the robbery that would make them look like local farmers, and Thomas Hayden gave a .32 caliber automatic pistol and ammunition to the stickup crew. They also made two different plans on how and where to meet after the robbery and divide the money. The Hayden brothers fed and housed the robbers and their wives from Monday through Wednesday morning.

On March 8, 1926, all four of the Toledo robbers pleaded guilty to robbing the Hadley bank before Judge Dingeman. Sentences were deferred until after the trial of the Hayden men which was set to begin on March 23. The coming trial was the talk of Lapeer and Hadley, and it was awaited with breathless anticipation.

It quickly became apparent as the Thomas Hayden trial opened that the confessions of the Ohio men were going to be used by the prosecutor as a battering ram to destroy any defense Hayden tried to mount. Under oath Benton Ford called Thomas Hayden the, "...brains of the job." [7] On the witness stand Franklin Todd admitted he robbed the bank because Thomas Hayden said it would be an easy mark and contained about $150,000. Todd also testified Thomas told him where to cut the telephone wires and supplied the pliers to do the job, as well as the wire to tie up the bank employees. And lastly, he admitted he and his friends drank heavily the morning of the robbery, and Hayden had given each of them a quart of moonshine before they left for the bank.

All of this was of course better and more dramatic than a radio soap opera, and the court room was usually crowded to the point of shoulder-to-shoulder standing room only with people spilling out into the hall. Many had planned ahead and packed lunches and either ate in their seats during the noon break or even standing up rather than go outside and gamble on giving up their place in court. A few took a chance and rushed outside to grab food out of the car and hopefully rush back inside to reclaim their spot. When you got right down to it, the trial was better than a three ring circus and nobody wanted to miss it.

When William Willard, a distant relative of the Haydens through marriage, took the stand on March 27, he stunned the courtroom by testifying Thomas Hayden had brought up the subject of robbing the local bank on Willard's first hunting trip to the farm five years ago. It never seemed far from Thomas Hayden's mind as the subject came up two more times on hunting trips. Willard also denied the Toledo gang brought any liquor north but observed, "We had plenty after we arrived at the Hayden farm." [8]

Through much of the testimony, Thomas Hayden appeared nervous and ill-at-ease. He continually wiped his forehead as if he was sweating and then pinched his checks and rubbed his eyes as if he could hardly stay awake.

Andrew Berry took the stand with his young wife sitting in the front row holding the couple's four-month-old child. While his wife openly wept, he recounted his part in the robbery and then identified the .32 Colt automatic Thomas Hayden gave him saying, "Better take it. You may need it." [9] Berry also identified the sack Hayden gave him in which to carry the loot and the clothes he told him to wear that would make him look like a local.

When Francis Hayden was called to testify, he recanted most of his confession but admitted he was threatened with murder if he talked and said he drove the Toledo wives. Asked if this was his first experience outside the law, he replied, "Yes sir, I have always been a square shooter and did not think any man could be such an ungodly liar as to tell the lies Tom Hayden told me. Of course it didn't take much persuasion in the condition I was in after drinking so much booze." [10] William Willard was the last of the prosecution's witnesses and revealed that Thomas Ledford, a half-brother to Willard's wife and a nephew of the Haydens had been the initial connecting link between the bank robbers and the bachelor brothers. He also stated that Thomas Ledford was the author of the letter to the robbers that the roads were in good enough condition to carry out the holdup. When Willard was asked, "What kind of liquor did you have to drink at Hayden's, moonshine?" The response was, "Was either that or dynamite."[11]

Finally, Thomas Hayden took the stand in his own defense and denied having any part in the robbery. He did admit he heard the men were going to rob the bank, on the day of the robbery, but didn't want to stick his nose into anyone else's business. Thomas Hayden's defense was brief and ended with two character witnesses. The jury took even less time, 35 minutes, to find him guilty. Judge Dingeman announced he would defer sentencing until the conclusion of the trials of Thomas Ledford, James Hayden, and Francis Hayden. The case against Francis Hayden was dismissed and the trials of the other two were anticlimactic as both were found guilty.

William Willard was sentenced to 7–15 years in prison. Benton Ford, Andrew Barry and Franklin Todd each received 10–20 years. Thomas Hayden also got 10–20 years while his brother received a lesser term of 1–5 years. Thomas Ledford, for his involvement in the crime, was sent to Jackson prison for 2–10 years.

1. Flint Daily Journal 1-14-1926 p1, c8
2. IBID
3. IBID
4. Flint Daily Journal 1-14-1926 p2, c8
5. Flint Daily Journal 1-15-1926 p1, c3
6. Flint Daily Journal 1-17-1926 p1, c4
7. Flint Daily Journal 3-24-1926 p1, c3
8. Flint Daily Journal 3-25-1926 p1, c2
9. Flint Daily Journal 2-25-1926 p3, c1
10. IBID
11. Flint Daily Journal 3-26-1926 p2, c4

Chapter 13

Crime & Punishment in Michigan as a Minute-Waltz

October 13, 1930

"...both armed robbers began furiously cramming greenbacks into their pockets..."

Seldom, if ever, in Michigan history has a major crime, apprehension of the guilty, and due process of the law and its half-sister retribution played out so quickly. Crime and punishment is usually an interminable Swan Lake legal ballet. The two robbers who walked into a Battle Creek bank on October 13, 1930, had no idea they were taking the first steps in a dance of crime and punishment that was to play out like a 60-second waltz.

At 2:05 PM on Monday afternoon, two men entered the Old Merchants National Bank & Trust branch bank. One walked up to bank manager Edwin Lean's window, one of two employees in the bank at the time, and said he wanted to open a savings account. Mr. Lean passed him an application card, but instead of picking up a chained-to-the-counter pen, the stranger had drawn a gun and aimed it at the manager. Obviously, there was going to be an illegal withdrawal. Three customers, Mrs. Buroker, Mrs. H. D. Clapper, and Tom Gierzak, had walked into the bank behind the robbers and became unwilling eyewitnesses.

Mrs. Clapper, 25, had no idea a bank robbery was in progress when she walked up to the second teller's window. Before she could even open her mouth, a man came up behind her and pushed her so hard she nearly fell and said, "Get over to that third window." [1]

Astonishment quickly turned to outrage, and the thought crossed her mind that if this was the way she was going to be treated then another bank could very well have her business. Mrs. Clapper was about to speak her mind, but swallowed her indignation when it dawned on her she was caught in the middle of a bank robbery and the cad who had pushed her wasn't a bank employee. The outrage and vexation instantly turned to bone chilling fear that only got worse when the man told her, "Look straight ahead through that window and don't move." [2] Turned to stone by fright, Mrs. Clapper later recalled, "I could have stood there a long time." [3]

Mrs. Clapper stood at the teller's window for only a few moments before the robbers marched the three customers and two employees to the back of the bank where one stood guard while the other crook began frantically grabbing money and stuffing it into a pillowcase. He worked with such unbridled enthusiasm he burst the seams of the repurposed pillowcase and the money spilled on the floor. The customers and bank employees all reported the robbers could hardly put two words together without at least one being so vulgar it could peel the chrome off a bumper. One can only imagine the blistering four-letter words aimed at the failed pillowcase when it was thrown on the floor and both robbers began furiously cramming greenbacks into their pant and shirt pockets.

After filling every pocket to overflowing, they herded the three customers and two employees behind the grilled door leading to the vault. There one of the bandits took a pair of handcuffs and accompanied by yet another tsunami of swearing tried to the use the cuffs to lock the grill closed with the five behind it. After several minutes of fumbling and enough cussing to open the gates of hell but evidently not enough to close and lock the grill, the exasperated robber asked Mr. Lean if the thing locked automatically when shut. Assured by the bank manager the grill locked when closed, the crook shut it, never tested it, and with his partner in crime, fled the bank spilling money from over-stuffed pockets. Once the robbers were out the door, the bank manager opened the unlocked grill door and sounded the alarm. The failed pillowcase, bearing the name of the Faust Hotel, was left lying on the floor.

Herbert Buroker had pulled up in front of the bank just behind a Hudson, and, along with the family baby, waited for his wife to run in and cash a check. He was becoming ever more aware that whatever was going on inside the bank didn't seem quite right. When two men ran from the bank with so much money jammed in their pockets they looked like scarecrows stuffed with cash, he realized the bank had been robbed. As the pair jumped in the Hudson and sped away, Buroker invited C.F. Radtke, who happened to be standing nearby, to climb in and chase bank robbers with him and the baby. Evidently, the weaponless Mr. Radtke just couldn't say no when asked to pursue armed desperadoes in a car in which the only thing that could possibly be loaded was the baby's diaper.

The car with two men and a baby aboard sped away from the bank and, like a beagle that flushed a rabbit, the Essex stayed on the heels of the bigger getaway car as it tried to outrun Buroker. The cars tore through town and out into the countryside, and at one point Buroker even pulled alongside the green Hudson intending to force the heavier car off the road, but thankfully came to his senses and dropped back. The chase continued until Buroker noticed the gas gauge on the Essex nudging empty and returned to town.

He did get the Hudson's license plate number which he gave to the police along with a description of the two bandits and the direction in which they were last seen heading—south. It would have been interesting to know what upset Mrs. Buroker the most, walking into the middle of a bank robbery or watching her husband, with her baby in the family car, speed after the armed bandits. The discussion between husband and wife on the wisdom of chasing armed bank robbers with the family infant along for the ride could have proven even more interesting than the robbery itself.

One of the robbers was described as 26 or 27, dark skinned, and dressed in the official bank robbing attire of the twenties and thirties, a suit and stylish fedora—in this case, a dark suit. The other man was thought to be of lighter complexion and wearing a tan suit.

When the police arrived at the bank, they quickly latched onto the Faust Hotel pillowcase as a major clue. Inquires made at the hotel concerning two men fitting certain descriptions who might have spent the previous night there came up with the names of Thomas E. Martin and James Gallagher. It was later discovered Gallagher had worked in the area for three months and during that time had banked with the Old-Merchant National Bank & Trust and decided it was ripe for the picking. Both Martin and Gallagher claimed Gary, Indiana, as home. The two had known each other about a year, and it had only been a week prior that Gallagher told Martin of his plans to rob the Battle Creek bank. Martin readily agreed to be the second man. They stole a car in Gary, then drove it to Fort Wayne on Saturday where they ditched it and stole the Hudson. They drove to Battle Creek on Sunday and registered at the Faust Hotel.

After losing Buroker and his Essex, the bank robbers turned toward Indiana and what they assumed would be safety, but the getaway was not going smoothly. Being chased out of town, even if by civilians, was not a good start.

The original getaway plan had been shredded by Buroker's dogged pursuit, and the bandits were hopelessly lost and confused. Out of sheer expediency and a psychological urge to flee, they drove the Hudson at top speed down randomly chosen or optimistically thought to be southbound roads. The pair made it as far as Leonidas when the Hudson objected to the hard driving and the radiator boiled over. They stopped, refilled the radiator, and drove on. It looked like their luck had turned when they hit M-78 which had just been paved and opened to the public except they were to discover not all the bridges had been completed and motorists had to make detours on rugged unpaved roads. On one of the detours, the Hudson stalled out either from engine problems or poor driving.

Considering the ripped pillowcase, the impromptu posse, and a Hudson with its own set of complaints, the bank job had not come up aces for the two bandits. In fact, they were holding losing hands, didn't know it, and were about to go all in on a senseless tragedy. The Michigan State Police Station WROS, which had been on the air all of two weeks, went on the air at 2:38 PM (barely a half hour after the crime occurred) with news of the bank robbery. The radio operator in East Lansing immediately began directing over twenty patrol vehicles, which only recently had the new radio receivers installed, racing to draw a net around the fleeing bandits. Cruisers from Jackson, Grand Haven, East Lansing, Tipton, White Pigeon, Bay City, and Paw Paw were vectored toward the probable escape routes, then directed to patrol specific roads and areas in hopes of eventually snaring the robbers.

As the two bandits tried to restart the stalled Hudson, State Trooper John Burke, who had been sent to patrol this stretch of M-78 on his motorcycle, pulled up behind the Hudson. Officer Burke was 24, had graduated from the state police training school just the previous spring, and had already proven fearless. He had recently responded to a domestic disturbance and wrestled a loaded shotgun away from a deranged man who had already shot a relative. Officer Burke was single, popular, and this was just another typical day doing a job he loved. He parked his motorcycle a few steps from the Hudson and walked over to question the two men when Martin pulled out a pistol and fired once. The bullet struck Burke on the left front side of his neck and exited on the opposite side near his back. He fell mortally wounded. The Hudson, almost as if it was complicit in the murder, restarted and the killers drove to Burr Oak then Sturgis heading for Indiana.

A Sturgis man found Burke's body, and at 5:15 PM the state police radio received and broadcast the news of Burke's murder. Trooper Dan Wurzburg from the Bay City post happened to be in Jackson that day having one of the new police radio receivers installed in his patrol car. Officer Wurzburg was also a rookie state cop who had graduated from the state police school in the spring of 1930, where he met and became fast friends with John Burke. With the radio installed, he was ordered to the Jackson post to join in the hunt for the bank robbers. At Jackson he was temporarily paired with Trooper Edd Freeman who had already become a living legend within the state police force.

Freeman and Wurzburg left Jackson on M-60 to patrol the Union City-Coldwater area when the radio receiver came to life, and the first message Wurzburg ever heard on the new device was news of his friend's murder. The two cops immediately headed to the general area southwest of Burr Oak, figuring it was the direction in which the killers would run. When Burr Oak was in their rear view mirror and they were only six miles from the state line, Freeman and Wurzburg began stopping and asking locals if they had spotted two men fitting the description of the killers or their car. They didn't let the state line stop them from bird-dogging their prey, and outside Howe, Indiana, a farmer told them he'd seen the two men on a country road making for Brighton, Indiana. No matter they were miles out of their jurisdiction, the two state troopers headed down the same road and soon found the Hudson. The gas tank was empty and the radiator was drier than a Southern Baptist Tent Revival. They didn't need to be bloodhounds to follow the two pair of footprints heading on up the road.

Later Edd Freeman recalled, "We followed the tracks about two miles and then we saw them. As we drove the car up even with them, they separated, one going one side and the other to the other side of the road. We stopped the car. I jumped out of the car and made for Martin with my gun in my hand. He reached for his pocket and brought out a gun. I fired and knocked it out of his hand. Wurzburg made for Gallagher and took care of him all right. He fired once at the ground to intimidate Gallagher. We got both guns and took them back to Sturgis." [4] Along with the two handcuffed killers, the troopers returned to Sturgis with all but $300 of the $4,000 the two had stolen from the bank. The $300 had probably fallen from their overstuffed pockets as they fled the bank.

So to recap: a pair of Michigan lawmen crossed state lines without, evidently, informing or asking for permission from Indiana, but it might count as OK because they were in 'hot pursuit' of the killers. Then like Roy Rogers, Gene Autry, or Marshal Dillon, when the killer pulled a gun on Freeman, he didn't shoot him; he shot the gun out of his hand. And finally, with the pair of bandits in handcuffs, extradition procedures amounted to driving them over the border and into Michigan without informing anyone possessing any legal authority in Indiana. One can only be left wondering if all legal hurdles and niceties were really that casual back in the day. Based on what happened next—yes, and then some!

Gallagher and Martin were taken to the Sturgis jail where they were questioned while a crowd of 300 gathered outside to get a look at the two killers. After initial questioning, the two were driven to the St. Joseph County jail at Centerville where they were again interrogated and the three customers who were present at the robbery were brought in and identified Gallagher and Martin as the bank robbers. No mention is made of the two being picked out of a line up.

An even dozen state troopers stood guard outside the jail during the night, and early the next morning Gallagher and Martin were brought before Justice William I. Ashley. Both men waved examination, and at 9:30 AM the two stood before Judge Warner in a circuit court packed with curious onlookers. First Martin and then Gallagher were individually taken into the judge's private chambers. Each spent no more than five minutes with the judge before returning to the courtroom where they were sentenced to life imprisonment. In total, the pair spent no more than 15 minutes in court, and newspaper accounts (does one dare call it a trial?) never mentioned defense lawyers.

Following sentencing, the two were delivered to Jackson State Prison at 12:30 PM where they were photographed, fingerprinted, given physicals, and placed in quarantine cells. They would stay in quarantine for two weeks before joining the general prison population. It is a deeply held principle of the American legal system that justice and due process should be swift, but when a bank is robbed at 2:05 PM on Monday, a state trooper is murdered during the escape, and the culprits are captured, sentenced, and in a state prison by 12:30 PM the next day, this is justice moving at the speed of light. At the very least, it is immodestly fast for someone who is blind and wearing an ankle length robe.

On Tuesday, a memorial service was held for Officer Burke, and that evening his body, accompanied by a two-man Michigan State Police honor guard, was placed on a train bound for Shenandoah, Pennsylvania. At the Shenandoah train station, Officer Burke's body was met by an honor guard from the Pennsylvania State Police who escorted the casket to Ringtown, Pennsylvania, the home of Burke's parents, where the fallen state trooper was buried.

1. Battle Creek Enquirer and Evening News 10-14-1930 p2, c7
2. IBID
3. IBID
4. Battle Creek Enquirer and Evening News 10-15-1930 p13, c5

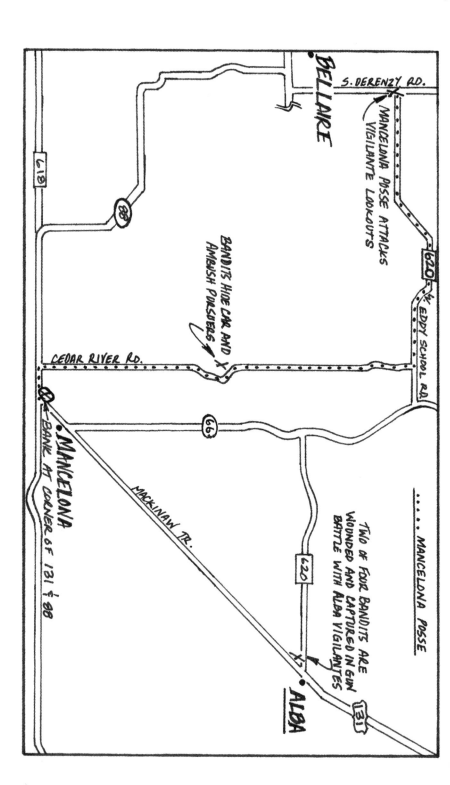

Chapter 14

The Great Antrim County Manhunt

June 2, 1930

*"...a blast from a sawed-off shotgun hit
Sullivan and knocked him off the car."*

*T*oday, the little village of Mancelona, located in
southern Antrim County astride U.S. 131, is usually a place you pass by on your way to someplace else. In
the 1930s it was a growing community with a pickle factory,
the Antrim Iron Company, its own two-mile-long railroad,
and one bank. On a beautiful late spring morning on June
2, 1930, it was the village's one bank, Antrim County State
Savings Bank, that became the center of attention in northern Michigan and where the starting gun was fired in the
Great Antrim County Manhunt.

At 9:30 AM a 1928 Chevrolet sedan rolled up to the
bank. Four men, all wearing bandanas covering them from
nose to chin and variously armed with a pistol, rifle, or a
sawed-off shotgun, alit from the car. One man stayed outside to guard the door while the other three rushed into the
bank. The bandits lined up assistant William Neeson and
cashier Ted Nelson against a wall and made the bank's four
customers lie face down on the floor. Outside, the bandit
guarding the door waved off approaching customers with his
shotgun. He ordered one man back in his car and told him

to drive off. When dentist Nothstine walked down the stairs from his second floor office, in the bank building, he was told to walk right back up the stairs.

What the robbers inside didn't know was that a director's meeting was taking place in the bank's back room, and they didn't see Sidney Medalie standing in the doorway of the conference room. Mr. Medalie saw the masked men enter the bank, ducked into the conference room, quietly shut the door, and told the other bank directors they were being robbed.

Cashier E. L. J. Miles immediately reached for the telephone and spun the crank. The central operator answered at once, was told of the robbery in progress, and flipped a switch on the community fire alarm. If a shrieking fire alarm wasn't enough to spook the bandits, the men in the back room began to make their own telephone ring off the hook. All the noise panicked the robbers who grabbed what little visible cash was lying around and ran from the bank as if it was on fire.

Across the street, Herb Sullivan, a sales clerk in the Medalie dry goods shop and a WWI veteran with a sharpshooter's ribbon, grabbed his rifle and stepped outside as the getaway car accelerated down the street. Sullivan got off one shot that hit the Chevrolet on the left side and clipped the driver's left leg. He was prevented from firing a second round when another car pulled between him and the getaway vehicle.

The dry goods clerk then ran and scooped up additional ammunition for his rifle. He and Lee Strickland, the manager of the community electrical company, asked Dr. L. G. Rifenberg to follow the desperadoes in his Ford coupe. The doctor needed no urging, and the car, with Rifenberg at the wheel and Strickland and Sullivan each standing on a running board and holding on for dear life, raced after the outlaws. Five miles north of Mancelona, the Cedar River

Road swings around a long curve. It was there that the bandits pulled their car off the road and waited for their pursuers to round the bend and come into view. When Rifenberg's car came abreast of the hidden robbers, they opened fire and a blast from a sawed-off shotgun hit Sullivan and knocked him off the car. Sullivan hit the ground and rolled off the road, scrambled for cover, and managed to stay hidden from the ambushers.

Rifenberg drove past the ambush point and stopped at the Larson farm. There he borrowed a rifle, called the local switchboard operator to give his location, and reported the ambush. The doctor and Strickland then headed back to the ambush site where they left the car and scouted around looking for any sign of Sullivan or the bandits. Finding neither, the pair went to the nearby Wildfong farm where they were told Sullivan had already been taken into town and the robbers had disappeared. In Mancelona Herbert Sullivan had buckshot removed from his head and upper body.

Within minutes of Rifenberg and Strickland pulling into Wildfong's farm, a large posse from Mancelona, led by Deputy Sheriff Barney Mitchell, sped north on the Cedar River Road under the assumption that it was the direction in which the gangsters would continue to flee. The robbers, though, had pulled their getaway car into a wooded ravine not far from the ambush site, and the posse flew by within yards of the crooks. The highwaymen had arranged to leave the Chevrolet at a prearranged spot along Cedar River Road where they would later be picked up by another gang member in a second car. The Mancelona posse continued north on Cedar River Road until they hit County Road 620. They still hadn't even caught a glimpse of the bank robbers, and whether they flipped a coin or the deputy sheriff counted on cop intuition, the posse turned west still hoping to catch up with the bank crew.

Word of the bank robbery spread across northern Michigan like an uncontrolled forest fire, and posses quickly formed in several northern towns and either headed for Mancelona or began searching for the thieves in their neck of the woods. In the town of Bellaire, northwest of Mancelona, a posse was hurriedly organized. One of the first things it decided to do was station lookouts at strategic locations on the outskirts of town as a kind of desperado early warning system. Dr. J. H. A. Gerves, 50, and his 22-year-old son Fred were sent two miles north of town to the corner of Derenzy Road and Eddy Road, also known as County Road 620, as pickets to keep an eye out for the bank robbers.

Dr. Gerves parked his car crossways on Eddy Road and stationed himself and his son in the front yard of Henry Lindmer's farmhouse. They had hardly settled into waiting before two cars with guns bristling from their windows roared toward them on Eddy Road. The cars came to a screeching halt in front of Gerves's car. The doctor and his son assumed the bank robbers had just driven up, and the posse from Mancelona thought they had finally caught up with the fleeing criminals. There was a momentary silence as both sides assessed the situation, and then somebody cut loose. No one is sure who fired the first shot, but it quickly turned into a very hot firefight. Ted Bonner, with the Mancelona posse, had a round crease his scalp as the air filled with bullets and buckshot that sounded like angry bees as they whizzed past ears. Joining the symphony of battle were the blasts from rifles and shotguns and the sharper crack of pistols.

The Gerves were heavily outnumbered and outgunned and beat a quick retreat to the Lindmer house. Fred made it into the house, but a round from Dr. Rifenberg's borrowed rifle struck Dr. Gerves in the shoulder. He fell only feet away from safety and lay in the yard unable to move. Fred Gerves, Mr. Lindmer, and his hired hand Louis Bandelang took shelter in the house's basement which was awash in two feet of water. The house above them was turned into a sieve as the Mancelona posse poured hundreds, if not thousands, of rounds into the building over the next two hours. The men in the basement were knee deep in water, and every time they peeked out a basement window they marveled at the growing crowd outside. Spectators showed up just to watch while others brought guns and joined in destroying the Lindmer house one bullet at a time. All the while Dr. Gerves lay wounded in the yard, and those in the house knew any attempt to help him was as good as suicide.

The Mancelona posse began the siege of the Lindmer house from the roadside ditch, but as the crowd grew to more than a thousand the house was eventually surrounded. As the day wore on, the rumor spread that Dr. Gerves and his son were being held as hostages in the farm house in which the robbers had barricaded themselves. The posse felt that anyone who tried to rush the house would be cut down, and it didn't help the situation that the police had tried calling the house several times and no one answered.

News of what was thought to be a dramatic standoff drew more and more gawkers until the crowd numbered close 1,500 of all ages who stood almost across the road waiting and watching for events to unfold. When word of the siege reached the state police, they dispatched cruisers to the site and sent a plane from Lansing loaded with six troopers armed with machine guns, tear gas bombs, and flares.

Mercifully, before the plane arrived and the house was assaulted with half a dozen Thompson machine guns and tear gas, former sheriff Bill Kittle edged up close enough to the back of the house and was spotted by Mr. Lindmer who yelled to Kittle and asked why they were being shot at. Kittle knew Lindmer, and the former sheriff walked up to the back door and entered the house. To the Mancelona posse, it looked like the bandits had finally surrendered, and they rushed the house only to find they had been shooting at innocent civilians for two hours. Dr. Gerves was sent to the Petoskey hospital where it was learned the one shot had paralyzed him from the hips down.

The Lindmer house had been riddled by thousands of rounds during the siege. In one two-square-foot space someone counted 38 individual bullet holes. The house, simply put, was a shambles, and so was the hunt for the bank robbers. The search had been suspended for two hours while the Mancelona posse tried to turn the Lindmer house into scrap lumber and gave the robbers, who were several miles away, a free pass to get out of the area.

The robbers squandered the gift. They had run the old Chevrolet into a wooded ravine where another car was to have picked them up and carry them to safety, but the second car never showed. After they grew tired of waiting, they couldn't get the original getaway car back on the road. To put it bluntly, and in words those from Mancelona would appreciate, the gang was in a pickle and indecisiveness wasn't much help. The gang moved farther into the woods and continued waiting for the second car to appear. As the afternoon wore on, it must have finally dawned on the four crooks that they had been left at the altar, and it was getting perilously late to make a clean escape.

Sometime during the early afternoon, the getaway car was discovered in the wooded ravine not far from the Sullivan ambush site. State and local police and a small army of volunteers raced to the area like hounds to a treed raccoon. The posse threw a tightly spaced picket line around the large tract of dense woods in hopes of sealing off the bank crew. In what was left of the daylight, airplanes circled overhead trying to spot the culprits while armed locals beat the edges of the wood. As night fell police drove the roads bordering the area with their cruiser's spotlights infiltrating the woods and marshes with cold-white cones of light. By 10 PM it was dark night, and for those on the picket line it became a job of staying sharp and waiting.

The latter paid off handsomely when a lone man quietly slipped out of the woods, walked down an embankment, and almost bumped into a car parked on M-66. The car's three occupants lit the man up with their flashlights and asked for some ID. The stranger proved to be 22-year-old Sylvester Elliott, an ex-con from Antrim County and more recently from Kalamazoo. And who were the three men in the car? Even for a bank robber it was like drawing three aces in a poker game. They were Lt. Earl Hathaway and troopers Earl Piechowiack and John Ruhl of the Michigan State Police. Elliott was taken to Mancelona, placed in the bank's back room, and grilled like a tough steak for more than six hours by Captain Lyons, deputy superintendent of the state police along with a tag team of other officers before Elliot confessed at four in the morning.

Elliot said the gang's plans broke down at the point where they had hidden their car and waited for the second car to appear. It didn't, and the crooks found they could not get the Chevrolet back out of the ravine. Elliott was caught when he finally decided to sneak out to the highway and try to catch a ride. He got one, just not the one he wanted. After his confession, he was driven to the county jail in Bellaire. He named the other robbers as his brothers Fred, 25, and Leonard, 19. The fourth name came as a real surprise. He was 25- to 40-year-old Fred Kelly, also known as Lawrence Marks and Loren Morrison—and a former Kalamazoo policeman. All three were still at large.

Fred and Leonard managed to slipped out of the woods and through the picket lines, then walked and hitch-hiked to the outskirts of Alba, which is northeast of Mancelona on U.S. 131, and waited out the night. Late in the morning, the two brothers left their guns just outside of Alba and headed for the town's nearest grocery store. They immediately raised suspicion among the alert townspeople who summoned Alba's vigilante committee. When the two brothers left the store and headed back to where they had left their guns, a group of more than a dozen men had materialized and followed them out of town.

When the Elliotts reached the edge of a cemetery, the brothers dropped out of sight in tall grass bordering the graveyard. It was the spot where they had hidden their guns, and the two waited and watched as the Alba vigilantes close in on them. When they got too close, the brothers stood and fired. The blast from one of the brother's sawed-off shotgun blew R.C. Bennett off his feet, but the tough, former banker sat up, leveled his gun, and shot and seriously wounded Leonard Elliott. It was the opening crescendo in a furious gun battle that spread across the cemetery. Fred Elliott had been lightly wounded in the leg during the getaway by Herbert Sullivan and was wounded again in the shootout. The Alba vigilantes simply shot up the Elliotts to the point they were no longer able to return fire and took them captive.

Leonard Elliott took upwards of 30 pieces of buckshot in his head and shoulders. The worst of his injuries was the loss of one eye and the near loss of the other. His brother Fred was also hit by buckshot in the head and a rifle round produced a flesh wound in his right shoulder. Both men were taken to the Petoskey hospital.

It was later learned that shortly after the ambush in which Sullivan was wounded, the Elliotts became convinced the fourth member of their gang was contemplating killing the brothers and taking the loot. They decided to act before he did and disarmed Kelly and then tried to slip out of the police cordon while leaving Kelly behind. Kelly later made his way to Alba and hid in the woods until Wednesday when he boarded a train in Alba bound for Cadillac. He was captured by the state police on his arrival in that town.

All four men stood trial and were given life sentences. Fred Elliot and Fred Kelly were sent to Jackson State Prison. Sylvester and Leonard got one way tickets to Marquette State Prison. The $4,000 reward was shared among several locals. Dr. Gerves continued to practice medicine until he retired but had to limit his practice because he was wheelchair bound for the rest of his life.

Chapter 15

The Daring Young Men in their Flying Machine

May 22, 1931

"Once aloft the plane staggered across the field like Charlie Chaplin imitating a drunk."

O n the early morning hours of May 22, 1931, Howard Hartung, owner of a small Detroit airport, awoke to the sound of an airplane engine kicking over and quickly accelerating to take off. Knowing there should be no airplanes at his airport taking off hours before dawn streaked the horizon, he rushed to a window and with growing disbelief glimpsed an open cockpit aircraft, with an engine that hadn't been properly warmed up, rumble down the runway and stagger into the air. The plane wobbled, dipped, and sideslipped toward the dark horizon as if it was held up by strings and manipulated by a really bad puppeteer. He quickly went to the phone and reported someone, who apparently could barely fly a plane, had just stolen one from his airport. Neither he nor the police could have guessed this was the opening act in a bank robbery that would play out like a strange mix of slapstick comedy and over-wrought soap opera.

A few hours later and a few miles away, six tellers working for the Pontiac Commercial and Savings Bank were going through their morning routines. One of which was that the six tellers went down to the basement vault a few minutes before opening, loaded a tray with money, and brought it upstairs. What no one expected to see were two masked men, one with two pistols and the other with one in hand, standing before the tellers as they left the vault. One of the gunmen, in what all described as a very youthful voice, stated the obvious, "This is a stickup and we won't stand for any tricks. All of you back in the vault." [1]

The tellers at first thought the holdup was someone's practical joke. One of the tellers even laughed until the crook carrying two handguns jammed them into the laughing man's chest and said, "Shut up and get those hands up." [2] Some of the tellers still didn't get this was the real thing and one fellow turned to another teller to say something but was threatened with having his brains blown out if he didn't shut up and lie down on the vault floor. As the last of the six tellers backed into the vault and lay down, the thief with the one gun pocketed it, pulled out a satchel, and started stuffing it with money from the nearest teller trays. Both robbers appeared nervous and a bit jittery which probably explains why the one grabbing the money bagged only $13,000 in two small satchels and left over $70,000 they could have easily added to their take.

Carrying two sacks of cash, the pair made it out of the basement without being seen by any other bank employees and exited the bank through a side door and drove off. Only one person on the outside saw the thieves leave the bank. He said they were lugging two satchels from which bills were overflowing. The first man out of the bank evidently wasn't moving fast enough to suit the fellow behind him because the trailing thief pushed the lead crook into the car and jumped in after him. The bandits then drove down East Alley toward Pike Street and disappeared.

While the robbery was in progress, none of the bank employees on the first floor, including the retired Pontiac

Chief of Police now employed as a bank guard, had any idea their work place was being held up. And just to make the sting hurt a little more, a traffic cop was busy directing cars hither and yon in front of the bank at the time. The bank also had more burglar alarm buttons spread around the first floor and the vault than loose change found in most overstuffed sofas. Not one alarm, all of which were directly connected to police headquarters just three blocks away, was tripped.

When the police did arrive, they noted the tire tracks in the back alley and knew, before interviewing the one person who saw the crooks leave the bank, the bandits had made their getaway by car. The word went out immediately to patrol officers to be on the lookout for two suspicious characters. They also discovered a significant piece of evidence. There, sticking out of the bank's back door lock was a key. To the police the key screamed 'inside job,' while bank officials were indignant at the suggestion an employee might have been involved. They all agreed the two pistol-wielding robbers were young and inexperienced.

Someone in the Detroit or Pontiac police force remembered a Mr. Pallister who walked into a Detroit police station the previous evening and reported at 10:30 PM he offered two men a ride home when they pulled guns and forced him from his car on Seven Mile Road. Police wondered if the hijacked car could have been used as the getaway car. At the time police found Mr. Pallister's story hard to believe and held him for the night. Now in the morning they began questioning him about a bank robbery of which he knew nothing. He was finally released.

The sheriff and state police had cruisers patrolling the country roads for any sign of the culprits. They were also searching for any abandoned car, including Pallister's, the robbers might have used. It had become the standard operating procedure for bank robbers to leave the bank in one car then change cars to throw off pursuit. About an hour into the hunt, Mr. Pallister's stolen car was found outside Pontiac on Opdyke Road. The police determined there was nothing mechanically wrong with the car; it had just been abandoned on a lonely stretch of road bordered by fields on either side.

Its very location had police warming to the idea that it might be the getaway car. But if so, who picked the crooks up, in which direction had they gone, and the police couldn't find any evidence of another parked car waiting for their arrival. It was possible but hardly probable that the crooks took off on foot across the fields, but just to cross every 't' and dot every 'i' in the investigation, detectives spread across the fields looking for evidence of any kind. They didn't have to walk far before a detective spotted three perfectly parallel groves in the grass that ran straight as a ruler for several hundred yards before they disappeared. You didn't have to be Charles Lindbergh to know you were looking at a field from which a plane had recently taken off. To make sure, detectives scattered across the area and asked residents if they had seen or heard a plane take off or land that morning. Nearly everyone had.

What really got folks attention was the plane's faltering engine. It coughed, sputtered, died, and then was reborn for another brief life before the cycle started anew. People sat up in bed, in the early morning hours, listening for the crash that never came. Those who saw the plane the morning after the robbery all agreed it sported an open cockpit. Detroit police broadcast the make and model of the plane and its registration number. Law enforcement agencies across southeastern Michigan were notified of the stolen plane and its possible connection with a bank robbery and asked to watch for it.

Leamington, Ontario, on the north shore of Lake Erie, was the first in with a sighting. The plane popped out of a heavy fog, circled the airport a few times, and came to earth in what looked more like a miraculously avoided crash than a planned landing. The landing was so obviously mishandled that an experienced pilot walked over to the plane and began questioning the flight experience of its two occupants. The veteran pilot got no answers, only evasions, and reported to the airport manager he thought the plane was stolen. The two daring young men in the flying machine didn't wait around to see what would come of the discussion between their questioner and the manager. The pilot of the craft poured on the power, and it rolled down the runway and into the air. Aloft and only a few dozen feet above the ground, the plane staggered across the sky like Charlie Chaplin imitating a drunk. It somehow stayed in the air as it headed north and disappeared into the fog.

The Canadian Mounties and the Ontario Provincial Police now joined the hunt for the stolen plane, but it was nowhere to be found. It wasn't until later in the afternoon that the case was broken open by a chambermaid in a Chatham, Ontario hotel. She had been sent to clean and ready a room for new guests. Among her duties was emptying wastepaper baskets, and when she upended the one in the room she was cleaning, out fell an old satchel containing 50 banded U.S. dollar bills. The basket also yielded several discarded wrappers from other bundles that had already been opened. They all were imprinted with the name Pontiac Commercial and Saving Bank.

What no one but the two bank robbers knew was after leaving Leamington the airplane ran out of gas and the in-experienced pilot for the third time in 24 hours brought the plane down for a landing, only this time on a rough field with a dead stick. The first-time pilot not only didn't kill himself or his partner, they weren't even injured. Pilots and police who later talked with the robbers couldn't believe the untried and barely trained young man piloting the plane hadn't killed himself and his partner. Police and air veterans chalked up the three safe landings to just plain crazy, dumb luck.

The plane had come down just a few miles from Chatham, and the two crooks had made it to the Pitt Hotel by the early afternoon. Soon after checking in, they went out and bought a suitcase in which to carry the money, but they had left no clue as to where they had gone. Chatham police fanned out across the city with a description of the two men and did what police do, asked questions and checked both the obvious and the obscure. Eventually and inevitably, a cop inquired at the railroad station if anyone had seen the two men fitting the description. The answer was yes; they had bought tickets and boarded the train for Toronto.

The train pulled into the Toronto station at 9:30 PM, and when the two unsuspecting robbers grabbed the single suitcase and stepped on to the station platform, they were greeted by a squad of Toronto's finest. Being met by six policemen with handcuffs resulted in a welcome wagon tussle in which the out-numbered crooks were presented with official welcomes—arrest warrants—and a short tour of the city that led directly to police headquarters. The two men who arrived in Toronto via train, plane, and automobile identified themselves as 20-year-old Louis Kish of Detroit and Adam Morgan of Pontiac, also aged 20.

If the pair of thieves, at first, exhibited a good deal of reticence in accompanying the Toronto police, once they arrived at headquarters they became very talkative and couldn't tell their story fast enough. They seemed to revel in the details. Morgan said he had approached Kish some six weeks prior to the robbery and suggested they take down Pontiac Commercial and Savings Bank. Morgan had been watching the bank like a stalker. He told Kish he had learned the morning routine for opening the bank, knew the vault was in the basement, and it opened a half hour before the bank opened at 9 AM. If done right, they would have only six surprised tellers in the basement to contend with. It was, in short, a piece of cake. Kish agreed and the two of them spent hours watching the bank from inside and out. They also tried more than 25 keys in the back door lock.

They told the Canadian police neither one could remember who first thought of using an airplane and the fact that neither knew the first thing about flying couldn't dampen the optimism of youth. Kish volunteered to take flying lessons, and it took both of the would-be robbers to come up with the flight school money. Kish didn't take naturally to flying, and behind the controls he was clumsy and heavy handed. His instructors repeatedly refused to allow him to fly solo. It made no difference if everyone who knew anything about flying saw Kish and instinctually knew that here was a young man meant to keep his two feet firmly affixed to the ground. Kish was supremely confident he was ready to take to the sky and convinced Morgan he could pilot any plane. Meanwhile, Morgan continued to observe the bank, watch the elevator come and go, and try keys in the back door.

The night before the heist, they hijacked a car and drove it to the field bordering Opdyke Road then took a bus to the airport. At 3 AM the pair made their way onto the runway apron, walked up to the first plane in line, and apparently without a ground check or inspection of any kind jumped in and took off. By 5 AM they landed the plane in the field next to the stolen car. Both said the takeoff from the field after the robbery was a little hairy with the plane just clearing the trees at the end of the field. Kish felt embarrassed at his own unprofessionalism in not checking the gas gauge but made no big thing over landing the out-of-gas plane a dozen miles from Chatham. It was a great story except for the fact it contained more horse dung than is shoveled from the streets of Mackinac Island at the height of tourist season.

The Pontiac police got transcripts of the Toronto confessions and told their Canadian counterparts not to challenge or question the men about any of their claims. While waiting for the two thieves to be extradited, the Pontiac police continued to investigate the robbery and the background of the two thieves. A look into Morgan's past showed he was a Navy veteran and after leaving the service studied accounting. As a child he had attended Sunday school and church regularly. He played the violin in the church orchestra. Morgan had a previous run-in with Pontiac police when an anonymous tip pointed the finger at Morgan as the perpetrator of a hotel and a restaurant stickup. He was brought in, questioned, and cleared. Not much later two men were arrested and charged with both crimes. And here was a real surprise: Morgan's Sunday school teacher was Gerald F. Grandson, a teller at the bank his former student robbed. It was also confirmed Morgan had been seen frequenting Grandson's home. Grandson was married with two children, a model husband, and was highly thought of at the bank. Grandson appeared so upright and straight-laced the police thought it unlikely he had anything to do with the robbery, but maybe Morgan on one of his visits had been able to make a copy of his Sunday school teacher's key to the bank's back door.

Questioned at police headquarters, Grandson readily admitted to a casual relationship with Morgan and utter shock that his former Sunday school student was involved in the robbery. On examining the teller's bank key, the police didn't think it likely to have been used to make a copy from a blank. It looked like Grandson had nothing to do with the robbery and was cruising through his interview with the police when his wife unexpectedly turned up at the station and passed the time of day with a detective while waiting for her husband.

The detective learned Mrs. Grandson did not care for Morgan and expressed no surprise he had slipped into crime. She then completely caught the detective off-guard when she told him the police had Morgan in their hands just a few weeks ago but let him go. By the longest of odds, the detective, who Mrs. Grandson was talking to, was the one who had taken the anonymous tip over the phone about Morgan. He immediately accused Mrs. Grandson of being the tipster. In a conversation with more surprises than an afternoon soap opera, Mrs. Grandson admitted, yes, she made the call, but it was because her Gerald had become romantically involved with, "…that girl…" [3]

Mrs. Grandson had been having a quiet conversation with one policeman, but the comment about 'that girl' was like a stone dropped in a pond. As the ripples moved outward, every cop in the room sensed a change in the direction of the case and moved closer to the origin of the ripples. The detective talking to Gerald's wife skillfully and gently poked and pried at the 'wronged woman's' pride, pain, marriage, sense of self, and what she knew of the robbery until an entirely new narrative and motive for the crime poured forth.

According to Mrs. Grandson, 'that girl' was a student at Ypsilanti State Normal College (its name later changed to Eastern Michigan University). The previous year temptation had sauntered across the path of the exemplary family man at a swimming party, and he couldn't have fallen harder if he'd been hit by a Joe Lewis upper cut. For the past year, the family man had gone off on long drives that often lasted all night or he left for brief trysts with the young lady. Mrs. Grandson considered divorce, but as she told the police, "…that would be selfish and I owed my husband the duty of standing by his side until his temptation had passed." [4] The good wife prayed and waited, but it seemed to have been for naught when even Morgan somehow found out about Gerald's infatuation. Mrs. Grandson learned Morgan knew of the ongoing affair when she overheard her husband and his former Sunday school student discussing money, and it wasn't the story of Jesus throwing money changers from the temple.

Mrs. Grandson confronted her husband with what she knew and had overheard. Gerald replied that Morgan was blackmailing him about the affair and threatening to make it known at the bank. It would, of course, ruin his career. Grandson said he was through with the other woman and would take care of the blackmail threat. All she had to do was remain faithful and say nothing to anyone. It wasn't long before the 'good wife' figured out the blackmail payoff probably involved robbing the bank. According to Grandson, Morgan promised to take the money and disappear from their lives. One is not sure how much moral teeter-tottering Mrs. Grandson put herself through before she decided the bank could take the financial hit and 'hallelujah and hands up' if it would save her marriage. Mrs. Grandson told the detective when Morgan learned she knew of the plans he threatened to kill her, and that's when she called the police. If he had been arrested and sent to prison, she could have saved both her marriage and the bank from being robbed.

Mrs. Grandson's story broke the case wide open and handed it to the prosecutor on a platter. The lead detective went to Kish and Morgan and related Mrs. Grandson's story but claimed it was, in fact, her husband's confession. He then painted a damning picture of the Sunday school teacher taking the witness stand and telling the jury of Morgan's multiple transgressions. The cops told Morgan that when he reached Marquette and was locked in a cell the guards would throw the key in Lake Superior.

The police expected Morgan, confronted with all the facts which supposedly came straight from Grandson's confession, to collapse like a bad soufflé. Instead, he exploded in anger and indignation. Yes, he said, he and Kish robbed the bank, but Grandson had planned the whole damned thing which included recruiting him to do the job. Furthermore, Grandson was still crazy in love with the co-ed and was considering eloping with her. Grandson was the one who thought of the plane as a getaway vehicle and paid for Kish's flight training. He had also given Morgan his key to the back door with which he had a copy made. When Mrs. Grandson stumbled into the imminent bank robbery, it was Grandson who thought up the idea of keeping her mum and in line by floating the blackmail scheme.

Grandson had only one job during the robbery and it was crucial. At the moment when the vault was open and just before the tellers were ready to walk out of it with the money, Grandson was to signal Kish and Morgan to enter the bank by putting his open hand on the back door window. Police later found the palm print and fingerprints on the window matched Grandson's. When the crooks had reached Canada and found a place to hole up, they were to call Grandson who would drive over and get his share of the take.

Determined to finally pin the tail on the right donkey, the detectives went back to Grandson and grilled him like a Porterhouse, but it wasn't until Mrs. Grandson personally pleaded with her husband to tell the truth that he confessed. Five days after the robbery, on May 27, 1931, Grandson changed his mind as he stood before Judge Frank L. Doty and pleaded not guilty. His wife visited him in jail and begged her husband to change his plea and take his medicine. She promised she and the two children would be waiting for him. He again stood before Judge Doty on June 1 and confessed his guilt.

There would be no young children waiting for Grandson when he got out; they would be middle-aged. The judge sentenced Grandson to 25–40 years in prison because, as the judge told him, "I am satisfied that you were the guiding mind." [5] Judge Doty sentenced Kish and Morgan each to 20 years in prison.

Days within the trio's sentencing, the Pontiac Commercial and Savings Bank president, Cramer Smith, committed suicide. He left a note saying ill-health drove him to the act. The suicide sparked a rush by depositors that grew so severe the state closed the bank.

And this is probably a gross injustice to Mrs. Grandson, but there is the nagging feeling that just maybe the reason she went to the police while her husband was being interviewed was as a means to make sure she ended the affair once and for all. After she stirred the pot to boiling, she was the one who talked her husband into confessing to the police and later changing his not guilty plea to guilty. She promised to wait for him with the almost-certain knowledge that a college co-ed would do no such thing. Her husband going to prison saved her marriage, and there certainly would be no elopement. And what's that saying about a scorned woman? Then again, maybe it was just 'standing by his side until temptation passed.' I would think temptation would pass quickly behind the cold gray walls on the shores of Lake Superior.

1. Taylor, Merlin Moore "The Key that Trapped Three." Real Detective v. 25, #1 3-1932 p11
2. Pontiac Daily Press 5-22-1931 p1, c8
3. Taylor, Merlin Moore, "The Key that Trapped Three." Real Detective v.25, #1 3-1932 p96
4. IBID
5. IBID

Chapter 16

'Dressed up Jimmie's' Last Bank

September 16, 1931

"I am not inclined to give you men life sentences..."

On September 15, 1931, it could proudly be stated that a Mount Clemens bank had never been robbed—but it was about to be. On Tuesday the fifteenth, two men drifted into town and did a thorough job of casing the town and the bank. The two well-dressed men approached Roy Shook, at the Powell and Schwork Garage at 110 New Street, about buying a car. They arrived at the garage in a Packard Coupe and dickered with Shook, looked over the cars for sale, and all the while kept an eagle eye on the bank noticing the amount of traffic and which streets seemed to give the easiest access. They stayed for more than an hour, and Mr. Shook thought they acted suspiciously starting with the fact they wanted to pay for whatever car they might buy with whiskey. It never crossed his mind the two could be bank robbers even after the salesman noticed bulges in the hip pockets of both men, bulges that he had a strong feeling meant the two men were packing guns.

At 25 minutes past noon the next day, two men drove up to the First National Bank of Mount Clemens in a Buick, cocked the front wheels away from the curb to facilitate a quick getaway, left the motor running, and walked into the bank. One carried a pasteboard box. They went to the counter and acted like they were making out deposit slips when one of the men filled his hand with a pistol and the one with the box opened it and pulled out a sawed-off shotgun while ordering the employees to, "Stick 'em up." [1]

There were no customers in the bank; a young boy had walked out as the men walked in, and one of the two employees proved uncooperative. Twenty-one-year-old bookkeeper Elden Valentine thought the men looked suspicious from the moment they walked in, and he was slowly backing out of a teller's cage when the bandits yelled the cliché heard in a hundred westerns. The raise your hands order had Valentine backing up even faster which drew a shot from the pistol-wielding thug that missed Valentine and buried itself in the vault door. The crack of the revolver might as well have been a starter's gun because the bookkeeper turned and raced for the basement which drew yet another shot that also missed.

The two gangsters turned their guns on Mr. Rosso while they picked up two large bags and scooped money into them. Rosso told police one of the robbers said, "Hurry up!" [2] to the other who replied, "We got all kinds of time." [3] The bandits took a couple of bundles of cash from Rosso, and with no more money in view, they ordered Rosso out the door ahead of them and into their car. As the assistant cashier, with guns pressed to his back, headed for the robber's Buick, the town's shoe store owner walked toward him as if to have a word. Rosso motioned him back with a shake of his head, fearing either he or both of them would be shot if he hesitated getting into the car. A witness to the robbery, hiding behind a car on the other side of the street, believed the robbers weren't in the bank more than four or five minutes. He took the car's license number as it drove away.

Fourteen-year-old Charles Kaltenbach was just leaving the bank when the robbers entered. He heard two men order Rosso and Valentine to raise their hands and the two pistol shots. The St. Mary's High School student peeked in a bank window, saw the two men holding guns on Mr. Rosso, and ran for the gas station a block away where he asked the attendant to call the police. Mr. A. P. Grim, president of the bank, had unknowingly followed the robbers into the bank. When he heard the bandits tell his employees to reach for the sky, he backed out of the bank and went next door to call the police except the store had no phone so Grim quickly made for the Co-operative Gas Station where he found the Kaltenbach boy had already summoned the law.

Patrolman Jack Perin took the call and wasted no time in grabbing the department's Thompson machine gun and calling Deputy Sheriff Ray Bush who rode to the bank with Perin. Finding no sign of the bandits, the two lawmen, on a hunch, drove north on North Avenue but never found the thieves or any evidence they'd taken that route. The police later would learn the robbers made it to Utica where they abandoned the Buick then took a car they had stashed there earlier and drove to Detroit.

The two desperadoes, $14,072 in loot, and Rosso sped west on Cass Avenue. The assistant cashier was taken as an insurance policy if the police got too close and was told if he later went to the police they would come back and kill him. As the car sped down Cass, Rosso later told police his kidnappers were constantly looking at every car on the street until they recognized a specific automobile and one crook said to the other, "Everything's all right now." [4] When Rosso turned to look at the car, he was slapped across the face and told to look straight ahead or die which leads one to believe the bandits must have had cohorts on the escape route who would have tried to stop any pursuit.

When the robbers passed over the Cass Avenue bridge, the Buick slowed and Rosso was pushed from the moving vehicle. The assistant cashier sustained several light injuries from hitting the roadway, but he was able to get to his feet.

Once the thieves were lost to view, he flagged down a ride to police headquarters. At the police department Rosso told Police Chief Arthur Rosso, his cousin, the kidnappers looked like they might be Italian. One was about 30 and the second 35. The most striking difference was their height which amount to a foot, with the tallest one hitting six feet. Rosso said the robbers were, "Both attired in racketeer fashion," [5] probably meaning they were dressed 'to the nines.' Back in the day, professional bank robbers wouldn't consider pulling a job without out-dressing the banker. The police chief called the state police, and within a few minutes of the holdup, news of the robbery was broadcast to every cruiser in southeast Michigan. For Rosso, the cumulative psychological effect of being kidnapped, thrown from a car, threatened with murder, the bank robbery, and watching his fellow employee being shot at took its toll later that day. He was ordered to bed under the care of a doctor.

It should be noted here that this holdup didn't spark an outpouring of armed citizens eager to hunt down the gangsters. No private citizen appeared the least inclined to grab a gun and give chase. No one rushed to the police station ready to join a posse.

In a column lying cheek by jowl next to extensive coverage of the robbery at the First National Bank of Mount Clemens was the report that the Macomb County Vigilante's Organization had disbanded and the time for vigilantes had passed. Mr. Henry Bohn, one of the organizers of the county vigilantes was quoted as saying, "Modern life is too fast, and bandits far too expert today for vigilantes." [6] Mr. Bohn was of the opinion that modern police forces with radio-equipped cars, motorcycle officers, long-distance telephones, fast police cruisers, and the new beefed-up police arsenal which included sub-machine guns and tear gas bombs made vigilante organizations antiquated. He pointed out the obvious—that the modern professional bank robber was not only better armed than the private citizen but had faster cars. The hunting down and arrest of the Mount Clemens bank robbers would be the result of solid police work. Vigilante organizations would continue to be an important presence around the state and take part in the pursuit and capture of bank robbers, but their importance and participation in fighting crime would steadily wane.

The Macomb county sheriff, the state police, and the Mount Clemens police spent the night searching county roads for the Buick sedan used as the getaway car. A fingerprint expert dusted the bank for prints and stood ready to do the same for the Buick if it was found. The police had three pieces of evidence they hoped would lead them to the thieves. There was the box used to carry the sawed-off shotgun into the bank and left on the floor, the steel-jacketed .38 caliber slug dug out from the vault door, and fingerprints from the bank. They also had the license number of the getaway car. The search for said car was called off at 6:30 AM the following morning.

The police thought they might have broken the case when they arrested two men on the evening of September 17 as they were entering a movie theater. The two strangers had been seen around Mount Clemens for at least a week and had been repeatedly seen driving around the city early in the morning. The two were arrested although they claimed innocence and said they were in town for the mineral baths. On searching their rooms, a .38 caliber pistol was found and a check with Ohio police revealed both men had criminal records, but neither man could be identified by witnesses.

Tracing the license number of the Buick showed that the car had not been stolen but purchased from a Gratiot Avenue used car lot in Detroit on Labor Day. The buyer fit the description of one of the bank robbers. He had put $10 down on the car and the next day returned with $325 to pay it off. Then, strangely enough, he left the car on the street in front of the used car lot for the rest of the day then took it to a garage where, records show, he stored it until the day before the robbery. The used car lot said the car was purchased by H. C. Colpin who supposedly resided at the Wolverine Hotel. A quick check showed no such name had been registered in recent months at the hotel.

Dogged police work finally paid off when the name of Colpin led to the name James Hall and an address on Old Town Avenue in Detroit. On Saturday night Detroit Detectives Edward Graff and Harry Schouw called at the house and arrested the three people there: James McCoy, Miss Dodds, and Mrs. Hall. James Hall wasn't home at the time, and the detectives staked out the house. On Monday a man claiming to be a lawyer came to the house wanting to speak with Mrs. Hall. When Detective Graff began asking the lawyer questions, he abruptly left the house. Graff waited a few moments and then trailed the mystery man to a house farther down the street. The detective followed the would-be lawyer right into the house where he discovered the man talking to an unknown individual. Inexplicably, the uniden-tified, mystery man took Detective Graff for a lawyer, and after a minute or so of inconsequential conversation, he took Graff into a side room and told him he and his pal—who had been arrested on Saturday along with the guy's girlfriend and his wife—had recently robbed a couple of banks. The just-confessed bank robber then told the detective it would be worth a lot of money to Graff, who he still mistook for a lawyer, if he could get the three out of jail and freed of any charges. It was at this point the confessed bank robber learned he wasn't talking to a lawyer but a cop, a cop who promptly arrested him.

The Detroit detectives took Hall downtown for further questioning not knowing they were in for a bit of a surprise themselves. Hall admitted the name was an alias and he was really James Overstreet, a notorious and quite famous western bank robber. Overstreet was born in Shawnee, Oklahoma, on March 3, 1904. He told the judge prior to his sentencing in Mount Clemens that he left home at the age of 18 when he was sentenced to 10 years at the Granite Oklahoma Reformatory for taking part in a labor riot. What he failed to tell the judge was that he was bombing houses in Shawnee during a railroad strike. The reformatory only managed to hold him for three months before he escaped and chose bank robbing as his career path. He made his way to St. Louis, Missouri, where he organized a bank robbery crew that robbed, depending on who you listen to, either 11 or 13 Illinois banks in 1922 alone. It is believed Overstreet's crew stole in the neighborhood of $150,000 from just the Illinois banks. His gang also attempted to rob a mail train in Salem, Illinois, with disastrous results. Many of his gang were captured and the attempt failed.

In 1924 the Shawnee, Oklahoma, boy returned home with four accomplices, stuck up the Shawnee Federal National Bank, and made off with $18,000. Evidently a clothes hound, he was variously called 'Dressed Up Jimmie' and the 'Jellybean Bandit.' After the Shawnee job, Overstreet went to Texas where he might have lived a mite too extravagantly because he aroused suspicion in Fort Worth when he tipped the hotel staff with 5 and 10 dollar bills. He was arrested and confessed to the Shawnee robbery and drew a 25-year sentence at Oklahoma's McAlester Penitentiary. There he met and became a fast friend of James McCoy. After six years and five months, Overstreet was ordered to paint the roof of a prison building; instead, he went over the roof and the wall. He fled to Detroit and wrote McCoy to join him there when he was released, which he did in 1931.

Detroit police brought Overstreet and McCoy to Mount Clemens on the afternoon of November 18, 1931, where they appeared before Justice Alton Noe. The two thieves waived examination and were held on $50,000 bond.

A half hour later they went before Circuit Court Judge Spier where the two were expected to plead guilty since Overstreet presented the Detroit police with a near complete resumé of his criminal career. He even admitted to killing two men. Instead, they stood mute before Judge Spier and had a not guilty plea entered for them. They were bound over for trial on November 24.

When Overstreet and McCoy were driven to Mount Clemens on the eighteenth, crowds turned out as if Kid Rock was making an appearance. A large crowd waited outside the courthouse, and more curious onlookers lined the building's staircase, packed the hall outside Justice Noe's courtroom, and stood shoulder to shoulder inside. When the pair was later taken to Judge Spier's court, equally large crowds awaited their appearance. Overstreet and McCoy were surprised and delighted by the large crowds that treated them as celebrities and happily traded quips with individuals in the crowd.

Sometime between November 18 and the trial date, both men had a change of heart and decided they did not want to be extradited to another state to serve a prison term and pleaded guilty to the Mount Clemens robbery.

In a packed and hushed courtroom, James Overstreet asked the judge to consider his youth when he committed his first offense and that he had become addicted to the thrill and adrenalin rush of robbing banks. He also said he was very much in love with his pregnant wife (he had been married the day before in his cell with the chief of police as a witness) and had planned on going straight for her. Overstreet's father was also present for the wedding and trial. Overstreet told the judge the Mount Clemens job would have been his last.

The famous bank robber had already realized bank robbing was a dead end career. Days earlier he told Detroit police that his 1922 St. Louis crew had numbered 19 at one time or another, and he knew that all but two or three were either dead or in prison.

Apparently, Overstreet's plea for leniency fell on deaf ears. Judge Spier made the following remarks before passing sentence on James Overstreet and James McCoy. "I am not inclined to give you men life sentences for the reason that such a sentence does not mean what it implies but allows you to be paroled after the serving of a few years. I think your offence entitles you to a more severe sentence and it is for that reason I am going to set a definite term that both must spend in the penitentiary."[7]

McCoy, whose only previous conviction was for the possession of narcotics, was sentenced to 25 to 50 years in Jackson. Overstreet received 35 to 60 years in Marquette. When Overstreet's son was born and the birth certificate filled out, under the father's occupation it read bank robber.

1. Mt. Clemens Daily Leader 9-16-1931 p1, c8
2. Mt. Clemens Daily Leader 9-17-1931 p2, c7
3. IBID
4. IBID
5. Mt. Clemens Daily Leader 9-16-1931 p1, c8
6. Mt. Clemens Daily Leader 9-16-1931 p1, c7
7. Mt. Clemens Daily Leader 9-21-1931 p1, c8

Chapter 17

Don't Mess With Yoopers

May 31, 1932

*"...robbing the Hermansville bank would be
just like going into a grocery store."*

*A*s of May 30, 1932, a bank had never been robbed in
Menominee County, Michigan. On May 31 four men,
two from Minnesota and two from Michigan, ended that
laudable streak by sticking up the First National Bank of
Hermansville. If you were going to rob a bank in Hermansville,
it had to be First National because it was the only bank in
the small company town barely a stone's throw off U.S. 2.
The little ink dot representing the town on a Michigan map
sat about halfway between Escanaba and Iron Mountain in
the western Upper Peninsula.

The question that begs answering is why rob this bank
when there were so many good reasons not to. It was highly
unlikely the First National of Hermansville could or would
produce a big payoff for robbers. The community was all of
four blocks long and four blocks wide, and the cash on hand
on any one day to serve its customers couldn't match a bank's
cash reserves in Escanaba, Iron Mountain, or Marquette.
Back then, in pre Mackinac Bridge days, a stranger in a
small U.P. community, especially in a four-block-square
town, couldn't be more obvious than a moose wearing a

glove on an antler playing second base for the Tigers on opening day. There was also the problem of an escape route. Getting away by going east or west on U.S. 2 was simply too obvious. There were a handful of county roads one could use, but the getaway driver better be as familiar with them as the back of his hand because they could lead seemingly—or actually—to nowhere.

The tiny dot on the map that was and is Hermansville was put there in 1878 by the Wisconsin Land and Lumber Company. The town was built and literally owed its existence to the hardwood flooring business and the company's innovative equipment that turned trees into tongue and groove flooring. The demand for hardwood flooring made Hermansville, for at least a few years, a boom town. When hardwood flooring went into hard times after the '29 Crash, a former worker came back to Michigan and Hermansville to rob its bank.

Frank Jacobinski, at 18 was the youngest member of the bank robber gang and its least experienced. Frank was recruited for the job by his brother John. Maybe because Frank had worked for some months in Hermansville in 1928 John mistakenly thought his younger brother would know his way around the Hermansville area. John would have plenty of time in the future to regret that assumption. Frank, like his brother, was originally from Amasa, Michigan, but of late had been living in Minnesota with John. The older sibling, for the month or so before the Hermansville bank robbery, had partnered with Edward and Rudolph (sometimes called John) Kunasiewicz in pulling off holdups and armed robberies in Minnesota. Although the Kunasiewicz brothers and John Jacobinski were all hardly out of their teens, each of them had police records going back several years, and all of them were suspected of murder. The idea for the Hermansville job may have sprung from the thugs' desire to absent themselves from their current land of illegal opportunity for a spell and allow the spirited pursuit from local lawmen to cool off.

The gang, with Frank as a new member, made a recon trip from Minneapolis to Hermansville in a stolen car then drove back to the Twin Cities. When they left town to pull the job, they stole a Chrysler, later mistaken for at least two other makes, and drove to Milwaukee the day before the robbery. The next morning the gang drove north, stopped briefly at Green Bay and Beechwood Resort, Wisconsin, where they gassed up at 8 AM. The car carried Minnesota, Illinois, Michigan, and Wisconsin plates.

At 10:30 AM three of the gang members described as, "three young men, moderately well-dressed," [1] walked into the bank with revolvers drawn and ordered the three bank employees to reach for the ceiling. To make sure they were clearly understood and got everyone's full attention, one of the robbers put a round through a bank window. The bank's cashier, assistant cashier, and bookkeeper were watched so closely and with the overt threat of violence still echoing in their ears bank personnel didn't dare trip a burglar alarm which would have filled the vault with tear gas.

One of the robbers marched cashier Chris Gribble into the vault and ordered him to open the safe. Gribble later reported, "I told him I couldn't open the safe because it was protected by a time lock until our closing time." [2] While the robber and Gribble were in the vault, the other two employees were told to lie on the floor. One bandit kept a gun on the two workers while the other thief began filling a leather bag with greenbacks and silver from the tellers' windows.

No customers had been in the bank when the robbers entered, but that changed when George Higden walked in midway through the robbery. He was immediately followed into the bank by the fourth robber who left the getaway car and entered right behind Higden. The unlucky customer was stunned by a blow to his head, had his watch stolen, and was pushed into the vault.

It took the robbers less than five minutes to intimidate the bank's employees, rough up George Higden, and make an illegal withdraw of roughly $5,000. The employees all agreed the four hoodlums were under the age of 25 and not a one of the bandits could open their mouths without a stream of obscenities pouring forth. Leaving the bank, the thugs piled into the getaway car and knocked the back window out in order to shoot at any pursuers and to make it easier to throw nails on the road as they drove out of town. The gang must not have had too many nails because as they drove toward Iron Mountain on U.S. 2 a Ford truck came speeding up behind them unimpeded by any nails and pulled out to pass the getaway car. The robbers mistook the truck as pursuit by vigilantes and opened fire, shooting through where the back window used to be. Luckily for the truck driver, who wasn't chasing anyone and didn't know the bank had been robbed, all the shots went wide of the truck. A bus arrived from Iron Mountain just 10 minutes after the holdup, and the driver reported he had not seen any cars fitting the description of the getaway vehicle. It didn't help that the make of the car was mistaken for either a Graham-Paige or an reddish-brown Oldsmobile.

The bank's burglar alarm was tripped the moment the gang cleared the bank. Angry and armed citizens quickly gathered and organized a posse. As in so many instances in the 1920s and '30s, it was a local telephone switchboard operator who played a major role in the pursuit of the bank robbers. Hermansville was so small their local telephone operator was half a dozen miles to the east in Powers, Michigan. Doris Behrend was on duty at the Powers switchboard the morning of the robbery, and her quick action was a major contributor to the robbers' capture.

The Menominee County Sheriff Edward Reindl was not in his office that morning, but Mrs. Behrend knew where he could be found and that was her first call. She then called the Iron Mountain State Police Post and then systematically spread word of the robbery in a widening circle of nearby towns and villages and told all to be on the lookout for the bandits. It was sometime later that morning when someone from the sheriff's department as well as the state police called the Powers' switchboard and requested notification of the robbery to be broadcast throughout northern Wisconsin and the western Upper Peninsula area. Mrs. Behrend proudly told both callers she had already done that some time ago.

The search for the bandits became focused across the state line in Wisconsin when reports were received that cancelled checks taken in the robbery were found on a Michigan county road leading to Faithorn, Michigan. Hardly more than a wide place in the road, Faithorn started out as a lumber town that back then and even today is miles from anywhere except the Wisconsin state line just a mile to the west. But from then to this day there neither was nor is a bridge at Faithorn over the Menominee River which marks the border between Wisconsin and Michigan. From Faithorn the gang was tracked to Nathan, Michigan, a dozen miles south, where they turned due west and made for a bridge on County Road Z that crossed the Menominee River and deposited them in the Dairy State.

The search then turned towards Pembine, Wisconsin, on U.S. 141 where the robbers could head south through sparsely settled Wisconsin countryside or north to Michigan and Iron Mountain. But the bandits didn't have much of a clue where they were. This was before detailed state maps and improved country roads. In the 1930s they were often poorly marked and in some cases not much better than the logging roads they started life as 30 or 40 years earlier. If you weren't a local, it was easy to get lost or turned around, especially at night. And if we're being honest, it's still easy to get lost in remote northern Wisconsin or the Upper Peninsula.

As night approached the gang became confused if not utterly lost near Pembine. When they asked a passing motorist how to get to Minnesota, the request for directions was less than successful. They either misunderstood the other motorist, misread road signs, or were given wrong directions because the gang drove hither and yon between Pembine and Niagara, Wisconsin, like they were caught an inescapable corn maze. At some point around 8:30 PM, the gang just gave up trying to drive out of the area. They were probably very sensitive to the fact they were still in the getaway car, made even more conspicuous by the absence of a rear window, and decided to abandon the car, split into pairs, and walk north.

One would think the brothers would stay together, but they didn't. Frank Jacobinski and Rudolph Kunasiewicz headed into a swamp, bushwhacked eight miles cross country, and hit the outskirts of Niagara, Wisconsin. They stopped at a barbeque stand to wolf down some food before stepping on the bridge over the Menominee to hoof it to Michigan. They made it to the U.P. but not on foot. The bridge was under watch by local police, and the pair didn't make more than a few steps toward Michigan before they were stopped, questioned, and arrested. The two robbers put up no resistance. Frank Jacobinski and Rudolph Kunasiewicz (who gave his name as John Dahl) completed the crossing of the bridge in the back of a police car that chauffeured them to Iron Mountain where they spent the night in jail.

Sheriff Reindl picked the two felons up at the Dickinson County jail the next morning and took them back into Wisconsin. They had agreed to show the sheriff where they had abandoned the Chrysler, but after exploring a number of roads and crisscrossing the country south of Niagara, the pair failed to lead the sheriff to the car, guess which road, or even identify the area in which it had been left. The two robbers did agree that the other pair—which they swore they knew only as 'Montana Blackie' and 'Pretty Boy' could have returned to the car and driven off. Giving up finding the car, for the moment, Sheriff Reindl drove the two thieves back to Hermansville where they were positively identified by the bank employees. The sheriff and his two prisoners were met by a large crowd who gathered to see the culprits and in many cases take snapshots. The sheriff also received a large ovation and much cheering. After the rousing welcome in Hermansville, Reindl took the two to Menominee and housed them in the county jail. The tireless sheriff then headed back north to lead an intensified search for the last two gang members.

On Wednesday morning, two men walked into a diner/filling station in Twin Falls. No longer on the map, Twin Falls was about eight miles north of Iron Mountain on U.S. 2 just before it bends to the west. On entering the lunch room, one of the men picked up a newspaper that featured a front page story on the arrest of Kunasiewicz and Jacobinski. Evidently neither man possessed a poker face because after quickly scanning the front page they threw the paper down and ran from the diner. The proprietor of the establishment had watched the two men panic when seeing the article and kept an eye on them as they ran across the highway and dove into the woods. The owner went to a phone, called the police, and reported what he had just seen.

Sheriff Reindl, his brother Deputy Sheriff John "Junior" Reindl, Corporal Donald Hoady of the Michigan State Police, and other police were soon patrolling the highway that ran north from Twin Falls and bordered the immense Sagola Swamp. The lawmen were sure the bandits were still hiding in the swamp, which at its widest was almost 15 miles of muck and sorrow. In spots, the water was dangerously deep with no sure footing on the bottom, and even on dry ground it was sometimes impassable where storms had created huge windfalls. If all that wasn't bad enough, the swamp harbored swarms of mosquitoes that could suck a person dry faster than Count Dracula.

As darkness fell Sheriff Reindl got tired of waiting and along with Deputy "Junior" Reindl and Corporal Hoady headed into the swamp after the outlaws. The trio didn't make it too far before they hit a railroad line cutting through the rugged area like an elevated highway. Figuring the fleeing men would also be drawn to the tracks and the ease of movement, the line allowed Sheriff Reindl to call a halt. The three lawmen spread across the roadbed and waited to see what might walk into their trap. It was a damp and drizzly night with poor visibility, and as the hours dragged by, the lawmen grew colder, wetter, and ever more miserable.

About a half hour before midnight, the deputies heard footsteps approaching and the low mumble of voices. The trio first saw just legs through the drizzle, and even as the men drew abreast of Sheriff Reindl's group, their features were still indistinct in the mist. Either the state cop or the deputy lit up the two men with his flashlight. When the two unknown men found themselves in a spotlight, no matter how dim, they drew guns and started firing. The three lawmen returned fire. Five men hardly more than an arm's length apart all firing as fast as they could pull the trigger sending lethal lead flying off in every direction and not a single gunman was even nicked. One of the culprit's pistols jammed, but the other one continued to shoot wildly as both of them turned tail and raced back down the tracks.

Sheriff Reindl emptied his pistol at the two desperadoes then rose to his feet and, with bullets still whining through the drizzle, began to run down the two gunmen. The sheriff had a riot gun in one hand, and when he got close enough to the slower of the two, he swung the gun like Babe Ruth hitting the ball out of the park. Reindl hit the crook so hard he broke the gun stock in two. He also knocked the crook down but not out because the man surrendered yelling, "Don't shoot me. Remember my mother." [3]

The other thief was still high-tailing it down the tracks when Deputy Sheriff "Junior" Reindl stood up and cut loose with a machine gun. Reindl's initial burst of 25 rounds failed to wing the fleeing man but out of sheer self-preservation drove the robber to leap from the roadbed and run for the swamp. Deputy Reindl was about to unleash another burst when the crook ran through a herd of cows, and fearing he'd hit one of the four-legged creatures, the lawman held his fire. The fourth bank robber was last seen wading through the swamp in waist-deep water before he disappeared into the rain and darkness.

Sheriff Reindl had captured Edward Kunasiewicz. The sheriff searched the new captive and found roughly $1,000 in folding money and another $500 in silver. Kunasiewicz was jailed in Iron Mountain for the night. The prisoner looked like he'd spent a miserable couple of days in the swamp. The bandits' clothes were reduced to filthy rags, and his appearance suggested he'd spent more time than a hog wallowing in mud. Even under all that dirt and mud, it was clearly evident the man had served as the main course in a feast for what Yoopers often refer to as "Keweenaw Eagles." Those from the Lower Peninsula call the critters mosquitoes until they're bitten by one.

Edward proved to be the most talkative of the gang. He told Sheriff Reindl that Frank Jacobinski had worked some time ago in Hermansville and told the other three members of the gang, "… robbing the Hermansville bank would be just like going into a grocery store." [4] Jacobinski also told them the Menominee sheriff's department had slow cars and the state police only had pistols.

The next morning fifty police officers were patrolling the roads in the neighborhood of the Sagola Swamp. It had been learned by then the fourth robber was John Jacobinski, 23, and like his brother, originally from Amasa, Michigan. The police thought he might be trying to return there to hide, but they also speculated John might have been wounded in the previous night's shootout and could have died from his wounds.

The getaway car had finally been found the day Sheriff Reindl was in the Twin Falls area. The Chrysler "75" was discovered two miles from Niagara where it had been run off the road into a swamp. A coat worn by one of the robbers was found nearby along with paper coin rolls belonging to the Hermansville bank. The thieves had thrown away the keys when they abandoned the car, so it had to be towed to Iron Mountain. The day after capturing Edward Kunasiewicz, the ever busy Sheriff Reindl had a mechanic hot wire the car and the sheriff drove it to Menominee. After the car had been towed away, curiosity seekers came to look over the site, and one of them found the watch stolen from George Higden lying in the dirt. The watch was returned to its rightful owner.

The three bank robbers now in the Menominee County jail were drawing lawmen from Minnesota. The sheriff from Duluth and a police officer from Minneapolis came to question the gang because Ed Kunasiewicz was suspected of murdering a county road foreman who had fired Ed the day before he was murdered. It was also revealed the Kunasiewicz brothers had served 85 days for assaulting a school bus driver. They were also suspects in the cold-blooded murder of a Minnesota grocer within the past month. The Duluth police left for home after getting admissions for several recent hold-ups in their town. The search for John Jacobinski dragged on for several more days; his parents' house in Amasa was being watched, and police were still in the field actively looking for him on June 5.

Justice might be blind but, on occasion, quick, and if not fast enough she could be prodded into moving with haste. Sheriff Reindl was lobbying for a special term of the Circuit Court to be held within in few days to pass sentences on the three captives. This, before they were even arraigned. On June 7, 1932, it was announced Circuit Court Judge Frank A. Bell was expected to open a special session of court to sentence the three armed bank robbers. Sheriff Reindl also made it known he was confident all three would plead guilty of all charges. Apparently, none of the three asked for or were asked if they desired legal representation.

Judge Bell's special session was called to order the very next day at the strange hour of 11:30 PM. The three defendants were brought into court handcuffed to a police officer while sheriff deputies guarded the court room doors with riot guns. Mrs. Kunasiewicz, the mother of Edward and Rudolph, had arrived from Duluth with her minister and a lawyer to speak for her boys. She prayed devoutly and at great length throughout the proceeding.

The three defendants did plead guilty, and before Judge Bell pronounced sentencing, he asked if any of the three would like to speak. This was the cue for Mrs. Kunasiewicz' attorney to rise and say he would speak for the brothers. And so began a lengthy argument for clemency that went on and on. The attorney pointed out that up until a month ago Ed had not been involved with any holdups until he came under the spell of the Jacobinski boys. Furthermore, the attorney argued Rudolph, up until the robbery, was an innocent—still a wet-behind-the-ears youth who had been corrupted by his association with the other three young men. The Minnesota lawyer might have been able to talk fleas off a dog, but he got nowhere in a Michigan courtroom. Judge Bell finally halted the speech and told the Minnesota attorney to sit down and then sentenced the three armed robbers to 15–30 years in Marquette with the recommendation they serve only 15 years.

John Jacobinski managed to walk out of the Sagola Swamp, evade capture, and simply vanished from the U.P. On August 16, 1932, he was arrested in Seattle, Washington, extradited to Minnesota, and charged with the murder of Nels Berglin in an April holdup. He was found guilty and was sentenced to double life in a Minnesota state prison. Frank Jacobinski was paroled in 1942 and lived quietly on a farm. The Kunasiewicz brothers came up for parole in 1941. It was denied. If and when they got out of Marquette prison, they faced Minnesota murder charges for killing Charles Sundell in 1930.

The Hermansville job remained the only bank robbery in Menominee County until 1941.

1.   Menominee Herald-Leader 6-1-1932: p1, c8
2.   IBID
3.   IBID
4.   Menominee Herald-Leader 6-3-1932, p2, c2

Chapter 18

Bank Robbing and the Pastoral Life in Lapeer County

July 16, 1932

"The house shook from a dozen booming shots."

*P*ontiac's Benjamin Dillon had his career path completely worked out. First and most importantly, he had chosen to be a career criminal majoring in armed robbery. The plan was to hold stickups throughout Michigan and the Midwest and between jobs retreat to a rural farm in southeast Michigan to enjoy the pastoral life. Yes siree, he would hide in plain sight from the police and public attention by living the life of a farmer. As Ben once told his mother, "I would rather be dead than poor." [1] By 1931 the teenager had added a number of robberies to his resume, the most notable being the General Motors Truck Company robbery in which he made off with $2,800 in cash. He pulled his first bank job on a warm Saturday night in 1932 when he hit the Clarkston State Bank. Ben must have been very happy with his career choice. Here he was, not even 21, and his employment opportunities were paying off faster than today's career promises made by online universities. Little did he know that his road to riches would soon go off a cliff.

Clarkston's downtown sidewalks were crowded on the evening of July 16, 1932. The town's stores stayed open past normal closing times on Saturdays to entice locals out of their homes and downtown to shop or at least window shop on pleasant summer weekends. Even the Clarkston State Bank stayed open late on Saturdays to serve their customers. It was a little before 7:30 PM when two young men parked their Chevy in front of the Clarkston barbershop and walked the few steps to the bank and entered through the front door unnoticed. They both pulled guns, and Ben's side kick, Leo Bogert, sprinted to the cashier's office where he found bank president David Taggerdine and cashier George King. The robber ordered the two to raise their hands and warned them both not to trip an alarm. The armed thug marched the two out of the office and into a back room where most of the other bank employees and four customers were also taken.

Meanwhile Ben, with surprising speed and ease, climbed over a ten-foot-high partition of bullet-proof glass and wire. He dropped into the teller's cage with a gun in hand and began shoveling cash, including seven rolls of pennies, into a canvas bag. It happened so quickly assistant cashier Ray Ainsley and teller Isabelle King stood in stunned silence and watched the young man fill the bag with loot.

Ben was apparently twitchy with adrenaline because a nervous trigger finger twitched once too hard, the gun roared, and a bullet disfigured a metal paperweight and blew apart a porcelain doodad that one wet their finger with when counting money. While he cleaned out the teller's cage, Ben kept up a running chat with Isabelle King, and after bagging everything worth taking, he thanked Miss King. Done with the cashier's cage, trigger happy Ben told Miss King and Ainsley to show him where the money was kept in the vault. He was in the vault and scooping up more money when the trigger finger twitched again and a bullet took a divot out of the concrete floor and whined harmlessly away.

The two shots announced to everyone on Main Street the bank was being robbed. With the crowd standing the entire the length of downtown and watching, a robber walked out of the bank with a pistol filling one hand and the loot in the other. He walked to the parked car, stood there until his partner emerged from the bank and walked to the Chevy. They both eased themselves into the car and drove away at high speed, but not fast enough to out-race Charles Huntly's 30-40 caliber army rifle. As the thieves sped away, he rushed out of his drug store with rifle in hand. He stopped in the middle of the street, raised the weapon to his shoulder, and fired twice. Both rounds smashed into the car and came perilously close to hitting Ben and ending his career then and there. The crooks returned fire or just fired their pistols in the air out of sheer excitement and exuberance because no one reported any lead came their way.

Oakland County Deputy Sheriff Ed Seeterin happened to be in town, and when he heard the gunshots he enlisted the aid of Charles Cutter and Irwin Baker. The deputy and Baker threw two rifles into Barker's car and, with Irwin at the wheel, the trio sped off after the bandits. The outlaws made a two-wheels-off-the-ground turn onto Sashabaw Road before Seeterin's small, one-car posse took up the chase. Trailing the out-of-sight car proved no problem. The posse just followed the dust kicked up by the fleeing robbers. Three miles out of town the pursuers passed through a wooded swamp in a series of S curves. The deputy figured he couldn't be more than a couple of minutes behind the robbers when the three-man posse realized they were no longer chasing dust. There was no car in sight and nor any evidence that one had just passed this way. They stopped at a farm to ask if a car had gone by in the last few minutes and got a no. So the three started backtracking their route through the woods and found a two-track, followed it for about a hundred yards, and discovered the abandoned getaway car.

The Clarkston telephone operator had notified the Flint and Pontiac police of the robbery before the robber's dust had settled. Within twenty minutes police from both cities, as well as the state police, were in Clarkston and soon at the site of the abandoned getaway car. It was quickly discovered the car had been stolen earlier that day in Pontiac.

Deputy Seeterin was certain the car had only been ditched moments before its discovery, and he felt there was an excellent chance the thieves were hiding in the surrounding woods and wetlands. The call went out for help, and sheriff deputies, municipal police, state cops from five different posts, and volunteers surrounded the four-square miles of woods and wetlands. Three police cars equipped with search lights were sent to the area's highest elevations and pierced the night with cones of light that swept the woods looking for the fugitives.

The robbery, pursuit, and huge search party amounted to just about the most exciting thing to ever happen in Clarkston. The place to be on that Saturday night was the picket line surrounding the woods were it was hoped the robbers were trapped. Parties broke up early or shifted party headquarters to one of the roads bordering the hunt. Gawkers arrived throughout the night and then stood around waiting for something to happen. And nothing did. At 5:30 in the morning, a picket line was established along Baldwin and Orion Roads while another line of officers and volunteers began walking through the woods and swamp where the car had been discovered. The search flushed no on and turned up nothing.

The thieves, Ben Dillon and Leo Bogert, had raced for the remote stretch of road east of Clarkston where they abandoned the Chevy. They then ran to where they stashed a roadster, changed into clothes working farmers would wear, and motored slowly home to Pontiac with $3,900 in loot. If the pair was seen, no one paid any attention to a couple of farmers driving to town in a Model A.

The two robbers had escaped, and the police didn't have a clue as to who they were or where they went. The police weren't even sure if there were two or three robbers. Some believed a third man had acted as the getaway driver, but no reliable eye witnesses came forward who could verify a third felon.

Frank Greenan joined the Oakland County Sheriff's Office in 1917 as a deputy sheriff. He served under four different sheriffs, and the current sheriff, Frank Schram, had appointed Greenan as undersheriff. That meant most of the high profile, unsolved cases ended up in Greenan's in-basket. During the summer and fall of 1932, the undersheriff spent long hours on the Clarkston robbery following up leads that never led anywhere and running down known criminals and ex-cons and clearing their names from his list of suspects.

That same summer Sheriff Schram had announced his retirement, and Frank Greenan ran in the Oakland County Republican primary for sheriff and won. As the summer waned, the leaves changed color, and the Clarkston case remained unsolved, Undersheriff Greenan spent less time on the campaign trail and more time on the July bank robbery.

Unknown to the police, Ben Dillon had begun implementing his career plans. Ben gave his mother $2,000 from the Clarkston job to buy a farm in Deerfield Township in northern Lapeer County. It lay less than ten miles from Lapeer. The farm was bought from an estate on August 22, 1932. Anybody who thought to ask where Mrs. Dillon got the money was told it came as an insurance settlement when her third son was killed in a plane accident.

Ben gave in to temptation and failed to follow his plan to live simply and inconspicuously when he bought a new car from a Lapeer dealer that sold Hudson and Essex cars—not an auto one would likely see on a northern Lapeer County farm. Ben was also always coming from or going to someplace out of town and continuously having his car's oil changed and tinkered with at a Lapeer garage. It can't be substantiated, but it's likely Ben was either casing banks for future jobs or committing armed robberies with person or persons unknown.

Undersheriff Greenan received yet another tip on November 1, just days before the election. He was told by a young man who occasionally worked for the Dillons when they lived in Pontiac the family had bought a farm near Lapeer. The farm was bought with cash, and they had attracted the attention of locals for their conspicuous, high-on-the-hog living. Greenan thought it would be just another dead end, but in police work you followed up on leads.

The next morning the undersheriff lined up deputies Harvey Tedder and Clare Hubbell to accompany him to Lapeer and check out the Dillon farm. When it was suggested he go to the farm in force, he rejected the idea and down played the chances this would be a lead of any importance. The morning of November 2, the three Oakland County police first drove to Clarkston and picked up two men who could identify the robbers, bank president David Taggerdine and assistant cashier Ray Ainsley. Their next stop was at the Lapeer County jail where they asked Lapeer County Sheriff Byron Courter how to get to the Dillon farm. Courter volunteered to show them the way and, neither expecting nor told there might be trouble, didn't take a sidearm.

The following account of events at the Dillon farm was drawn from several eye witnesses. Like any after-action report of a life and death fire fight involving even a small unit and which took only seconds to play out, the accounts of the participants can differ greatly. The huge adrenalin rush of fighting for your life and trying to save others and the unique perspective from which one viewed or took part in the event can dramatically alter what one thought they saw or did. What follows is a best effort to meld differing accounts into one narrative.

The trip to the Lapeer County farm was made in what, at best, could be called good duck hunting weather. It was a cold, dreary day with the sky blanketed in low-lying clouds. If it wasn't spitting rain on the muddy roads and sodden fields, it snowed. When the two police cars reached the farm, they slowed and turned into the long driveway. Ben Dillon and his brother Scott were in back of the house chopping firewood. As the car pulled closer to the home and the two men came into view, the bank's assistant cashier instantly recognized at least one of them and shouted, "That's them." [2] The three Oakland County police jumped from the cruiser as Ben looked up, saw the police, and broke for the house.

Greenan and Tedder drew their guns and got off a couple of shots at Ben before he ducked into the farmhouse. Undersheriff Greenan entered the house not ten feet behind Ben with Tedder following closely behind. When Dillon flew through the house's side door, he grabbed a loaded shotgun from a virtual arsenal kept at the ready and immediately whirled and fired. The house shook from a dozen booming shots. At least one shotgun blast hit Greenan in the arm and chest, and the undersheriff staggered back toward the outside door.

Before the echo of the gunshots faded, an older woman flew through the front door, jumped from the steps, and started running. Sheriff Courter happened to be in her way and grabbed the woman. As Courter held on to the woman, Deputy Hubbell emerged from the tool shed with Scott Dillon in an arm lock. Hubbell handcuffed Scott to the car bumper, and the Oakland County Deputy and Sheriff Courter turned to look at the farmhouse and saw Greenan stagger out the side door, fall down, and rise again to his feet. Courter and Hubbell watched as Greenan pointed toward a window with a bloody hand. The undersheriff raised his gun, pointing it at the window when another blast came from within the house and the pistol flew from Greenan's hand as it dissolved in a mist of red.

Courter and Hubbell raced to Greenan's side, picked him up, and carried him to a car. They put the critically injured man in the back seat and told the stunned bankers to drive like hell for the nearest hospital. Another resounding boom had rocked the house as the two lawmen were getting Greenan into the car. As the cruiser backed down the driveway, Hubbell handed Courter his extra gun and they headed for the house.

When they reached the kitchen door, the two men found a young woman sitting on the steps sobbing. When Courter noticed she didn't have a weapon, he grabbed her by the arm, spun her around, and placed her in front of himself as a human shield. He shoved her first through the door then followed her inside. Hubbell entered just a step behind Courter. The girl's sobbing slackened, and she clearly didn't want to go any farther into the house. Sheriff Courter ordered the young woman to tell the shooter she was coming in the house. In a fear-shrouded voice she called, "Don't shoot, Ben. It's me Marion." [3]

Courter pushed his human shield into the living room where she came to a shuttering stop. When the sheriff looked over her shoulder, he saw Deputy Tedder face down near the stairway in a pool of blood. In a house suddenly as quiet as a tomb, a moan escaped Tedder's throat. Courter pushed the girl to a door on the left which he figured was the room from which Greenan was shot. When Marion got to the doorway, she screamed.

Ben Dillon lay on the floor partially resting against a bed. The pump shotgun lay by his side. His face was a mask of blood and gore. Ben had accidently shot himself while reloading the gun. One can only wonder if it was the result of another twitchy finger. Surprisingly, he was still alive though unable to speak.

Hubbell and Courter carried Officer Tedder to a car, and Hubbell rushed him to a hospital and once there requested an ambulance for Dillon. While waiting for the ambulance to come for Ben, his brother played dumb and asked Courter why the police had come to the house and opened fire. Courter told Scott his brother was one of the Clarkston bank robbers. Scott turned to his brother and asked if it was true. Unable to speak, Ben nodded yes and grunted in the affirmative. Hubbell returned to the farm soon after the ambulance left with Ben and took Scott Dillon and the two women in for questioning.

Several other deputies from Oakland and Lapeer counties and the state police arrived, as well as reporters and photographers. Even from the outside, the house looked like it had been through a battle. Most of the windows were shattered or blown out, doors hung open, and the steps up to the side door were painted with blood. Inside, the walls were riddled with bullet holes and shotgun blasts. Blood splattered the walls and pooled on the floor.

The police began searching the house and found it filled with newly purchased or stolen merchandize. There were a variety of new appliances, clothes, several short wave radios, and six canaries in cages. Sergeant Curran of the Oakland Sheriff's Department focused on looking for photographs, letters, and documents. He went through dressers, closets, and tables and walked out of the house with his pockets stuffed with papers and snapshots to sift through later.

That evening, it was learned that Ben Dillon died shortly after the ambulance delivered him to the hospital. Deputy Tedder, 42, the father of ten children, died en route to the hospital. One month to the day after her husband's murder, Mrs. Tedder delivered the couple's eleventh child. Frank Greenan was taken to the Mayville hospital where doctors worked feverishly to save his life. A blood transfusion and early work to stabilize the officer's condition led to a glimmer of hope, but he began failing as night fell and died at 11:30 PM.

The police were convinced Scott was the second robber, but under intense and repeated questioning, he maintained his innocence. Scott swore he was in Chicago when the Clarkston bank was robbed but finally admitted Ben told him in late July he had robbed the bank. Scott told his brother he didn't want to know any of the details, but a few days later Ben bragged he was the one who leaped into the cashier's cage and scooped up the money. Scott also admitted he had bought five guns in Chicago and transported them to Michigan. Reluctantly, the police were swayed by Scott's apparent sincerity and his forthright manner in answering questions and concluded Scott probably wasn't involved with the robbery.

The police next grilled the mother of the two men. Mrs. Dillon surprised everyone in the room when she told them she used to be a bareback rider in the circus, but she was tight lipped when it came to her son Ben and the Clarkston bank robbery. She repeatedly swore she knew nothing, saw nothing, and admitted nothing.

Mrs. Dillon went back to a cell, and Marion Halliday was brought to the hot seat. She was clearly scared and, even in a pair of bib overalls, very easy to look at. Ben's sweetheart was seventeen with blond hair, blue eyes, full lips, and with all the right curves in the right places. Marion said she'd been injured in a motorcycle accident while riding with Ben. Mrs. Dillon had invited her to stay at the farm while she recuperated. Marion claimed when asked that she slept in Mrs. Dillon's bedroom, but the police had found all her clothes in Ben's closet or scattered on his bedroom floor. She denied any knowledge of the bank robbery but reported she and Ben were engaged.

The questioning of the three turned up no useful information, and the police decided to put Marion in a lineup to see if she might be identified as the second bank robber. No one picked her, so the detectives decided to turn up the heat and go another round with the three. Mrs. Dillon finally broke down and admitted Ben told her he robbed the bank and gave her money to buy the farm. She swore he never told her the identity of his partner but spilled the news that what money was left over from the robbery was buried in the cow pen. A sheriff's deputy was given the unpleasant task of digging through an enclosure that was ankle deep in cow manure until he unearthed a glass jar containing $178 in paper currency and $3.55 in coins.

The identity of the second bank robber was still unknown when Sergeant Curran began to sort through the pile of documents, checks, and snapshots he'd taken from the farm. He found nothing that led to Ben's accomplice in the letters or papers, so he turned to the snapshots. He noted one photograph of two couples. One of the young men looked like Ben Dillon, and the blond next to him could have been Marion. Curran had no idea who the other couple was, but the possibility lingered that it could be Ben's partner. The sergeant then came across another photo of Ben and Marion, with their arms around each other, standing beside a roadster. Curran wondered if it was the second getaway car and who owned it? He grabbed a magnifying glass and slowly scanned the photo; there was the car's license plate number 472-771 clearly visible. A call to the Secretary of State told him that car had been owned by Ben then sold to Leo Bogert who, just before the robbery, transferred ownership back to Ben.

Curran wrote down Bogert's address and with six heavily armed Oakland deputies in two cars headed north. At Lapeer they were met by two state cops who added their cruiser to the convoy. On the north side of town, they checked with a man who lived near the Bogert address given on the Secretary of State's registration form and learned the suspect had moved to North Branch. At North Branch one of the Oakland deputies slipped into town and made some discreet inquires as to where one might find Leo Bogert only to learn he had moved again. This time he had reportedly moved to Vassar where he was living with his brother.

The lawmen must have begun to wonder whether they were on a wild goose chase as the convoy neared the Tuscola County town. Once again, the task force waited outside the village while Curran and another officer slipped into town and asked someone in the know where the Bogerts lived and if the younger brother also lived there. Curran got the Bogert address and was told Leo was living there and driving a gasoline truck. If the truck was at the house, Leo would be too.

The task force drove to the address, and although the gasoline truck wasn't there, the roadster with the 472-771 license sat in the front yard. The three police cars drove around town and out into the country and circled back several times before the gasoline truck sat parked in front of the house. The police armed themselves with tear gas and rifles before surrounding the house. With the back door under surveillance, several cops quietly stepped up on the front porch and knocked on the door. They waited a heartbeat then burst through the door with guns drawn and found a young man standing frozen on the stairway. The police rushed the individual, checked to see if he was armed, and asked if he was Leo Bogert. The answer came back affirmative and that he wouldn't give them any trouble. He confessed in the car on the drive to Pontiac and pleaded guilty to armed robbery before a judge. He was sentenced to 25–40 years in prison.

Mrs. Dillon and Marion Halliday were eventually released and faced no charges. Rumors abounded that Scott Dillon had taken part in several area holdups, but nothing could be proved. Even more damning than rumors was a letter from Illinois that arrived at the farm after Ben's death. The anonymous letter writer told Ben that if Scott didn't agree to take part in future bank robberies the writer and Ben had enough dirt on Scott to send him to prison. Apparently, Ben was considering blackmailing his own brother. The letter spurred police to renewed efforts to pin something on Scott. The only thing they could find and charge him with was having an unregistered firearm in his possession. Scott was brought before Justice Glenn Hollenbeck and surprisingly the charges were dropped—but with a catch. Scott Dillon had to agree to leave Michigan within 36 hours. One can only wonder how someone can be banished from the state for not being guilty.

It was reported the Dillon family did not have the money to bury Ben and his body was given to the University of Michigan Medical School.

1. Francis Patrick Arthur Mason McGuirk Family Home Page http://familyfreemakermaker.genealogy.com/users/k/i/r/Merrily-R-Kirchen/WEBSITE-0001/UHP-0134.html
2. "Official Vengeance," by Sgt. J.H. Curran Real Detective Mag. March 1937 p15
3. IBID p17

ROUTE OF BANDITS FLIGHT FROM HOLLAND

MRS. BEASLY RUNS HEAD ON INTO LEAD GETAWAY CAR AND LOCKS BUMPERS.

RIVER ST.

OIL STATION

BUMPER-LOCKED CARS PUSHED ASIDE BY BANDITS WHO ESCAPE IN AUBURN.

LEFT BANK AT REAR ENTRANCE AFTER ROBBERY.

BANK

7th STREET

WARM FRIEND TAVERN

CENTRAL AVE.

8th STREET

HOLLAND

OTTAWA COUNTY
ALLEGAN COUNTY

ROBBERS FLEE FROM CITY PURSUED BY POSSE.

TRUCK STOPPED BY ROBBERS & USED TO BARRICADE ROAD; GUN FIGHT ENSUES.

DRENTHE

OUTLAWS SEED ROAD WITH ROOFING NAILS.

POSSE LIMPS INTO BURNIPS ON SHREDDED TIRES, BANDITS ESCAPE.

16th STREET

LINCOLN ST.

TURNED SOUTH ON LINCOLN ST., THEN TURNED EAST ON 16th ST.

W

N

S

E

Chapter 19

"Brave Little Holland"

September 29, 1932

"I could feel bullets whistling past my legs..."

The gunmen burst through the doors of Holland's First State Bank like an invading army. They came in fast and hard, brandishing Tommy guns and hand guns. The gang possessed an unmistakable air of violence, and their shock value proved so great they took immediate control of the bank. Later, the victims couldn't agree whether there were five or seven bandits. The leader of the mob, a large, beefy man with an oval face cut by a moustache, had enough of a presence that all the witnesses could later describe him, but then again who wouldn't remember the guy who shouted, "This is a holdup."

Eddie Bentz was the man all the witnesses remembered, and if there was an air about him, a certain memorable but indefinable presence, it might be attributed to Eddie's belief that men who shared his line of work—robbing banks— were the royalty of the criminal profession. And in Eddie's world you didn't become royalty by birth but through cold-blooded devotion to detail, imaginative and original research, plus a ruthless disregard for the safety or wellbeing of bank employees or anyone else who got in the way. Bentz was smart enough to realize a well-planned daylight robbery had a better chance of success than going about it haphazardly, so he became a student of robbing banks. Eddie planned heists with precision, and like a soldier planning an attack, he wanted to intimately know the battlefield. He often cased a bank by posing as a major investor or a new businessman in town and asked for a bank tour. He could read bank employees and know who might threaten the success of the job and who, under pressure, would fold like a wet paper towel. Bentz visited public libraries, studied American banking practices, and came up with a system for figuring out when a specific bank would have the most cash in its safe.

No one can be absolutely sure why Eddie Bentz picked Holland's First State Bank as this gang's target. Eddie was apparently familiar with the area (he and Baby Face Nelson would rob a Grand Haven bank a year later). He probably knew the City of Holland had a small police force, and the town—founded a century earlier by the Dutch—had a reputation for being a quiet, peaceful place that wouldn't be expected to offer any resistance. Bentz, always the tactician, decided to hit the bank and the town with overwhelming force and cow the bank employees and the citizens of Holland. It was 9:30 AM on September 29, 1932, and Eddie Bentz was about to learn you don't intimidate a hornet's nest.

After Bentz's four little words that no one ever wants to hear in a bank, the gang herded the employees and customers to the center of the room and made them lay face down on the floor. The banker's cashier, Cornelius vander Meulen, was ordered to open the safe. When he said he couldn't, a gang member slapped him around. Assistant cashier William Westover was then told to open the safe and proceeded to do so. Whether it was a case of nerves or he wanted to delay the robbers, Westover did not rotate the tumblers fast enough to suit the gang. They whacked him over the head a couple of times thinking it would encourage a faster response.

The crew had been in the bank less than ten minutes and everything was going according to plan until Ben Hamm walked down the street and turned to enter the bank. A member of the gang stationed outside the front door told the salesman to raise his hands. At that moment the robbery went from under control to out of control. Instead of meekly complying with the gangster's order, Hamm turned and ran down 8th Street like Jessie Owens in the Berlin Olympics while breathlessly shouting the news that the bank was being robbed. Fred Beeuwhes and Ray Knooihuizen, both bank employees, were walking toward the bank when they met Hamm and they added their voices to Ben's in spreading the word.

Holland's Police Chief, Peter A. Lievense, just a few days shy a year since being named the city's top cop, recounted his part in the robbery from a hospital bed. "I was in the Boston restaurant on Eighth Street talking to Dick Van Kolken when George Overwege ran up to me shouted that the bank was being held up. I told him to quit kidding me, but when he persisted I knew he was not joking.

"I ran to the doorway at the west side of the bank that leads to the offices of Diekema, Cross and Ten Cate above the bank. I waited there with the idea of halting the men when they came out of the bank. But I happened to think the bandits might have finished the job and had escaped through the rear. So I decided to find out and moved over to the bank entrance. Stepping past the screen door, I saw about 15 people laying on the floor, a man with a submachine gun and another man at the rear of the bank.

"I noticed this last fellow just as he raised his gun to fire at me. I jumped to the side, but the bullet struck a steel clip on my gun holster and was deflected into my left side. The slug stopped at the lower rib… The wound made me mad. I ran behind a car parked near the drinking fountain at the bank corner. Determined to get the fellow who hit me, I crept along the east side of the bank under the windows with the idea of jumping up near the rear of the bank and firing through the window.

"As I neared the rear of the bank, I noticed a man with a machine gun as he poked the weapon through the side of a car parked on the west side of Central Avenue near the alley at the rear of the bank. I opened fire but do not know whether I hit him. Then I ducked and ran diagonally across Central as he started firing. I could feel bullets whizzing past my legs…"[1]

At the same time, H. G. Taussig, a traveling salesman from Chicago, walked out to his car after spending the night in the Warm Friend Tavern, slipped behind the wheel and cranked the starter. Taussig might have been ready to start his day, but his car wasn't, and as he tried to fire up his reluctant transportation, the battle between the chief of police and the gangsters erupted. Rounds from a submachine gun, once the trigger is pulled, often give the distinct impression of willfully disregarding the intended target and going where they damn well please. Although not directly in the line of fire, the gang's attempt to kill Chief Lievense drew fire toward the traveling salesman. Taussig said, "One shot whistled past me as I got out of the car and ducked behind it."[2]

Hoping the car's body would keep him out of the line of fire, Taussig ran for better cover in the Warm Friend Tavern's kitchen only to witness a bullet penetrate the hotel and fall spent at the feet of a woman employee. A half block down the street, the roar of the submachine gun and the bark of Lievense's sidearm brought meat cutter Peter DeJongh, 45, out of the shop where he was working to see what the ruckus was all about. He had hardly come to a standstill when a machine gun round struck him in the chest. The police chief thought DeJongh was probably hit by a stray from one of the machine gun rounds chasing him across Central Avenue.

After running the gauntlet of submachine fire, Chief Lievense said, "I found shelter behind a car in front of the Tavern drug store and worked my way to the front of the car and fired at the man with the machine gun. He replied with a spray of lead that splattered the side of the Tavern. I ducked back, and when I fired again he responded with another volley of bullets. At that time Henry Rowan, a sergeant in the national guards, appeared at my side and began firing. The two of us drove the man out of the car and down the alley." [3]

Officer O'Connor was the second lawman to appear at the scene, and with Chief Lievense they worked to a position from which they could fire down the alley. A block down Central Avenue, Ben Lievense, brother of the police chief and owner of a garage, heard the sound of gunfire, grabbed his rifle and ran to the corner of 8th and Central and joined the growing fight. Other Holland citizens picked up guns and headed toward the ever-increasing sound of battle. Inside the bank, the gang realized simply from the rising crescendo of gunfire Holland hadn't laid down and turned belly up. If not outgunned, the mounting incoming fire from all directions certainly meant the scales were tipping and not in the bandits' favor. Bentz and his crew knew that if they were not presently outnumbered they soon would be and it was past time to hotfoot it out of Holland.

Nick the Greek, owner of the Columbia Hat Shop a few doors down from the bank, stepped out his back door armed with a shotgun at nearly the same moment the gang exited the bank into the alley where they'd stashed two getaway cars. Nick opened fire at the robbers only to be met by withering submachine fire that swept the alley. The haberdasher dove for the ground and continued to blast away.

While others joined the fight, Chief Lievense's wound forced his withdrawal. He called headquarters to let them know he was hit and had reached the stage where he was unable to continue. A man helped him into a room in the tavern where a doctor looked at the wound and ordered him to the hospital. There he was X-rayed, and the bullet along with pieces of clothing were removed from the wound.

Back in the alley, the robbers piled into the getaway cars amid a hail of bullets and buckshot, and the lead car, a big Studebaker, barreled down the alley headed for River Street. Yards from where it would make a right on River, Mrs. Vance Brailey—who one can only conclude somehow remained oblivious to the raging firefight through which she drove—turned into the alley and hit the Studebaker head-on. The two cars' bumpers locked on impact, and the bandits in the Studebaker, not realizing the two cars were hung up, yelled at Mrs. Bailey to back up, which only made the automobiles even more difficult to separate. All the yelling directed her way from the Studebaker upset Mrs. Brailey, who thought the men she hit had been hitting the bottle too much. She yelled back expressing her low opinion of a carload of drunks. Unfortunately, there is no record of what Mrs. Brailey thought or how she reacted when she finally and belatedly discovered the true situation into which she had driven.

When the gangsters realized the cars had snagged bumpers, they piled out of the Studebaker and jimmied, coaxed, and swore both creatively and at length at the lip-locked cars, all to no avail. Tired of dodging bullets and trying to separate the vehicles, they shoved both cars to the side of the alley and ran for the backup car. The second getaway car, an Auburn, with all the bandits aboard shot out of the alley onto River Street, turned right on 7th, drove several blocks to Lincoln where they turned right again. When the crooks reached 16th Street, they took a left and sped out of town with the Sheriff's Deputy Charles Jackson in close pursuit with his car full of posse members. The second getaway car escaped the gauntlet of downtown Holland and the threat of being fired at from any direction by any citizen who had a gun apparently unscathed. Sixteenth Street led out into the country where the robbers might have sighed with relief except for Deputy Jackson and his ad hoc posse that included Chief Lievense's garage mechanic brother Ben. The state police were also racing to join the hunt and not far behind.

Eddie Bentz's gang must have felt some faint stirring of concern about not being able to break contact with their pursuers when the answer and means—George Boerman and his gravel truck—appeared before them. George had no idea what he was heading into as he drove west on 16th Street a couple miles outside of Drenthe until a car full of heavily armed gunmen stopped him at gunpoint. They ordered him to park the truck broadside to the road, effectively blocking it, and then made him lie down on the road in front of his truck. The desperadoes warned him if he tried to crawl away or even move they would kill him. The bank robbers then opened fire on the approaching police car. Outgunned, the posse retreated to the home of George Hulzenga with machine gun fire licking at their heels. The house was ventilated by the Thompson, but no one was hit—and neither was Boerman who lay out on the road as a torrent of gunfire whistled overhead.

With the police out of the car and taking cover in the house and unable to return fire because their shotguns and .38 caliber revolvers couldn't reach the bandits, they finally allowed Boerman to scramble into a roadside ditch. The bank crew then covered the road with roofing nails, climbed back in the Auburn, and headed for Drenthe. Boerman got a good look at the crooks, but even he was not sure whether there were six or seven of them, but he clearly saw one had been wounded in the neck. When the Auburn disappeared down the road, the posse mounted up and gave chase but was soon doing so on flat tires while taking fire from a Thompson submachine gun.

The Auburn blew through Drenthe and then turned southeast for Burnips Corners. The growing line of pursuers, including state police, tried to follow, but the robbers continued to salt the road with roofing nails. By Burnips Corners the chase came to a halt on shredded tires. News of the bank robbery had raced ahead of the Auburn, and an impromptu group of farmers had grabbed their guns and gave the car and its occupants both a very warm welcome and send off as it passed through town. As the Auburn raced from Burnips Corners and was lost from view, it would be the last time any adult saw the bank robbers.

State police officers from the Grand Haven post spent 48 hours searching for any trace of the bandits. They received reports from school children walking on rural back roads that an Auburn slowly cruised by and the bank robbers waved to them as they passed. The trail of roofing nails disappeared near Gun Lake which prompted the state police to perform several house-to-house searches in the area and to send out a posse of 400 to beat the woods and fields hoping to flush the crooks. Eventually, all the leads grew cold, all the trails disappeared, no one was ever caught, and no one was even identified as a possible suspect.

Police believe the robbers slipped through the police cordon shortly after passing through Burnips Corners and were safely back in their hideout or in Chicago while police were still looking for them in the Holland area. The state police used radio dispatch to coordinate their hunt and seal off areas, but the police strongly suspected the crooks had a radio receiver in the getaway car and used it to stay a step ahead of the law.

Today, Holland is known as a destination that draws thousands for the annual Tulip Festival and other attractions reflecting the city's cultural heritage. In the weeks after the bank robbery, throngs descended on the town to 'ooh' and 'aah' at the pockmarked buildings. The area around the bank

Stick 'em Up... by Tom Powers

looked like a war zone. Automobiles on Central Avenue were riddled with bullet holes from both the gangsters' submachine guns and the citizenry's small arms. One car had only the rear window whole, and almost 150 bullet holes could be counted in the body. The Warm Friend Tavern was chipped and gouged from machine gun rounds, and several second floor windows had been shot out. The alley from which the gang made their escape with guns blazing became a popular part of the walking tour. And invariably, many a small Dutch boy, instead of putting a finger in a leaking dike, got the up-'til-then thrill of a lifetime by sticking his finger in a bullet hole.

The total haul of the robbery came to $47,164.10 of which $12,000 was in cold hard cash. Insurance reimbursed in full everything taken by the gunmen, and the bank reopened for business an hour after the robbery with replacement funds from Grand Rapids. The only thing not covered was the bullet hole in the front door window.

The getaway car the robbers abandoned in the alley had been stolen from Oak Park, Illinois. The Studebaker's contents included radio equipment, an automatic rifle, a machine gun, ammunition for pistols and automatic weapons, road maps, a gray hat, leather jacket, and license plates from Illinois, Missouri, and Wisconsin. The Auburn was never found.

Chief Lievense was on the mend within days of being shot, but butcher Peter DeJongh remained in critical condition. A third man bloodied by the bandits had received a minor cheek wound at the 16th Street barricade and was treated on the scene. DeJongh died on June 16, 1953, at the age of 66. He had never completely recovered from the chest wound and had undergone several surgeries at the University of Michigan hospital which included the removal of several ribs.

The violent robbery and the crooks' escape proved to be a glaring example of how the local and even state police were not equipped to deal with heavily armed desperadoes driving automobiles that could outdistance police vehicles. An editorial that ran in the *Holland News* a week after the robbery read in part, "We know one thing—Holland did not lack brave men. They marched right up to danger and possible death, inadequately armed and without flinching. Our experience, and this is not said in the way of criticism has taught us that our police department should be provided with arms and ammunition if not superior at least equal to what highwaymen use." [4]

An editorial in the *Grand Rapids Press* and reprinted in the *Holland City News* read in part, "The thugs seem to have made their getaway, at least temporarily. But there is nothing of which Holland need be ashamed; 'Brave little Holland' has taken on a new meaning in Michigan." [5]

1. Holland City News 10-6-1932 p1, c2-3
2. IBID
3. IBID
4. IBID
5. IBID

Chapter 20

Crossing the Finnish Line in Kaleva

January 5, 1933

"A sawed-off shotgun proved to be a can't-argue-with-that deal sealer."

*K*aleva is and was a quiet, little, out-of-the-way village some 18 miles northeast of Manistee founded in 1900 by Finnish settlers when the land was covered with nothing but white pine stumps in any direction one looked. If you were searching for a place to put down roots, raise a family, and avoid the clamor and glamour of a big city, this was it. Kaleva was not a place that expected to make news or where the unexpected occurred. Then tragedy and change came to the peaceful, close-knit town on Thursday, January 5, 1933, and it had nothing to do with the sudden death of former president Calvin Coolidge that day.

At about 11:30 AM that morning, a black Buick sedan stopped beside the Bank of Kaleva, and three men—later described as 25–35, well-dressed, and clean-shaven—jumped from the car and entered the bank. They found three men in the bank: customer Wellington Hones, cashier Ellsworth Billman, and assistant cashier Frank Wilson. As the three dapper men hurried into Bank of Kaleva, the driver stopped Weikko Pihl, a village youth who happened to stroll by, and persuaded the kid to tarry a while beside the Buick. A sawed-off shotgun proved to be a can't-argue-with-that deal sealer.

Inside the bank, the three men from the Buick drew guns and told customer Hones to move to the rear of the bank as each of the gunmen walked up to one of the three tellers' windows. The gang's leader, wearing a light gray suit, overcoat, and cap and looking like he'd just stepped from the pages of GQ, confronted Billman at the cashier's window and said, "You know what we're here for, I suppose," [1] pointing his gun at the banker.

Billman's foot was only inches from the floor alarm, and a loaded Colt .45 revolver lay temptingly close, but he reached for neither and probably surprised the gunman when he abruptly took a step back from the window, not an unnatural reaction to having a gun pointed at you from only inches away. The gang leader apparently misread Billman's move. The gunman accused Billman of either sounding the alarm or trying to and fired a bullet into the cashier's chest. Ellsworth Billman, the son of the man who founded the bank, died before his body hit the floor. One of the other bandits then ran behind the tellers' row of windows and at gunpoint told Frank Wilson to lie on the floor. The crook mistook a nearby light socket for an alarm and ordered the assistant cashier not to touch it.

The shooting of Billman seemed to rattle the gunmen. The killer ran to the vault but somehow failed to find any money, so he turned his gun on the assistant cashier. He ordered the cashier into the vault and to come up with some money. When Wilson handed over a single stack of bills, the killer shouted, "Is that all you've got?" [2] If unsatisfied, the robbers settled for the solitary stack of greenbacks plus a handful of gold coins they scooped up as the gang fled the bank and jumped into the getaway car. In their hurry they failed to notice $1,500 in cash lying in plain sight. As it was, they left the building with $1,500 in non-negotiable securities and $2,800 in cash.

Well aware of the Michigan State Police post only 15 minutes away in Manistee, the bank robbers decided to cut the telephone wires running to that town. This presented a challenge because the bank crew had not thought to bring wire-cutters, pliers, or even a knife. They finally resorted to the "Neanderthal method," pounding the wire between two rocks until it broke. They mistakenly cut the telephone line between Kaleva and Brethren leaving the line to Manistee open.

Most of the village was fully aware that a bank robbery was underway before the crooks fled the bank, and news of the fate of Ellsworth Billman spread through town almost as fast as the gang's getaway car. Moments after the robbers sped away from the bank heading south to Brethren for M-55, a car full of locals gave chase. And the Buick didn't get out of town unscathed. As the Buick raced down the street, Einar Hagelburg stood in front of the village hardware store, calmly waited for another auto to move out of his line of fire, and shot once as the car rounded a corner. When discovered, the abandoned car had one bullet hole in the side. Hagelburg had scored a hit.

The instantly organized posse from Kaleva stayed with the getaway car for a few miles before being out paced. Until lost from view, the pursuers reported seeing the Buick several times taking sharp curves so fast two wheels left the pavement. The state police were soon on the scene in Kaleva where they organized a large, well-armed posse and resumed what was to become a relentless hunt for the desperadoes. After finally shaking the locals who had followed them out of town, the robbers raced through Brethren, Wellston, and High Bridge. Near the village of Peacock, they stopped because of unspecified car trouble but couldn't find a mechanic and were seen limping out of town in stops and starts. Just a few miles outside town, the Buick breathed its last and was abandoned.

Ellsworth Billman had been highly thought of in the little community and the wider area, and his murder both stunned and angered the village. Billman had been prominent in the political life of the village, served as the bank's cashier for eleven years, taught Sunday school, taken an active role in town meetings, and knew virtually everyone in his community by name. If he knew everyone, everyone knew and liked him. Dead at 55, he left three daughters, two of whom were married, a son, and a grieving widow. His body was moved to the back of the bank until Coroner Ray Bradford arrived and had it transported to the Bradford Funeral Home. After the autopsy, the body was taken back to Kaleva where it would lie in repose from 12–2 PM at the Finnish Lutheran Church on Sunday January 8 with funeral services beginning at 2:30. The entire town was in mourning, and everybody wanted to be a part of catching the killers.

By Thursday evening the state police had strung a network of road blocks and watchers in a large triangle from Baldwin to Reed City and south on U.S. 131 to Big Rapids. Early on Friday the police feared the robbers might have slipped through the net, but hope of catching them was renewed when the abandoned Buick was found. Police learned the Buick had been stolen from an Indianapolis garage. The garage owner was robbed and kidnapped, and Indianapolis police had engaged in a running fire fight with the bandits before they escaped. The car was also identified as being used in a hold up of a Kalamazoo gas station on Wednesday night. There was no doubt among the cops and volunteers that the men being hunted were experienced, hardened desperadoes who were extremely dangerous. A bullet-proof vest and the non-negotiable securities stolen from the bank were found in the Buick. The car attracted local and state police and carloads of volunteers. Locals in the area were warned that the bank robbers were on foot and might try to steal another car.

The news came too late for P. A. Holenbeck of Lake County. He found three men at his door demanding the keys to his Chevrolet, and in exchange they tossed him a few dollars. On the move again and in a different car, the gang must have felt pretty good about their chances. The optimism was short lived. State police radio had sent cruisers to likely choke points, and shortly after 9 AM Friday morning, a state cop nine miles south of Baldwin spotted the bandits and gave chase. Shots were traded and Mr. Holenbeck's car soon sported a bullet hole. Once again the gang disappeared and was thought to be somewhere northeast of Big Rapids. The gangsters knew the state police and every other cop in the area would soon have a description of their new getaway car, so six miles from the brief shoot out, they ditched the car and headed west across northern Newaygo County in dress shoes and suits. One would think they would have stuck out like pigs in bowler hats and spats, but they disappeared.

On Friday night the state police threw a net around the Baldwin-Big Rapids area, sure that the outlaws would try to make a break for southern Michigan on the second night after the robbery. Everyone in Manistee County with a radio listened for state police reports from East Lansing, and there was hardly an adult male left in Kaleva because they were out with the volunteer posse hunting the killers of one of their own. Volunteers from Manistee also joined the hunt. Manistee County sheriff deputies and the municipal police from several communities added up to a small army on the lookout for the crooks. On Friday night 42 state police cars plus sheriff patrol cars blanketed a 40-mile area around Baldwin and turned up nothing. In spite of not a single new clue turning up, police still believed the gangsters were holed up somewhere in the area.

All day Saturday the once-dapper but now bedraggled outlaw gang wandered through the backwoods and marshes of northern Michigan looking for a place to hole up and stay out of sight. They somehow stayed cleared of all the police and posse patrols, but on Saturday evening a call came into the state police from a woman living near Colfax swamp with the news that she watched four men walking across her land. While the police rushed to her home, local farmer Ben McGahan, near Walkerville, heard the police report of the sighting and realized the men must be near his place. Mr. McGahan grabbed his rifle and walked outside into a light snowfall and almost immediately spotted the men heading across his field toward a large swamp. McGahan tried to cut off the men before they reached the swamp but lost them. He wandered around until he ran across their tracks in the snow and within moments spotted them some distance ahead. He yelled at the gangsters to stop. Instead, the gangsters began running, and one of them turned and shot at McGahan. In return the local farmer, at the length of a football field, in failing light and falling snow, fired at the fleeing crooks. He didn't know if he hit anyone as he returned to his house and called the police.

Within minutes state police pulled up to McGahan's house, and the farmer led them to where he had taken a shot at the felons before losing sight of them. The police set off in the direction the gang was last seen and soon came on their tracks in the lightly falling snow. The police had barely made a hundred yards when they heard moaning and groaning, followed the sound into the bush, and discovered a critically wounded bandit McGahan had unknowingly hit. The man was carried out of the woods and transported to a hospital where he was guarded around the clock.

It was a freezing cold night with the ground muddy enough to lose a shoe in, and a dry spot in which to take shelter was harder to find than an unhappy fly fisherman on opening day. The police slogged on through the cold night following the tracks in the snow until about 10 PM when the searchers' flashlights played across the faces of three clearly miserable, hungry, tired, and very muddy bank robbers. They quickly and meekly surrendered. Two of the men were bare-foot, and none of the three had eaten in two days. Wayne Robertson, the man taken to the hospital, admitted he was one of the bank robbers. Elmer Zeller, 28, Henry Shelton, 25, and Robert Veneman, 25, all asked for something to eat as they were taken to the White Cloud jail for the night.

Questioned on Sunday they admitted to robbing the bank, and Veneman confessed to shooting Billman but claimed he didn't do it on purpose. The gun went off by accident. Robertson remained in critical condition. McGahan's 30-30 caliber bullet passed diagonally through the bank robber, fractured into pieces after hitting the body, clipped the man's pelvis, punctured the bladder twice, and pierced the small intestine 10 times. A full recovery was expected, but it would take time.

The capture of the robbers was owed, in a large part, to the hundreds of volunteers who reached for their shot-guns, rifles, and handguns and joined the largest northern Michigan manhunt in history. They were everywhere and did nearly everything. Volunteers manned checkpoints and roadblocks and helped police anyway they could. A squad of four volunteers from Manistee guarded a roadblock only 50 yards from where the thieves were captured. Frankly, it was the professionalism and effectiveness of the volunteers that surprised the state police. Corporal Colburn Munger from the Manistee post was barreling down U.S. 10 from Baldwin on Friday night when a bright, waving light appeared in the middle of the highway. As he grew closer, he could see it was a man standing in the middle of the road waving a lantern with one hand and a rifle in the other. The state cop had to either stop or run the man down. He stopped, and when he looked to either side, he spotted armed men pointing guns at him. When the man with the lantern saw the state police uniform, he lowered his rifle, had a few words with the statie, and waved him on. Volunteers like these closed off nearly every avenue of escape.

Mrs. Earl Hathaway had accompanied her husband to Manistee when he came for a scheduled inspection. When news of the robbery reached the Manistee post, Officer Hathaway and every other state policeman from the post left for the manhunt. Mrs. Hathaway wasn't going to sit idly by. She manned the post's desk answering phones for three days straight. Her voice grew hoarse; she became sleep deprived, caught a few hours of sleep, and was back on the job until the crooks were in custody.

On Sunday most of those who came to view the Ellsworth Billman body remained for the service. The church filled to overflowing, and some 250 stood outside in the cold. A family service was held at the Billman home later in the day, and the body was escorted by a state police car to Traverse City where 30 cars met the funeral cortege and followed it to Oakland Cemetery where Ellsworth Billman was laid to rest.

On the afternoon of January 9, 1933, in a packed courthouse with people crammed into stairwells and corridors, the three healthy bandits appeared in a Manistee County court and pleaded guilty to armed robbery before Justice Hal L. Cutler. The judge sentenced them to life imprisonment and during sentencing said he regretted capital punishment was not the law in Michigan. Through it all the three robbers stood before the court without emotion or any sign of distress or regret. They would later be charged with murder, but the charge would be held in abeyance because it might result in a long and costly trial. The county sheriff and state police officers would transport the three convicts to Marquette State Prison the next day. Robertson's arraignment would wait until he was well enough to appear in court.

1. Manistee News-Advocate 1-5-1933 p1, c8
2. IBID

Chapter 21

The Grapes of Wrath and Then Some

July 20, 1933

"...the barrel [of the deer rifle] looked like a stove pipe..."

*F*ennville, on the western side of the state, was a place one neither heard much about in the 1930s nor seldom traveled through or to. It sits, then and now, on a state highway all of fifteen miles long and for more than half that length the road cuts through the Allegan State Forest. The nearest town of any significance, Saugatuck, is only six miles away if a crow was traveling between the two places, but nearly twice that if the crow took a car. In the 1930s it was a quiet farming community in which, it would be fair to say, not much ever happened.

By 1933 the country, the state, and even Fennville were neck deep in the Great Depression, and for people all over the country, desperation led to desperate acts. On July 19, 1933, in Fennville, love, hunger, and financial calamity collided like particles in a nuclear cyclotron to produce a short, 25-minute, violent event that changed lives and made the news from New York to California. If for only a brief moment, Fennville was on the front page of newspapers all over the state and nation. It was a story that would not been out of place in Steinbeck's *The Grapes of Wrath*.

Life for Mrs. Grace Austin, 45, of Bravo, Michigan, (some four miles north of Fennville) never, even in its best moments, came within pit-spitting distance of being 'just a bowl of cherries.' Her childhood was an unhappy one and as she told it, "All I ever knew was hate. My near relatives did not show their liking for me. Hired help took care of me when I was little. I don't think my father hated me, although I was never sure." [1]

Her first marriage ended in divorce when she became the victim of physical abuse. When Grace moved back to Michigan after the divorce, she met and fell in love with Edward Austin. They were like two pieces of Velcro, simply made to be together. She said of Ed, "My husband is the only person I ever loved or whoever loved me. He is an angel. I have no one else, not even friends." [2]

The newly married couple bought a small farm in Bravo and literally poured every cent they owned and earned into paying off the bank. They even went without food to pay down the mortgage. By mid-1933 the couple was still very much in love and in all other matters very near the breaking point. They were starving and penniless. As she later explained, "We were destitute. No the county did not help us. We owned a home. That is, we had only one more payment to make. The county won't help people who own property, and no one would lend us the money to make the last payment." [3]

And that's how Grace Austin came to find herself sitting in the couple's clapped out Essex on the morning of July 19, 1933, waiting for Edward to rob the Old State Bank. Fennville, for the moment, was still quiet as a barn on a foreclosed farm in Kansas, but it was about to erupt into a half-hour of blood-letting violence.

At 4 AM Edward Austin, 45, jimmied the lock on a back window of the bank, opened it, crawled through, and hid. When the aged janitor, Dewitt Steanberg, walked in the door, Austin jumped the old man, tied him hand and foot, and locked him in a bathroom. The next to arrive at 7:50 AM was assistant cashier Marion Hutchinson, who failed to notice the absence of Steanberg as he went about his job of opening the bank for business. Austin stayed in hiding until the time lock turned off and confronted Hutchinson as he swung open the vault doors. Austin, with pistol in hand, forced the assistant cashier into the vault, then spread a big sheet of paper on the floor and ordered the banker to make a pile of money on it. Hutchinson was having none of it. As he recounted later, "I went into the vault noticed he was alone and very nervous so when he glanced at the paper to see how much money was there I tackled him and tried to take the gun." [4]

The two men fought for the possession of the firearm until Austin hit the banker over the head with either the revolver or a blackjack. While the dazed assistant cashier was regaining his senses, the now panicked Austin grabbed an armful of money, ran out the bank's back door, and jumped into the family getaway car.

At virtually the same time, Hutchinson staggered out the bank's front door on wobbly legs—probably suffering from a concussion—and bleeding from a scalp wound. He was still sharp enough to notice the getaway car head west on a back street as he made for the Express Office where he knew a revolver was kept. Either the gun wasn't there or the manager, no matter who was asking, wasn't about to give a hand gun to a battered, bloody man who looked half dazed. Hutchinson hurried to the hardware store and asked for a rifle and was given a .22. He made it out into the street with the rifle only to see the old Essex round a corner and head south. Standing in the street with a rifle and bleeding all over himself, someone finally went up to him, took the gun away, and helped the wounded man find someone to treat him.

Member of the village council, garage owner, and organizer of the town's vigilantes, Kenneth Jackson was having a morning cup of coffee in Orthers' restaurant when a man burst in and announced the bank was being robbed. It was as if the Batman light flickered on over Gotham. Jackson sprang into action. He sent a man to fetch his Chevrolet from his garage while he ran to get a shotgun. Jackson was armed and ready when Russell McKellups drove up in the Chevy and, with about twenty other vigilantes in assorted automobiles, set off after the robbers who were last reported heading west on M-89.

The posse with Jackson and McKellups still in the lead quickly closed on the Essex with Grace Austin at the wheel. When the pursuers got within shotgun range, Jackson opened fire and, intentionally or not, shot out both of the Essex's rear tires. Considerably slowed by two flat tires, McKellups pulled abreast of the Essex, and when he did Edward Austin raised up from the Essex's back seat with his deer rifle. Jackson later remembered the moment and said, "From where we were the barrel looked like a stove pipe. We shot at the same time." [5] Austin was hit in the right cheek and hand by buckshot. A single bullet from Austin's rifle clipped Jackson in the ear then hit McKellups above the right eye. Instead of penetrating his skull, the bullet burrowed around his skull and came to rest at the back of his head just under the skin. When McKellups was hit, the Chevrolet skidded out of control and ran off the road and slammed into a ditch. McKellups was loaded into one of the following cars and rushed back to Fennville while the stubborn, single-minded Jackson had to be talked out of the car and to give up the chase. The cars that took over the pursuit easily caught up to the limping Essex and kept a steady rate of fire on the Austins.

One can only imagine the desperation, panic, and down-right terror experienced by Mrs. Austin. She was no gun moll, no sister-in-arms with Bonnie Parker, but just a very scared, middle-aged woman talked into what was supposed to be a sure thing, would harm no one, and bring a little economic solvency to the family. Instead, she was driving a car down a highway while being shot at, and the only man she ever loved had been shot in the face. She turned the Essex off the road and drove a half-mile through an apple orchard then stopped the car.

James Michin, now in the posse's lead car fired several shots over the Essex hoping it would convince the Austins to surrender. Finally, Ed Austin with rifle in hand stepped from the car and turned to face his pursuers. Michin fired one shot hitting Austin in the shoulder. The bank robber dropped the rifle and gave up.

The criminals might be in the bag, but as far as Fennville knew, the hunt was still on and the emergency procedures, put in place and practiced so diligently by the vigilantes, was just gathering steam. The telephone operator had called the sheriff's department, the state police, and all the surrounding towns to inform them of the robbery. The effectiveness of the calls was clearly evident on the streets of Fennville. Before the Austins were brought back to town, more than a hundred armed men had flocked to the village, and more had been sent west to back up the original twenty who had followed the bank robbers out of town. The Allegan County Sheriff, the Holland Chief of Police, three of his officers, and troopers from the state police post in Paw Paw were all in town. Dr. R. J. Walker from Saugatuck went to Fennville in case they needed a doctor and arrived in time to treat Hutchinson, assess McKellups' condition and send him to the hospital in Allegan, and then treat Jackson.

Ed Austin was the last to be looked at by the doctor. Dr. Walker partially patched him up, stopped the bleeding, and sent him to the hospital in Allegan. There he was given an anti-tetanus shot and was reported in just fair condition. Doctors reported Austin was suffering from loss of blood, shock, and that his general physical condition was listed as poor. The latter was a testament to he and his wife's struggle to survive over the past few months and their poor health as they slowly starved. Mrs. Austin was taken to the Allegan County jail while her husband remained under constant guard at the hospital.

The stolen money was found in the couple's Essex along with most of their belongings. The man who was asked to drive it back to Fennville kept as close as possible to the lead posse car because he was afraid some uninformed vigilantes might take a shot at him.

Grace Austin spent her nights in a rocking chair in the women's wing of the county jail telling anyone who would listen that for the couple it had come down to either rob the bank or starve. She also swore that her husband only shot at the vigilantes to protect her. Reflecting back on the bank robbery and chase she said, "…I wish I had been killed…" [6]

From his hospital bed, Ed Austin worried about his wife. He repeatedly asked about her and said, "I hope she doesn't worry and have a nervous breakdown. She's been a real pal. My marriage with her is the only thing in my life that has turned out successfully." [7] Austin steadfastly claimed his wife had nothing to do with the robbery and that he had not wanted to shoot or kill anyone and didn't fire until the posse's car pulled up beside the Essex. Asked if he was worried now, Austin said, "I am not worrying. I'll let the law worry. I know my personal liberty is gone but that's life's destiny." [8]

Mr. and Mrs. Austin had no previous criminal record. Evidently, neither one was represented by a lawyer when less than two days after Edward and Grace took $2,000 from the Old State Bank they appeared in court before Judge Fred T. Miles of Holland. Edward received a sentence of life imprisonment in Jackson State Prison. Grace received 10–20 years in the Detroit House of Correction. She fainted on hearing her sentence. Grace was paroled in 1938. There is no record of if or when her husband was paroled and if they were ever reunited.

1. Holland City News 7-27-1933 p1, c4
2. IBID
3. IBID
4. Lane, Kit., Fennville, village to city, Fennville Herald c1985, Fennville, MI p150
5. IBID
6. Holland City News 7-27-1933, Section 2 p1, c6
7. Holland City News 7-20-1933 p1, c8
8. IBID

Chapter 22

The Day Baby Face Nelson Failed his Final Exam in Grand Haven

August 18, 1933

*"...the little man reached into the basket, pulled out
a submachine gun and yelled, 'Hands Up.'"*

*A*ugust 18, 1933, was a sleepy, summer afternoon in
the Lake Michigan tourist town of Grand Haven,
Michigan, until Baby Face Nelson's gang drove into town.
Nelson picked the Grand Haven bank for his first "professional" bank job after he and his gang had been tutored in
the finer points of bank robbing from a crook with a PhD
in armed robbery. It would be an inauspicious and violent
debut that turned the local undertaker into the hero of the
day. Even when taught by the best, some crooks couldn't
overcome bad karma, unexpected heroism, or their own innate stupidity.

If some babies are born with a silver spoon in their
mouths, then Lester Joseph Gillis, later known as Baby
Face Nelson, came into this world sucking on a Thompson
submachine gun. He was also endowed with a hair-trigger
temper and a penchant for violence that got him into trouble
with the law early and often. By age twelve he led his own
gang of preteen hoodlums who spent their days committing petty crimes and stealing cars until Nelson landed in a

reformatory after accidently shooting another child with a pistol he found in a stolen car. Reform school proved hardly more than a hiccup in Nelson's life of crime. Driven by his passion for stealing cars and joy riding, he became a repeat offender within days of his release. Auto theft returned him to prison in 1922 and twice in 1924. In 1928 he worked in a gas station that served as a cover for his gang of thieves that stole tires. As a hoot he raced stock cars.

By 1930 the gang had worked up to burglaries, home invasions, armed robberies, and a couple of amateurish bank robberies that were more smash and grab than planned heists. During home invasions, his gang would hold a family at gun point while they looted the house of cash and jewelry. Gillis also took to robbing well-heeled women on the street when they flashed high-priced bangles. On one celebrated occasion, he stole $18,000 worth of jewelry from the wife of Chicago's mayor. It's been said she told the police her attacker, "...had a baby face. He was hardly more than a boy...," and hence his nickname. It was probably acquired more normally because, as an adult, Lester Joseph Gillis came up short and topped out at 5'4" tall. This less-than-imposing stature and his youthful appearance probably accounted for the famous moniker.

The young hot head and brazen crook rose up through the ranks of Chicago's criminal who's who and even worked for Al Capone until Gillis became so violent and unpre-dictable the Chicago crime boss cut ties to the youthful gangster. The string of robberies and home invasions earned Gillis an arrest warrant and forced him to assume the alias George Nelson, soon to be generally known as Baby Face Nelson. The name change did not prevent him from being arrested and convicted in 1931 of armed robbery for which he received a one year to life sentence at Joliet State Prison. In 1932 a handcuffed Nelson was transported to Wheaton, Illinois, where he stood trial for another robbery and received a second one year to life sentence. On the taxi ride back to Joliet, which was beginning to look like his long-term residence, Baby Face produced a pistol (no one knows from where or whom), forced his lone guard to unlock the cuffs, and escaped.

Nelson spent nearly a year in Reno, Nevada, before returning to the Chicago area and renting a house in east Michigan City, Indiana, on Lake Michigan. It appears he had made up his mind to become a bona fide bank robber and looked to build a solid reputation for conducting and participating in by-the-numbers heists that ran as smoothly as a Swiss watch. And who should live right across the street but Alvin Karpis, the Midwest's premier bank robber. Nelson approached Karpis about joining his gang. If Baby Face was looking for R-E-S-P-E-C-T, all Alvin Karpis saw was a man who wouldn't think twice before trying to knock down a dynamite-filled piñata with a lit blowtorch because a roll of dimes might be inside. Even keeping Nelson at arm's length was too close for Karpis' liking, so the master crook steered Baby Face to Eddie Bentz, the bank robbing partner of Machine Gun Kelly for an advanced workshop in bank jobs.

Bentz approached robbing a bank as if it were a military operation and showed Nelson and his newly recruited gang how to select a pigeon to be plucked, estimate the take, how to case a bank prior to the real thing, and how to conduct oneself once the gang entered the bank. According to Bentz, each member of the crew who walked into the bank had tasks so specific and detailed they could be written up with as much minutia as a government job description. Bentz also explained that the getaway, or the "get" in robber parlance, had to be thoroughly planned out by the crew member driving the getaway car. In that day and age, there were few reliable maps showing secondary roads and, more often than not, even fewer signs at crossroads naming the intersecting roads. The "get" driver had to actually run the back roads out of the target town in order to discover the fastest route that got the gang the farthest away from the robbery and any potential roadblocks. He then had to write down the directions in detail. It was also the driver's responsibility to buy boxes of roofing nails to throw behind the getaway car in hopes of slowing pursuers. Lastly, the getaway driver served as a "cleaner" which pretty much meant just that, cleaning the street or keeping the law and armed citizens at a distance until the crew came out of the bank and piled in the car. The broom used to "clean" the street was either a Thompson submachine gun or a Browning automatic rifle, preferably the former. Either one usually left the police outgunned. In Eddie Bentz's world, a professional heist was as carefully choreographed as a Broadway musical, and in the case of Baby Face Nelson and his untested crew, Bentz was handed a sack of feral cats and told to teach them how to dance. Fur was about to fly in Grand Haven.

People's Savings Bank of Grand Haven was picked as the crew's graduation exercise probably because Bentz was familiar with the area and not much of a police presence was expected. When casing the bank, they learned it stood at the corner of Washington and Third Street facing Washington. A furniture store sat next door and shared a back alley that emptied onto Third where the bank had a second entrance. Across Third stood Grand Haven's answer to Macy's, the popular McLellan Department Store where the fashionable came to shop.

On graduation day, outside of town, Bentz went over final details with the inexperienced troupe. Bentz had previously agreed to drive the getaway car, but now, at the last minute, Nelson was having second thoughts. Baby Face didn't like it that with Ed outside there wouldn't be an experienced robber inside, and Nelson worried that they would miss or overlook a big payoff or couldn't get anyone to open the bank safe. The old bank robber didn't like the idea of leaving a wet-behind-the-ears getaway man on the street but reluctantly agreed to the change in plans.

Shortly before 3 PM on August 18, four of Nelson's gang entered Grand Haven's People's Saving Bank with the first three spreading out to keep an eye on every corner and person in the bank. The fourth, carrying a picnic basket and the most visibly nervous of the quartet, walked to the teller window farthest from the door manned by Art Welling, handed him a twenty and asked for $2 in nickels. After 40 of the five-cent pieces were meticulously counted out, the man then asked for $2 in dimes. Bentz must have begun to wonder if Nelson had decided to nickel and dime the bank to death rather than rob it when the little man reached in the basket, pulled out a submachine gun, and yelled, "Hands up!" If the 5'4" bank robber didn't get people's attention, the submachine gun surely did.

Invented in 1918, the Thompson was meant to rain death on German trenches during World War I. The Thompson was nicknamed the "Trench Broom" or "Trench Sweeper," but the weapon never made it to the battlefield before the war ended. In the 1920s, gangsters took to the Thompson like Lois Lane took to Superman, and it soon became one of the iconic symbols of the Roaring Twenties, Prohibition, and pre-World War II gangsters. It proved most popular among Chicago criminals who called it a "Chicago Typewriter" and a "Chicago Piano." In the hands of any criminal, it was a frightful, death-dealing machine.

Nelson ordered the bank employees and customers down on the floor while another robber lowered the Washington Street window shades but, maybe out of nervousness, failed to close them completely. The last two bandits went from teller to teller sweeping up coins and bills while Bentz told the head cashier to open the safe. When the vault's door swung open, the old pro began stuffing money and securities into a laundry bag. It was at about this time that the getaway driver pulled a Buick up to the side of the bank, near the mouth of the alley.

When Mr. Welling's hands went up, one foot had gone down tripping a silent alarm. It rang in the police station and, of all places, the next door furniture store. When furniture salesman/owner and town mortician Edward Kinkema heard the alarm, he rushed out the front door, took a quick look around, then glanced in a bank window that hadn't been completely shuttered and saw a gunman scooping up money at the teller's window. He told everyone within hearing the bank was being robbed then ran back into his store and told his partners in the business to get the police. Kinkema grabbed his shotgun and stepped into the back alley. Immediately noticing a Buick parked on Third Street near the bank door, he was convinced it was the getaway car. Kinkema said, "I put my gun to my shoulder to shoot, but by that time there were too many women in the street and I did not dare to." [1] When the young man in the Buick found himself looking down the barrel of a large-bore gun held by a man who looked as solemn as death, it brought a brilliant new clarity to his recent career choice and he sped off.

With the getaway car on the lam, Ed Kinkema hurried down the alley, crossed Third, and slipped into the nearby Elks Temple where he told the scattering of members to grab their guns, bandits were robbing the bank. The announcement was taken as a joke. If, in comedians' terms, "he killed the room," Kinkema surely found nothing laughable with what he had said and returned without a posse to Third where he continued to spread the news of the robbery. There it met with a lot less hilarity than in the Elks Temple, and an orderly and quiet afternoon rapidly came unhinged. Folks hurried away from the corner and panic began bubbling up between heart beats while the small town mortician with the receding hairline and friendly, gentle face, turned into

Gary Cooper's character in the movie *High Noon*. Alone and armed with only a shotgun, Ed Kinkema stood opposite the end of the alley on Third confident the gunmen would leave by the side door. He didn't have long to wait.

Inside the bank Ed Bentz left the vault with a bag full of loot and went to a window for a quick look on Washington. He found the street nearly deserted and those still there in a hurry to join those who had already left, which meant to the veteran Bentz that the alarm had been sounded. He told the gang things were "getting warm"[2] outside. The robbers herded the employees and customers to the Third Street door and then used them as human shields as, one by one, they left the bank holding a hostage in front of them. All hostages later remarked how every single order from the gunmen in the bank was delivered with a staggeringly rich abundance of swearing, but it was nothing compared to the outpouring of profanity that erupted when the crooks stepped outside and discovered their getaway car had left without them.

Nelson emerged first using a cashier as a human shield, which evidently gave Kinkema not an iota of concern for the employee's safety because whatever part of Nelson's 5'4" frame peeked out from behind the cashier the undertaker immediately drew a bead on and pulled the trigger. In return Baby Face let loose with the Thompson. The submachine gun fire blew out windows and pockmarked buildings up and down the street. Eddie Bentz pushed another human shield out onto the street as the Thompson roared, and the old-timer added to the mayhem with blasts from his sawed-off shotgun. The last two gang members then made it onto the street with their hostages and added their revolvers to the mix. As the last two robbers joined the fray, two policemen rounded the corner of Washington and Third, drew side arms, and added their minor melody to the symphony of gunfire.

Third Street instantly became a free-fire zone with bullets and buckshot shattering glass, chewing away buildings, turning parked cars into Swiss cheese, and adding the whine of ricochets to the buzz of passing cartridges. Across Third Street machine gun fire riddled the McLellan Store, bursting plate glass display windows, shredding walls, ripping apart a display case, trashing merchandise, and sending shoppers into screaming pandemonium. Strangely enough, people on the street, who just moments ago had been fleeing the scene, now rushed toward the sound of gunfire and stood watching as bullets stitched the air around them. The tight-knit ball of thieves and human shields started to break up as the fire fight erupted. Miraculously, no one died. Peter Van Lopik, the manager of Grand Haven Oil and a bank customer, took a round of buckshot from Bentz' sawed-off shotgun and collapsed against the side of a building. He received multiple buckshot wounds in his back from neck to thigh and one pellet buried itself in his jaw. Amid the gunfire, people rushed to his aid. Sergeant Julius Pleinies, U.S. Army retired, took a machine gun round in the back; the bank's assistant cashier was grazed in the side by a pistol round. Art Welling threw himself under a parked car and escaped injury, but as William Pellegrom tried to sneak away from the robbers, he was shot in the foot.

With no getaway car, the robbers began running down Third, away from Washington, and toward Franklin Street. At this point cashier F. "Ted" Bolt decided he'd had enough and grabbed the nearest robber and wrestled him to the ground. The bad guy ended up on top pointing his gun at Bolt's chest when the redoubtable Ed Kinkema rushed to the rescue. The mortician was out of ammo, but that didn't stop him from wading into the scrum and wielding the shotgun like a club, knocking Bolt's assailant to the ground. Was Kinkema the kind of man who would kick a man when he was down? Yes, and then some. When the clubbing and kicking failed to take the fight out of the crook, the undertaker grabbed the felon's revolver and shot him once in the hand and once in the head. With the gunman sufficiently pacified, Ed and Bolt, with the help of others, dragged the robber off to an ambulance that rushed him to jail instead of a hospital. It was discovered at the jail the robber was wearing a bulletproof vest.

Totally obvious to the chaos unfolding only a block away, Mrs. Louis Bonema was driving her Chevrolet down Franklin Street and became a part of the unfolding drama. The other occupants of the car included her baby and her friend Mrs. Joe Miller with her four children. It was just rotten luck that the Chevy with its car full of women and children reached the intersection of Third and Franklin at the same time as the bank robbers. Mrs. Bonema only became aware of trouble when she saw three armed men run into Franklin pointing guns at her. She slammed on the brakes as a short, machine gun-toting man ran up to her door and ordered her out the car. When she refused, the man opened her car door and yelled, "Get out or I'll plug you" [3] then grabbed a handful of dress and pulled the woman from the car.

As the crooks climbed into the car, a distraught Mrs. Bonema shouted, "I must have my baby." [4] When that didn't seem to register with the bandits, she screamed, "I want my baby!" [5] Meanwhile, Mrs. Miller didn't need any urging as she and her children bailed out the other side. The other two crooks threw bags of loot in the car, ditched the stunned hostages, jumped into the Chevy, and, just before speeding off, handed Mrs. Bonema her baby. Being the original getaway driver, Ed Bentz was behind the wheel and vetoed Nelson's suggestion they go back and rescue the captured gang member. Even though Bentz had driven the roads and planned the getaway, he couldn't remember his written directions—they were in the getaway car—so Ed headed straight south on U.S. 31. The gang had barely gotten four miles out of town when they discovered the Chevy's gas gauge bouncing on empty.

Oscar Varneau of Grand Rapids, his wife, son, and dog were summering at a cottage on Lake Michigan and had gone out for an afternoon drive in the country when they stopped at the farm of Ernest Behm to buy strawberries. Mrs. Varneau stayed in the car as her husband went to the farm door. She became aware of three suspicious looking men approaching the car and called to her husband, but the trio of desperados arrived first and told her to get out of the car and began physically pulling her from the Chrysler when she didn't move fast enough. Mr. Varneau rushed to his wife's aid only to face the business end of a submachine gun. Any demands quickly turned into simply begging the three to take anything he had except his wife and child. The gangsters quickly threw the loot into the Chrysler and took off leaving some $300 in loose money in the Chevy. The fate of the dog remains unknown.

Nelson's gang's troubles were not yet over because their second hijacked car promptly blew a tire and ran off the road. In what was beginning to look like a storyline from a Laurel and Hardy movie, the crooks flagged down a passing car that held four college students, threw them out, and drove off. They finally reached their Lake Michigan hideout near dawn the next day.

Back in town the firefight had drawn people from miles around, and as soon as the shooting stopped, curious onlookers rushed the bank to gawk at the scene of the crime but got there just seconds after thoughtful bank employees locked the doors. With nothing to see there, the ever-growing crowd sped off to the jail to get a close-up look at the bank robber. The captured bandit gave his name as Harry Harris, but that turned out to be an alias; his real name was Earl Doyle. He sat in his cell with blood flowing from head and neck injuries and a broken leg he evidently suffered during the tussle with Ed Kinkema. Doyle had nothing to say other than his alias and he was from Chicago. He was seen by a physician who bandaged him up and put a cast on his leg. Those of the public who were allowed near his cell were usually treated to a smile.

State and local police scoured the county but never even got close to capturing the crooks. The original getaway car was discovered the next morning south of Holland, Michigan, and led to speculation the robbers might be somewhere in the dunes, but an extensive search turned up nothing but sand. The getaway car contained 100 rounds of ammunition and 35 pounds of roofing nails. Nelson and his gang made off with less than $2,500, but when the gang's various expenses were deducted, each member of the crew pocketed around $600.

Eddie Bentz began his banking career as a safe cracker, which could be hard work, and he soon shifted to the new style of bank robberies made possible by fast cars and improved roads. It might be more dangerous to rob banks in broad daylight and then outrun the police, but it was a lot easier than hauling around a cutting torch and all its equipment.

The 36-year-old master criminal married an 18-year-old woman prior to the Holland bank job and had planned to retire after the robbery and only work as a consultant. He loved to collect rare books and coins, travel, and visit museums and historical sites. He was also an amateur photographer and loved the theater. After the Grand Haven job, he did retire and moved to the Northeast where he ran a legitimate toy business, but old habits and the lure of easy money proved hard to shake when the business ran into financial trouble, and on July 4, 1934, he and a crew robbed a bank in Danville, Vermont. He was tracked down and arrested in Brooklyn. He refused to name anyone else in the crew and drew a twenty-year sentence. Eddie asked to be sent to Alcatraz because that's where his friends were. He was paroled from the famous prison in San Francisco Bay in 1948 and died in Tacoma, Washington, on October 31, 1979. Bentz was thought to have taken part in more than a hundred bank robberies during his career. The only two he ever admitted to were the Danville and Holland robberies.

It was rumored that the faint-hearted driver of the getaway car was murdered in Chicago less than a week after the Grand Haven robbery. The rumor has never been substantiated.

Edward Kinkema was hailed as the hero of the day and the man who single-handedly saved F. "Ted" Bolt's life. What few, if any, in town knew was that eighteen months earlier Edward Kinkema was in Lansing, Michigan, when he walked into a bank-turned-slaughterhouse. A deranged man walked into a bank Ed was in, drew a gun, and shot five people. The bank guard standing beside Ed was shot and killed. It can never be known if that horrible experience is what prompted Edward Kinkema to step forward a year and a half later in his hometown and prevent another mass killing. Ed Kinkema never talked about the Lansing shooting or his part in the Grand Haven bank robbery. His own son knew nothing of his father's part in the day Baby Face Nelson came to town because he never spoke to his son about it. He learned about his father's heroic actions through a scrapbook his mother kept.

Baby Face Nelson's criminal career would last only seventeen more months, but in those few months he would kill more FBI agents than any other single American, and he is believed to have been involved in the murder of six law enforcement officers. He committed several more bank robberies, three with John Dillinger, and briefly made top billing as the FBI's "Public Enemy No. 1." On November 27, 1934, the FBI received a tip that Nelson was seen driving a stolen car near Barrington, Illinois. Two FBI agents spotted Nelson, his wife, and a gang member in the car and gave chase. A high-speed gun battle ensued in which Nelson killed the two agents but was mortally wounded in turn. An anonymous phone call led to his body being found the next day near a Niles Center, Illinois, cemetery. At the time of the Grand Haven bank robbery, no one knew it was Nelson's gang that had robbed the bank and shot up the town.

1. Grand Haven Daily News 8-8-1933 p1, c1
2. IBID
3. Grand Haven Daily News 8-9-1933 p1, c1
4. IBID
5. IBID

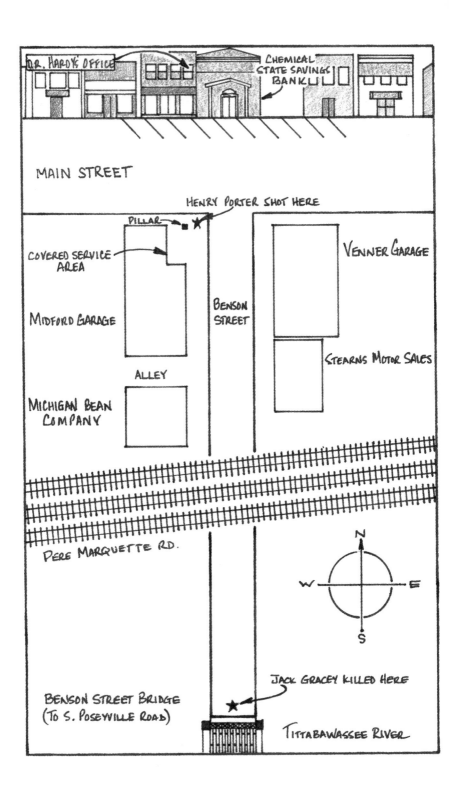

DR. HARDY'S OFFICE

CHEMICAL STATE SAVINGS BANK

MAIN STREET

HENRY PORTER SHOT HERE

PILLAR

COVERED SERVICE AREA

MIDFORD GARAGE

BENSON STREET

VENNER GARAGE

STEARNS MOTOR SALES

ALLEY

MICHIGAN BEAN COMPANY

PERE MARQUETTE RD.

N
W   E
S

BENSON STREET BRIDGE
(TO S. POSEYVILLE ROAD)

JACK GRACEY KILLED HERE

TITTABAWASSEE RIVER

Chapter 23

Chemical State Savings Bank:
A Formula For Death

September 27, 1937

"It's not a nice thing to see a man die—
or have a part in executing him."

*B*efore the days of paychecks or automatic deposits, employees of most companies received their pay in the form of cold, hard cash slipped into pay envelopes. Every other Wednesday, Dow Chemical deposited $75,000, in cash, in an account at the Chemical State Savings Bank in Midland to cover their company's large payroll. As far as bank robbers were concerned, it made the Midland bank about the biggest, juiciest peach on the tree ready to be plucked. The money came into Midland by train, and on the appointed day, bank president Clarence Macomber walked to the train station empty handed and returned toting a money bag containing the $75,000 in cash. It is unclear, but apparently a bank guard didn't even accompany Macomber.

Chemical State Savings Bank wasn't just known within the state's criminal community as a mouth-watering target. Word had passed through the bank-robbing grapevine that it was a tempting and easy mark. That was what brought Ray Hamilton, 19, and Jean O'Darr, 22, to the area from Oklahoma where they were members of Bonnie and Clyde's gang. In

1933 the two men stepped off a bus in Bay City and decided it made a good home base for casing the Midland bank and familiarizing themselves with the area. They thought reconnoitering and planning from Bay City would make them less conspicuous and took an apartment on Adams Street.

Their next move was to go to Midland, find the bank, and look it over, but you just can't stand around and study the employees and the layout. It looks too suspicious. One of them went up to a teller and asked for change for a twenty. There was something about the two strangers that didn't sit right with the bank employees. Whether it was the way they eyed the bank, their general demeanor, or just seemed out of place, the pair raised the bank's wariness to the point where one of the employees called the police. A quartet of state troopers, two Bay City detectives, and the Midland County sheriff took the suspicions seriously enough to track down the two men. The law caught up with the Oklahoma duo at a Bay City roller rink where they were arrested after a brief scuffle in which it was necessary to subdue Jean O'Darr by the application of a pistol to the side of his head. This in turn required a brief stop at a hospital for stitches before the two men were jailed. A quick look into their backgrounds revealed Hamilton and O'Darr were members of the notorious Barrow Gang, and both men were wanted for murder in Texas. They were held until Texas authorities arrived and escorted them back to the Lone Star State.

Bonnie and Clyde engineered Hamilton's escape from a Texas chain gang in 1934 which was a prelude to a cross-country crime spree. Bonnie and Clyde met their bloody end in the same year when they and the car they were riding in were shot to pieces. Hamilton was rearrested later and executed for murder by the state of Texas.

The failed attempt at robbing the Chemical State Savings Bank didn't even make it past the planning stage, but it did alert the police, the bank, and the citizenry of

Midland that even outlaws halfway across the country had the Midland bank in their crosshairs. A group of downtown businessmen was organized and baptized as vigilantes by the county sheriff, and its members remained alert and sensitive to the possibility, if not probability, of another try at the $75,000. Dentist Frank Hardy joined the group and brought his hunting rifle to his office on the second floor of the Arcade Building next door to the bank. Every morning Dr. Hardy set the loaded rifle next to the window overlooking the bank entrance.

$ $ $

Five years later, on the morning of September 29, 1937, Jack Gracey, 28, and Tony Chebatoris, 37, drove north up the Poseyville Road and into Midland. The road ended at a football-field-long bridge that carried traffic over the Tittabawasee River and onto a very short Benson Street that crossed the tracks of the Pere Marquette Railroad before climbing a gentle hill and ending at Main Street. Chebatoris drove the Ford Tudor up the hill heading right at Chemical State Savings Bank which stood on the north side of Main and looked straight down Benson Street to the longest single-span bridge in Michigan. At the intersection of Benson and Main, the Ford turned left on Main and went around the block. Back on Main, Chebatoris passed the bank, pulled into an angled parking spot in front of the Arcade Building, and the two men got out of the car.

Gracey wore a pair of glasses without any lenses, a fedora, and a long overcoat that hid a sawed-off shotgun. He had also dyed his hair blond. Chebatoris had on a gray hat and a denim jacket with a .38 Smith & Wesson stuffed in a pocket. At a little after 11:30 AM, the two bank robbers entered the bank and walked into Michigan's history.

The two men were habitual, failure-prone criminals. They first met in Jackson State Penitentiary where Jack Gracey was serving a second sentence for armed robbery. His first arrest was for stealing bicycles and cars and got him a jolt in the Boys' Industrial School. He escaped from the reformatory and graduated to armed robbery. Gracey had also served time in Marquette after authorities uncovered a plan to escape from Jackson.

Anthony Chebatoris emigrated from Poland and had served time in his homeland before coming to the United States. He was sent to prison here in 1920 for robbery, won parole in 1926, but was soon back in jail for another robbery. He was finally released from Marquette State Penitentiary on December 14, 1935. He was 35 years old and had spent 40% of his life behind bars. When Chebatoris walked into the Midland bank, he was already listed as wanted for bank robbery and felonious assault in Pennsylvania and had spent fifteen of the previous seventeen years of his life in prison.

Gracey and Chebatoris reconnected in early September 1937 when they happened to meet in a Hamtramck pool hall. Gracey had already robbed a number of banks in the past year and had only recently cased the Chemical State Savings Bank. The two men talked, and invariably Gracey brought up the rich piece of fruit begging to be picked in Midland. He asked Chebatoris if he wanted to partner-up for the job. The answer came back yes and little more than two weeks later the armed pair walked into the bank.

Gracey was the first of the two to enter while Tony hung back by the entrance. Jack walked directly to the 65-year-old bank president Clarence H. Macomber who was helping a customer and, without saying a word, jammed his shotgun in the banker's ribs. It was Macomber's bad luck, or maybe Gracey's, that the bank president was even in the building. He was supposed to go to lunch with his daughter, who was standing next to him, but had stopped to help a woman complete a transaction.

With the business end of a sawed-off shotgun stabbing his ribs, Clarence Macomber did the unexpected. He grabbed the barrel of the gun and pushed it down toward the floor. When the struggle for the shotgun started, either the woman Macomber was helping or his daughter screamed. Unbelievably, the 65-year-old began wrestling the 28-year-old toward the front of the bank and away from his customers and employees.

Chebatoris had remained near the front door, and when he saw his partner and Macomber fighting over the shotgun, Tony stepped in front of a customer and shot the bank president. The bullet cut a shallow crease across the left side of Macomber's chest. The blast also brought the bank's cashier Paul Bywater rushing to his boss's assistance. Tony saw the man step toward his partner and calmly shot Bywater from about three feet away. The .38 round penetrated the man's left side, and he immediately collapsed on the floor seriously wounded and his life in doubt. Macomber dropped the barrel of the shotgun which he had held on to even after being wounded and went to aid Bywater.

Gracey and Chebatoris immediately ran for the bank's front door. They stepped out on the street brandishing their weapons and yelling 'hold up' in hopes of clearing the street and making their escape. As soon as the two left the bank, Macomber hurried to the front door and locked it.

The two hoodlums ran to the Ford, and Chebatoris jumped behind the wheel. Gracey might have cased the bank a few weeks ago, but he never mapped out the quickest way out of town. The only sure route he knew was back down Benson Street, over the railroad tracks, and across the bridge spanning the Tittabawasee to the Poseyville Road. Unfortunately, the crooks had angle parked their getaway car facing west on Main Street and past the intersection with Benson Street.

It slowed the getaway down considerably that Chebatoris had to back out of the parking space and then continue backing down Main Street until they reached Benson. For accomplished bank robbers, this was like going out of the world backwards, and the two ex-cons were late, way too late to make a clean getaway.

In his second-floor office, Dr. Frank Hardy heard the shots and screams coming from the bank, went to the office window overlooking Main, and drew back the curtain. He quickly spotted the two armed men waving their guns and yelling before they whirled about and fled to the Ford Tudor. For five years the dentist's deer rifle—he was an avid hunter and outdoorsman—sat leaning against the wall next to the window. Positive he was watching robbers escape from the bank, Dr. Hardy grabbed the rifle, punched out the window screen, and drew a bead on the getaway car that was passing in front of his office as it backed toward the Benson Street intersection. Hardy pulled the trigger, and the round plowed downward through the car's passenger door burying itself in Gracey's right leg. As Gracey bent over and screamed in pain, Hardy chambered another round and loosed it at the Ford. His second shot bored through the passenger side window, missed the bent-over Gracey, and tore into Chebatoris's left arm.

Tony managed, even one-handed, to shift the Ford into forward and make the turn onto Benson Street. He then floored the automobile and found he couldn't control the vehicle with only one good arm. The car veered to the left, struck a parked car, and rammed the guard rail. As the car struck the guard rail, yet another round from Hardy's .35-caliber rifle puckered the Ford's left rear fender.

Chebatoris grabbed a rifle from the shot-up car and stepped out on the street. Gracey also was in a rush to exit the car that was attracting so much lead, but with his first step, he landed on his wounded leg and went down. Tony raced around the Ford and helped his partner to his feet while he scanned the surrounding buildings, doors, and windows looking for the marksman who was shooting them to pieces. With the rifle in one hand and supporting Gracey with the other, he started his partner down Benson toward the railroad tracks. While Gracey half limped, half hopped away from the bank, Chebatoris stood in the middle of the street still searching for the shooter. As he scanned to the left, he spotted a man standing by a pillar that supported the second story of the Midford Garage on the west side of Benson and across Main Street from the bank. The man wore a short, form-fitting jacket and chauffeur's cap with a plastic visor and a badge easily seen pinned to the front of the hat. Chebatoris saw, in the chaos of the moment, what looked like a cop and instinctively adjusted his stance and shot from the hip. The bullet struck Henry Potter in the abdomen, and the 55-year-old truck driver who was wearing the company uniform fell critically wounded.

Irene Stolsmark had business that morning at the county courthouse that sits to the west of the bank on Main Street. Finished with the necessary paperwork, she loaded her two-year-old son in the family Essex Coupe and, somehow remaining oblivious to the gunshots reverberating across Main and Benson streets, drove east on Main and turned south on Benson just as, or moments after, Chebatoris shot Henry Potter. As the Essex passed Tony, he stepped on the car's running board and told Irene to keep driving until she reached the railroad crossing. When she stopped at the railroad tracks, Jack Gracey appeared at the car's driver-side window, pointed the shotgun at Mrs. Stolsmark, and told her to get out. She grabbed her son and ran.

Dr. Hardy held his fire until Mrs. Stolsmark was clear of the car then put a round through Gracey's elbow as the fleeing man climbed into the car. Wounded in the arm and leg, Gracey was now unable to drive. The dentist's unnerving accuracy and continuous volleys had both men jumping from the Essex and making toward the Tittabawasee on foot and what might have looked like salvation. A Nehil Lumber Company pickup truck had stopped at the north end of the bridge because the abandoned Essex blocked Benson Street.

Gracey hobbled up to the truck's right front window, pointed the shotgun at the driver, Levi Myers, and told him to back the pickup back across the bridge. Accounts differ, but either Gracey was about to step on the truck's running board or already had when Dr. Hardy's shot from one-and-a-half-football-fields' distance put a bullet through Gracey's head. He was dead before he hit the ground.

Tony Chebatoris saw his partner fall and, still carrying the rifle, ran down the Pere Marquette tracks. Where the tracks crossed Ashmun Street, he forced a woman and her baby from a car but couldn't figure out how to operate the new semi-automatic transmission and was once again out and running. When he reached the Pere Marquette depot, he ran into a small parking lot where he stole a car but in pulling out of the parking space rammed a parked car. The owner of the just-hit car, Richard Van Orden, saw what happened and confronted Chebatoris who tried to pull away. Van Orden jumped on the car's running board and began struggling with the bank robber. While trying to drive the car, Chebatoris attempted to shoot Van Orden with the rifle. In return Van Orden choked Tony. With Chebatoris's attention diverted from steering the car, it ran into a pile of dirt and stalled while the two men continued to fight over the rifle. Van Orden yelled for help, and Ira M. Smith, the Midland County Sheriff, just happened to be in the area looking into the theft of construction tools. What is left unexplained in all accounts is how Smith heard Van Orden yell but didn't hear half a dozen blasts from a deer rifle. Anyway, he arrived at the car in time to open the passenger door, drag Chebatoris from the car, pin him to the ground with a knee on his head, and handcuff the thug. The Midland police appeared shortly thereafter and transported the prisoner to jail.

The second attempt at robbing the Chemical State Saving Bank was as unsuccessful as the first but much more bloody. Clarence Macomber had a flesh wound from a bullet that scored his ribs but never penetrated the rib cage. Paul Bywater was in serious condition from a bullet that entered his left side and shredded his intestines. Henry Potter, the trucker who looked like a cop, was also in serious condition from a rifle round that hit his hip bone and wreaked havoc in his lower abdomen. Bank robber Jack Gracey had been shot three times by a high-powered rifle, the last of which proved fatal. Tony Chebatoris, although wounded, was taken to the county jail and treated there.

Dr. Hardy was hailed as the man of the hour and was everyone's hero, but he liked neither the spotlight nor the adulation. He said, "Don't make a hero out of me in this thing. I like to hunt, and I like to play bridge. Today, I'd say I liked bridge better. You know it's a funny thing, but that parked car the bandits ran into is owned by Violet Venner. Her father was the sheriff who got me to taking my gun to work." [1]

There was never any doubt that Tony Chebatoris would be charged and tried for a federal crime, not for breaking a state law. To meet and hopefully stem the rising tide of bank robberies sweeping the country in the early 1930s and the evermore dangerous outlaws who committed them, the National Bank Robbery Act was passed in 1934. The law gave jurisdiction in any robbery of a bank that was a member of the FDIC or the Federal Reserve System to the U.S. Federal Courts. The Chemical State Bank was a member of both. If an innocent person happened to be killed during the course of the robbery, the law allowed for the death penalty to be imposed. With two critically injured victims of the robbery barely hanging on to life, the death penalty became a topic of almost daily conversation. When Henry Potter died of his wound on October 11, 1937, at Mercy Hospital in Bay City, the death penalty became a distinct possibility in a state that disavowed capital punishment and had not had a state-sanctioned execution since 1830. When Michigan's revised code of 1847 limited the penalty for murder to life imprisonment, it became the first state and the first English speaking government in the world to abolish capital punishment.

The federal trial of Tony Chebatoris opened on October 26, 1937, in the U.S. District Court in Bay City with Judge Arthur J. Tuttle presiding. John C. Lehr served as the federal prosecuting attorney. As a former congressman, Lehr had helped draft the National Bank Robbery Act of 1934. There was no doubt in anyone's mind that the prosecutor would seek the death penalty for the accused, and to those who closely studied the trial, it appeared that the prosecutor shaped and framed the charges against Chebatoris so the National Bank Robbery Act fit the accused like a hand-tailored suit.

It is highly unlikely there was an iota of doubt to be found in any jury member as to Tony's guilt before the trial even got underway. Chebatoris's two lawyers seemed to act more as spectators than defense attorneys. In the three-day trial, the prosecution called 34 people to the witness stand. The defense didn't call anyone. Granted, the case against Chebatoris seemed as air tight as a steel-belted radial. The accused never took the witness stand, and his demeanor gave no hint of remorse or regret nor a soupçon of gentleness let alone compassion. It's a given Chebatoris could have also killed Macomber and Bywater, but it still seems a man facing the death penalty is due a minimally credible defense.

When the defense rested and the final closing arguments were made, the guilty verdict was almost anticlimactic. In his closing statement, Prosecutor Lehr asked for the death penalty and labelled Chebatoris a "…brutal, ruthless killer, [and a] human beast…"[2]

After the guilty verdict, the jury retired to pass sentence. It was not a speedy, easy, or emotionally painless process for the seven women and five men in the jury room. On the first ballot, eight of the twelve voted for the death penalty. It took seven ballots for the jury to reach a unanimous verdict. It was after 8 PM when the court was convened. At 8:28 the foreman read the verdict. "We find the defendant guilty as charged and direct he be punished by death."[3] Several jurors were quietly crying as the verdict was read. Tony Chebatoris stared straight ahead and showed no emotion.

Throughout the trial the defendant had been held in the Saginaw County jail. Early Friday morning and what amounted to just hours after he heard the verdict and sentence on Thursday night, Tony somehow got possession of a rusty razor and slashed his wrists and throat. Guards flooded into his cell and wrestled the razor away from the prisoner. The condemned killer was rushed to the hospital where he was stitched up. It was never determined how he got the razor.

Judge Tuttle on November 30 formally sentenced Anthony Chebatoris to death. The judge set the date for July 8, 1938, and named the federal detention farm in Milan, Michigan, as the place of execution. That allowed the condemned seven months for filing appeals, but Chebatoris had already been told by his law team there was no money or grounds for appealing the verdict. The two lawyers walked away from a penniless client.

$ $ $

U. S. Marshal John J. Barc was handed the job of carrying out the execution. One of Barc's first acts was to name G. Phil Hanna as hangman. The 64-year-old Illinois farmer had never charged for his services in the 71 hangings he had officiated. He said he became a hangman out of a desire to be merciful. Forty years earlier he had been witness to a hanging that had gone horribly wrong. Instead of a quick, merciful death, the condemned man slowly and painfully strangled at the end of the rope. Hanna vowed to make sure executions were done properly and with as little pain as possible for the condemned. He had special rope made for hangings and ran tests on the length of the drop along with the weight that would pass through the trapdoor. Traditionally, a hangman's noose had 13 coils in it, but Hanna varied the number according to his own formula to ensure a quick snap of the neck.

In the weeks before the sentence was carried out, a covered gallows was built. The platform with its large steel trapdoor stood ten feet above the prison yard and was covered by tar paper and canvas. The platform was lit by four electric lights strung overhead. Directly beneath the trapdoor, a hole three feet deep and four feet in diameter was dug. This was done so Chebatoris's legs would hang in the hole and allow doctors to examine the body and check for a heartbeat without having either to cut the body down or make the doctor climb a stool or ladder to perform his official duties.

While the execution date neared, the debate over the first execution in Michigan in nearly 100 years became heated. Michigan governor Frank Murphy was adamantly opposed to capital punishment and thought it had no place in his state or civilized society. He spoke out against the death penalty repeatedly and argued that only the poor and the lower class were executed and those with money escaped the gallows. Two weeks before Chebatoris's scheduled date with the hangman, Murphy asked President Roosevelt to carry out the sentence in some other state. Illinois even volunteered to dispatch the condemned in their electric chair.

The problem for Murphy and those not wanting to reintroduce capital punishment to the state was an obscure

Michigan law that called for the death penalty for treason. It didn't matter if the law or the penalty had never been invoked; it was on the books. The National Bank Robbery Act said capital punishment could be sentenced and carried out in any state where the death penalty was already in the criminal code.

Roosevelt referred the matter to the U.S. Attorney General Homer Cummings who passed it on to Judge Tuttle with the understanding the judge would write an opinion on the governor's request. Judge Tuttle noted the obscure law stating, "...that Michigan has a statue providing the death penalty by hanging, [and continued] I have neither the power nor the inclination to change the sentence." [4] Governor Murphy was powerless to stop the execution, and at the time of Tuttle's ruling, it was only a week away.

In his last 24 hours before he met his end, Tony Chebatoris probably exhibited more decorum and less bravado than at any other time in his adult life. Tony told the prison chaplain he did not want to meet with him because he was an atheist. On his last night his divorced wife, daughter, granddaughter, and his three siblings spent time with Tony. He declined any special last meal and ate what the other prisoners had for supper.

The warden removed all the inmates from the cells which Chebatoris would have to walk past on his way to the gallows and created a new door in a brick wall to bypass other cells and shorten the passage from Tony's cell to the place of execution. At one in morning, those appointed as witnesses began to appear at the prison gates. They were searched, passed through a metal detector, signed a register, and led to a waiting room. Dr. Harding had declined to serve as a witness.

A few minutes before 5 AM, Marshal Barc and Warden John Ryan arrived at Chebatoris's cell. Barc asked if the prisoner wanted to make any final statement. Chebatoris replied in the negative, then stood up and held out his hands so Barc could handcuff him. The U.S. Marshal and Warden Ryan then led the way out of the cell with Chebatoris, a prison guard at his side. A Catholic priest trailed behind them praying quietly. The prisoner wore a white shirt, black pants and shined brown shoes. He was freshly shaved and his hair was combed.

Witnesses joined the procession as it made its way down the corridor and through the newly created doorway that opened onto the small yard holding the gallows. Chebatoris climbed the 13 steps to the top of the platform and walked to the center of the trapdoor. Midland County Sheriff Ira Smith had been asked if he would spring the trapdoor on the gallows and accepted the invitation. When Chebatoris stepped on the trapdoor, Sheriff Smith removed the security bolt from the lever.

Chebatoris looked at the man standing nearest him on the platform and asked if he was Mr. Hanna. When the man answered in the affirmative, Chebatoris said, "Then I know it will be a good job." [5] Guards wrapped leather straps around the prisoner's arms, knees, and ankles. A long black hood was pulled over Chebatoris's head that reached to his waist. Mr. Hanna stepped up, placed the noose around Tony's neck, adjusted the coils up against his right ear, and firmly snugged the loop around his neck. Hanna then stepped off the trap door and said the last words Chebatoris would ever hear, "God be with you, Chebatoris." [6] Hanna then nodded at Sheriff Smith who pushed the lever springing the trap door. It was 5:08 AM; Chebatoris dropped almost six feet before the rope went taut and the knot snapped his neck. He either died instantly or was unconscious just as quickly. Witnesses said his body never even twitched. Attending doctors waited several minutes before checking for a heartbeat and pronouncing him dead.

What no one but the warden knew was that just hours before the hanging Mr. Hanna and a trio of friends, all of whom were intoxicated, arrived at the prison. Hanna demanded his drunken friends be allowed to witness the execution or he would walk out and take his equipment with him. Ryan tried to reason with Hanna and reminded him only official witnesses were permitted to view the legal killing of a condemned man. Hanna wouldn't budge, so Ryan called the director of U.S. prisons who gave Ryan little help or comfort. The director told Ryan if Hanna wouldn't do it, the job fell to Ryan. The warden shot back he was against capital punishment, the prison was on edge, the state hadn't had a hanging in almost a hundred years, and concluded with, "You and the Attorney General can have this job right now." [7]

Ryan finally decided to tell Hanna his friends could watch, but the warden felt the hangman was too far in the bottle to notice his friends were not in the room. Ryan said OK to Hanna's demands then barred the three drunks from the execution site. The incident speaks of the terrible pressure Warden Ryan must have been under if he would allow a man so drunk he couldn't tell if his friends were in attendance to handle the execution. And what a toll seventy-some executions must have taken on George Phillip Hanna. The man who just wanted to make sure a hanging was a quick, painless death must have borne a terrible weight if he had to get drunk to carry out his self-appointed job. Hanna once said, "It is not a nice thing to see a man die—or have a part in executing him." [8] It is not known if Chebatoris was his last work as a hangman but extensive research can't find any record of Hanna taking part in another execution after 1937.

Guards cut down the body, loaded it on what's called a 'dead wagon,' and wheeled it outside the prison to a waiting hearse. Chebatoris's remains were taken to Milan's A.C. Stevens Mortuary where it was placed in a pine box and the funeral home waited for someone to claim the body. When no one stepped forward, a grave was dug in the potter's field section of the Marble Park Cemetery on West Main Street less than a mile west of Milan. The grave diggers waited for the pine box to arrive, but the sun set without it being brought to the cemetery.

That afternoon a woman called the funeral home and told Mr. Stevens she was Tony's mother and would pay for her son's burial. The woman arrived at the funeral home that evening, picked out a casket, and paid $75 for the box and funeral services. Mr. Stevens volunteered himself and three other men whose discretion he could trust to act as pallbearers.

The secret funeral was set for 2 PM on Saturday July 9, 1938. There were a handful of spectators present in addition to a reporter and photographer from the Ypsilanti Daily Press. Police kept them at a respectful distance as Father Lee Laige performed the burial service. Three men, two women, and a young girl were in attendance. The woman claiming to be Chebatoris's mother at the funeral home was obviously too young to be the deceased's parent, and Funeral Director Stevens never said if that woman was one of the two female mourners at the burial.

As of this writing, Anthony Chebatoris was the last person executed in the State of Michigan.

1. Veselenak, Aaron, The Execution of Anthony Chebatoris. Michigan History Magazine May/June 1998 p36
2. IBID p37
3. Hobey, Jack, The Lawless Years: Tony Chebatoris & Jack Gracey Story. Meadowbrook Books, Midland, MI 2012 p242
4. Veselenak, Aaron p38
5. Hobey, Jack, Lawless Years p234
6. IBID
7. Veselenak, Aaron, The Execution of Anthony Chebatoris p39
8. IBID p37

Afterword

*T*he 1920s and 30s proved to be a unique era in the history of bank robberies in Michigan and the nation. The robbing of banks didn't cease in the 1940s and succeeding decades, but the manner in with they were robbed and the characteristics of the robbers certainly did. There were two main reasons for the sea change in how banks were robbed and by whom.

The Federal Bank Robbery Act of 1934 made the robbing of a national bank a federal crime and gave jurisdiction for tracking down and capturing the bank robbers to the FBI. In the 1930s the Justice Department estimated there were 5,000 professional bank robbers in the country, most of which were loosely associated in large bank-robbing syndicates. Ruthless, well-armed, and highly proficient at their craft, the syndicates or gangs were literally serial bank robbers who traveled from state to state and knew the police in one state could not pursue them into a neighboring state. Until the FBI was tasked with tracking them down wherever they went, it was like pushing a reset button every time a gang moved to a different state. The 1934 act only covered national banks, and small town banks cried long and loud that the law would simply make the professional bank robbers turn their attention from big city national banks to small town banks. The 1935 Federal Bank Robbery Act extended protection to all banks insured by the FDIC. It also gave the FBI jurisdiction over all bank robberies.

Prior to the 1934 act, the American Bankers Association reported an average of 16 national banks robbed per month nationwide. With the FBI relentlessly hounding the professional robbers, the average had fallen to 6.4 a month by the end of 1935. Old pro Eddie Bentz was unlucky enough to have knocked off a national bank in Danville, Vermont, just after passage of the 1934 act. He and his crew were hunted down and arrested in Brooklyn by the FBI. From his cell Bentz complained that with the FBI making arrest after arrest most of the old-time 'yeggs' (criminal term for bank robbers) had gotten out of the business because you just couldn't get away with robbing banks any more. The FBI's pursuit, killing, and/or capture of the era's most famous bank robbers broke up the professional gangs, made the agency famous, and endowed J. Edgar Hoover with enormous political power and influence.

By the 1940s police departments had become better trained and better armed, and police cars were routinely equipped with two-way radios. All of which meant that local law enforcement had become more professional and better equipped to hunt down bank robbers. Vigilantism also died out in the late 1930s, and gun-toting mobs no longer commonly shot it out with bank robbers.

Lastly, World War II and the draft swept the streets clean of apprentice bank robbers. Young men who might have flirted with crime as teenagers and naturally moved from petty crime to armed robbery before graduating to bank robbery were snapped up by the military. The draft wiped out bank-robbing apprenticeships. In addition, there were plenty of well-paying jobs for those who were classified as 4-F, not acceptable for military service.

The bank robbers of the 1920s and 30s were a unique and short-lived breed. They were violent, deadly, amoral killers. They didn't wear masks and didn't pass a note and a sack to a teller informing him or her this was a stickup and fill the sack with money; rather, they walked into a bank with guns drawn and took what they wanted. Almost routinely, they shot anyone who got in their way. The robbers then counted on either outrunning the cops in faster cars or outgunning them in a firefight. Their kind are not likely to pass this way again.

Bibliography

BOOKS

Bruer, Willam B. *J. Edgar Hoover and His G-men*. Westport: Praeger, 1995.

Burnstein, Scott M. *The Detroit True Crime Chronicles*. Philadelphia: Camino Books, 2013

Burrough, Bryan. *Public Enemies: Americas Greatest Crime Wave and the Birth of the FBI, 1933-34*. New York: Penguin Books, 2004

First Hand Account of Life in Mancelona in the 20th Century. Mancelona: Mancelona Historical Society, 2002.

Hobey, Jack. *Lawless Years: The Tony Chebatoris and Jack Gracey Story*. Midland: Meadowbrook Books, 2012.

Kavieff, Paul R. *The Violent Years: Prohibition and the Detroit Mobs*. Fort Lee: Barricade Books, 2001.

Lane, Kit. *Fennville, village to city*. Fennville: Fennville Herald, 1985.

Longtine, Sonny. *Murder in Michigan's Upper Peninsula*. Charleston, S.C. History Press. 2014

Myers, Robert C. *Historical Sketches of Berrien County*. Berrien Springs: Berrien County Historical Association, 2009.

Newton, Michael. *Encyclopedia of Robberies, Heists, and Capers*. New York: Facts on File, 2002.

Rogers, D. Laurence. *Ghosts Crimes and Urban Legends in and around the town of Bay City, Michigan USA*. Bay City: Historical Press, 2006.

INTERNET

Francis Patrick Arthur Mason McGuirk Family Home Page
Letters of Note
Murderpedia.org

MAGAZINE ARTICLES

Bell, Anthony M. "State Treasures—Michigan." *Lost Treasure Magazine* (February 2011) .

Curran, Sgt. J. H. "Official Vengeance." *Real Detective* (March 1937).

LaMarre, Virgil. "Smashing Michigan's Bank Robbing Mobsters." *True Detective Mysteries* (October 1939).

Taylor, Merlin Moore. "The Key that Trapped Three." *Real Detective* (March 1932).

Veselenak, Aaron J. "The Execution of Anthony Chebatoris." *Michigan History Magazine,* May/June, 1998.

NEWSPAPERS

Acorn (Three Oaks)
Cass City Chronicle
Chicago Tribune
Clarkston News
Detroit Free Press
Detroit News
Dowagiac Daily News
Flint Journal
Grand Haven Daily
Grand Rapids Press
Holland City News
Ironwood Daily Globe
Jackson Citizen Patriot
Lapeer County News
Menominee Herald-Leader
Mt. Clemens Daily Leader
New-Palladium (Benton Harbor)
Pittsburgh Press

About the Author

*O*ne of the charms, or burdens, of writing for a small press is that the author gets to write his own author bio, so here goes:

Because the word "retired" sounds to me like I bought a new set of Goodyears, let's just say I worked for the Flint Public Library for 32 years before exiting public service and I turned to writing books instead of selecting, collecting, and preserving them for the public good. To date I've written better than a half dozen and am proud of every single sentence in them except one found in the early pages of *Michigan Rogues, Desperadoes and Cut-throats*, and I'm not telling which one.

My abundance of character flaws include spending an indecent amount of time fly fishing, refurbishing bamboo fly rods, being a hockey fanatic, piddling around (it's an art), reading, and an excessive fondness for Up North Michigan. On the plus side I am blessed by an incredible family that leaves me in awe of their talents, accomplishments, humor, and unadulterated love. My crowning achievement is to somehow have found or been found by a woman who has loved me and been my steadfast partner for over fifty years. If I made any small contribution to the success of this wonderful joint venture, it is that long ago I realized a husband is always a work in progress.

And finally, I do so love both writing and the written word. There is something magical about placing two words together on the page and instead of one plus one equals two they add up to so much more. Admittedly, it doesn't happen often when I'm stroking the keyboard, but when it does it almost makes you feel better than eating a piece of Jesperson's coconut cream pie in downtown Petoskey, Michigan.

The neurons willing and the creek don't rise maybe I'll be lucky enough to write yet another book on my home state.